PATRIOTS TWICE

Former Confederates and
the Building of America after the Civil War

Stephen M. Hood

Savas Beatie
California

Library of Congress Cataloging-in-Publication Data

Names: Hood, Stephen M., author.
Title: Patriots Twice: Former Confederates and the Building of America
  after the Civil War / by Stephen M. Hood.
Other titles: Former Confederates and the Building of America after the
  Civil War
Description: El Dorado Hills, CA : Savas Beatie, [2020] | Includes
  bibliographical references and index. | Summary: "After the American
  Civil War, former members of the defeated Confederate military attained
  prominent positions in the reunified nation. Former rebels served in the
  federal government, the U.S. Army, founded colleges and universities,
  and became presidents of several national professional societies.
  Patriots Twice reveals many of the high-achieving former Confederates
  who helped build postwar America."— provided by publisher.
Identifiers: LCCN 2020013913 | ISBN 9781611215151 (hardcover) |
ISBN 9781611215168 (ebook)
Subjects: LCSH: Veterans—Employment—United States—History—19th century.
  | Veterans—Employment—United States—History—20th century. |
  Veterans—Confederate States of America. | United States—History—Civil
  War, 1861-1865—Veterans. | Veterans—United States—History—19th
  century. | Veterans—United States—History—20th century. | United
  States—Politics and government—1865-1877.
Classification: LCC UB357 .H54 2020 | DDC 973.8092/697—dc23
LC record available at https://lccn.loc.gov/2020013913

First Edition, First Printing

Savas Beatie
989 Governor Drive, Suite 102
El Dorado Hills, CA 95762
916-941-6896 / www.savasbeatie.com / sales@savasbeatie.com

Savas Beatie titles are available at special discounts for bulk purchases. Contact us at sales@savasbeatie.com or see our website for details.

Proudly printed in the United States of America

To my granddaughter,

Harper Elizabeth Hood

Table of Contents

"[I do not] despair of the future. The truth is this: the march of Providence is so slow, and our desire so impatient, the work of progress so immense, and our means of aiding it so feeble, the life of humanity is so long, that of the individual so brief, that we often see only the ebb of the advancing wave and are thus discouraged. It is history that teaches us to hope."

— Robert E. Lee to Charles Marshall, September 1870

Author's Note: Sources and Methods

This book was inspired by the current cultural, political, and scholastic movement of reassessing historical characters and causes, removing symbols, monuments, and memorials, and renaming buildings and landmarks of those deemed unworthy by current social values. When this book was being written (2018-19) the imperiled monuments were primarily those related to the Confederate States of America. This issue has also spread to historical characters and causes before and after the 1861-65 American Civil War. Many historical personages, from fifteenth century to today (from European explorers to the Founding Fathers) are being reassessed and reinterpreted based upon ever-changing social and cultural standards.

The Confederacy's brief life during the Civil War, although vitally important, was only a chapter in the lives of those who survived the conflict. When the controversy over the modern interpretation and portrayal of the Confederacy erupted in the mid-2010s, I became curious about what former Confederates did after the war and how they lived their professional lives in a country that had been torn apart by such a bloody war. It had been reunified, but had the nation, at least for the most part, truly reconciled?

Biographies of prominent Southern soldiers and politicians typically include something about their prewar lives and of course their wartime service, but in most cases their postwar lives are consigned to footnotes or a short postscript. After

viii   *Patriots Twice: Former Confederates and the Building of America*

writing this book, it is now clear that the dearth of postwar coverage shortchanges these men, as well as modern Americans who read about them and live in the country they helped to create *after* the guns fell silent.

In late 2016 during the early months of the national controversy over Confederate memorials, I decided to research former Confederates and study, as much as possible, their postwar lives and careers. Before my work began the bulk of my universe of knowledge in the arena of former soldiers who attained postwar prominence consisted of a slim handful of Confederate Army generals like Joseph Wheeler, Fitzhugh Lee, Thomas Rosser, and Matthew Butler (all of whom served as U.S. Army generals during the Spanish-American War), Stephen D. Lee, the former Confederate general who became president of Mississippi State University, and Robert E. Lee, who assumed the presidency of Washington College in Lexington, Virginia.

What I discovered during my research was, in a word, fascinating. Eight—not four—former Confederates became U.S. Army generals during the Spanish-American War. Starting in 1869 with Ulysses S. Grant, a total of ten postwar U.S. presidents appointed dozens of former Confederates to fill high-ranking federal government positions—some at the highest pinnacles of various parts of our government, including chief justice of the Supreme Court. Ex-Confederates also presided over national professional societies and institutions outside of government, including the American Medical Association, the American Bar Association, and the Sierra Club. Former soldiers who had donned the gray founded many colleges and universities and became presidents and chancellors of many more—not just in the Deep South (as one might expect), but in such unlikely locales as California, Colorado, Missouri, Maryland, and West Virginia. These men also taught at universities and colleges in the Union states and territories of California, Colorado, Wisconsin, Vermont, and Massachusetts. Many were elected or appointed to state, territorial, and local political offices in the old Confederacy, but this also took place in Alaska, Colorado, Oklahoma, California, Montana, Wyoming, New Mexico, Minnesota, Utah, Kansas, the Panama Canal Zone, and West Virginia, which had seceded from Virginia in 1863 to fight against the Confederacy.

I did not investigate, analyze, or render opinions on the personal politics, opinions, or values of any of these former Confederate because that was beyond the scope and purpose of this work. Whether a man deserved his position at the time, and/or his subsequent historical notoriety—if any—are better left to other researchers. *Patriots Twice* does not analyze, accuse, condemn, glorify, or criticize any of them. Instead, I identified and chose men based solely on their tangible professional accomplishments and the fact that (in most cases) they were welcomed into their positions by men who had worn blue uniforms and fought for the Union. If those who had crossed bayonets with these former Confederates and had suffered the most during those four long years could welcome, work with, and share the benefits of the professional contributions of these men, why are people 155 years removed from the war so virulently opposed to even a marble or bronze likeness of a Confederate soldier or a name on a building?

Any history book should be titled or described as "a history of" rather than "the history of" because new information will always be discovered and historians must constantly decide what material to include or exclude. This book is no different. More than a million men served the Confederacy. I limited entries to those whose postwar successes will be readily understood and hopefully respected by present-day Americans.

The sources of information I used for this book deserve some discussion. The bulk of its content is almost exclusively biographical, though finding the information was not always simple or straightforward. Getting reliable biographical information on individuals who lived a century or more ago is often difficult. Administrative records like birth and death listings, places of birth, death, residence, marriages, divorces, children, parents, and military service rank often conflict with public records, memoirs, diaries, obituaries, or engravings on tombstones. For example, General John Bell Hood's tomb in Metairie Cemetery in New Orleans claims his birthplace was Owensville, Kentucky. In fact, there is no such place. There are cities named Owingsville and Owensboro in Kentucky, but no Owensville. Similarly, obituaries and published tributes often contain inaccurate information and, perhaps inevitably, embellished accomplishments, of the deceased. Even the accuracy of military ranks can be problematical. Sometimes, especially late in the war as the Confederate government was unraveling, recommended promotions passed into history unconfirmed by the Confederate government.

Another problem was the nineteenth century custom of bestowing honorary titles to older gentlemen. For example, popular culture offers up "Colonel Sanders" of fried chicken fame, and "Captain" Rhett Butler from *Gone with the Wind*. Other situations involved former officers on both sides who attained one rank during the war but were given higher official ranks later in state militias or National Guard organizations. One example of this was former Los Angeles Mayor Cameron Thom, a staff officer in the Confederate Army of Northern Virginia whose commission as an officer cannot be located. In later life he was acknowledged as a former Confederate captain, but was sometimes called "Major

Thom," presumably a reference to his service in the postwar California State Militia.

My primary interest during research was to verify whether an individual actually served as a Confederate soldier, sailor, or government official and, as best I could to ascertain his official rank or position. If I found conflicting ranks, I chose the one I believed most likely to have been the case.

Another issue entails determining the military units in which a soldier served. In a vast majority of cases, a soldier enlisted or enrolled in a company and went on to serve in multiple companies, regiments, and brigades as the armies organized and reorganized as the war dragged on. Likewise, officers would be promoted and their commands changed from regimental to brigade, division, corps, and, in rare cases, full army command. For an enlisted man, I typically listed the first unit to which he was assigned, and, in some instances, the unit in which he served the longest. Otherwise, I identify a soldier's unit with the most readily available credible source. For senior commanders, mostly generals whose historical records are more complete, I assigned their highest rank and the unit with which they are most notably identified. Consolidation of regiments presented another problem. In the Confederate Army, especially later in the war, regiments were combined as the number of effective soldiers diminished. In such events I usually attach only one regiment to a man who may have served in several.

Searching for biographical information can be a tedious exercise. Wikipedia's reputation is not pristine, but most researchers recognize its basic utility and employ the online encyclopedia more than they care to admit. I often used it as a *starting point* and found it a valuable source for raw first-search information, which I almost always tried to confirm in other sources if I wasn't already sure of it. Thankfully, Wikipedia does not cloak a man's Confederate service by identifying him as simply a "Civil War soldier." This is not true for many college and university websites, whose "history" pages omit a founder's or past president's Confederate service altogether, or state only that he was a "Civil War" veteran. In other instances, the word "South," "Southern," or "Southerner" is used in lieu of "Confederate" or "Confederacy." Wikipedia does not do this (at least not yet), which made it a valuable initial search device for identification and basic biographical information. In most instances Wikipedia posts also provide additional links to sources so I could better verify, corroborate, or find additional information about the man in question.

Other primary online sources included the outstanding www.findagrave.com unpublished database "Confederate Physicians . . . who Served the Confederacy in a Medical Capacity during the American Civil War," by F. T. Hambrecht and J. L.

Koste. I also relied heavily upon U.S. government web sites for the president, both houses of Congress, and the departments of Justice and State. Official web sites for individual states were also useful. The most helpful print sources included, but were not limited to, *Crimson Confederates*, *Yale's Confederates*, *Generals in Gray*, *Staff Officers in Gray*, and *The Corps Forward*.[1]

I decided to eschew the use of extensive footnotes. This is not a detailed battle or campaign history, or a biographical study comparing particular actions, decisions, ideas, and controversies. Anyone with an interest in a particular man covered here can easily type in their name on the Internet and find more than enough to satisfy his or her curiosity and confirm the basic facts about his postwar accomplishments. Indeed, I urge you to do so. In many cases it will be hard for you to resist researching some of these characters, many of whom led nothing short of extraordinary lives and left real contributions in their wake that have touched and influenced many of us.

*   *   *

Necessarily subjective criteria governed the selection of Confederate veterans included in this book. In fact, as I discovered increasing numbers of high-achieving veterans, I was forced repeatedly, and regretfully, to raise the bar of qualification for inclusion. As a result, many former Confederates who attained unqualified postwar success could not be included. My perusal of several thousand biographical profiles identified about 850 prominent veterans, which I whittled down to some 220, either in the main narrative or listed in the appendices.

Former Confederates who served in postwar United States government positions often were difficult to locate, but there was no doubt they needed to be included in this book. Other categories, however, were not so simple. In higher education, for example, defining and confirming the founders of colleges and universities frequently required a degree of subjectivity. If an individual provided funding or land or organized and began the operations of a college—as was the case with Clemson University, Texas Christian University, Coker College, and others—I could confidently credit him with the establishment of the school. Other

---

1 Helen Trimpi, *Crimson Confederates: Harvard Men Who Fought for the South* (U. of Tennessee Press, 2009); Nathaniel Cheairs Hughes, Jr., *Yale's Confederates: A Biographical Dictionary* (UOT Press, 2008); Ezra Warner, *Generals in Gray: Lives of the Confederate Commanders* (LSU Press, 2006); Robert E. L. Krick, *Staff Officers in Gray: A Biographical Register of the Staff Officers in the Army of Northern Virginia* (UNC Press, 2003); William Couper, *The Corps Forward: The Battle of New Market* (The Mariner Companies, Inc., 2005).

founders and institutions are not so cut and dried. The creation of public schools often resulted from the efforts of powerful legislators or governors who forcefully advocated the establishment of an institution and produced or signed into law the required legislation. In all cases, I designated a founder or co-founder of a college or university by credible sources, such as records from the school itself or the state's official historical department or bureau.

Presidents or chancellors of a university are also easily identified, with the rare exception of the few schools (the University of Virginia in the nineteenth century had a faculty committee or senate preside over the institution). Members of governing boards were likewise straightforward, although institutions variously name their governing bodies: board of directors, board of trustees, board of governors, or board of visitors. For college and university teachers, I included veterans who instructed at a school and often use the term "professor" as a generic reference to those who taught at a college or university, as opposed to an instructor at a primary or secondary school.

For simplicity and consistency with the numerous military ranks and grades in armies and navies, I most often use the common salutatory form of the ranks: "sergeant," for example, whether the soldier was a sergeant, first sergeant, staff sergeant, master sergeant, color sergeant, etc., and "private" and "corporal" whether a veteran was a private first class or a first or second corporal. For officers I use "lieutenant" instead of designating them by their various levels, and "colonel" for both lieutenant colonel or full colonels. For general officers I usually designate the specific grade—brigadier, major, or lieutenant—but will also refer to them on occasion generically as "general."

For medical personnel I consistently use the rank and title "surgeon" even if the veteran formally served as an "assistant surgeon." Finally, in the diplomatic corps, different nations used the term "minister" or "ambassador" to designate the highest-ranking diplomat. I use the U.S. government's term "ambassador."

Acknowledgments

Although my research involved innumerable sources, because of the nature of my book, much of my data comes from a handful of publications and online databases.

The splendid Findagrave.com biographical register of physicians who served the Confederacy in a medical capacity, for example, provided data for most of the former Confederate physicians and surgeons. Robert E. L. Krick's respected *Staff Officers in Gray* (2003) was an essential resource for veterans who were non-medical professionals, along with *Crimson Confederates* (2010) by Helen P. Trimpi, *Yale's Confederates* (2008) by Nathaniel Cheairs Hughes Jr., William Couper's *The Corps Forward* (2005), *Generals in Gray* (1959) by Ezra J. Warner, and Bruce S. Allardice's *More Generals in Gray* (1995). The extensive research of these dedicated historians provided the foundation for a work like mine.

As with my two previous books I relied heavily on my publisher and friend Theodore P. Savas. Beyond the typical professional guidance one might expect from an adroit publisher, Ted also provided brotherly advice and, on more than once occasion, reassurance and encouragement. Thanks also to his outstanding staff, especially the two marketing Sarahs (Sarah Keeney and Sarah Closson), Joel Manuel for helping proof the manuscript, and photo editor Jane Martin and Cindy Bucher of Copper Penguin LLC.

When I began research, I sent numerous emails and private messages to individuals involved in Civil War and Confederate history, asking for distribution of my appeal to their acquaintances and, if possible, the identification any obscure, yet high-achieving Confederate veteran they might know of. I also contacted many Civil War and Confederate history organizations soliciting this information.

In response to my public appeal the following individuals provided either guidance, or in many cases specific biographical and historical information on Confederate veterans included in this book. Some of these respondents I know personally, and others I do not, but to all I offer sincere thanks: James Bonk, Samuel J. Broh, Larry Burford, Joe Byrd, Heidi Crabtree, Jan Croon, Jimbo Dear, Chris Dempsey, Frank Eggen, Laura Elliott, Ed Ernewein, Ashley Hamilton, Michael Hardy, Lana Henly, Tom Hiter, Mike Hollingsworth, Terry Klima, Mike Landree, Frank Leatherwood, Alan Lerwick, Phil Logan, Mike Majors, Daniel Mallock, Phil Maxson, Bruce Merritt, Lauren Miller, Joe Owen, Bill Payne, Ran Pickell, Fred Ray, Sanford Reed, Kyle Reichle, Joseph Ricci, Patricia Ricci, Jessie Riggs, Ben Sewell, Brett Schulte, Steve Smith, Pete Snyder, Ken Sumner, Paul Taylor, Tom Unkle, Paul Williams, and J. R. Wolfe.

Personal friends who answered my call and provided needed assistance and encouragement include Greg Wade, one of Franklin, Tennessee's prominent Civil War educators and preservationists, and all-round good guy. My "Tennessee mom" Betty Callis of Hendersonville was as always, and in every way, a reliable source of inspiration for me. Another of my go-to Civil War history friends, Len Riedel, director of the Blue and Gray Education Society, also proffered assistance, advice, and encouragement. My cousin Oliver C. "OC" Hood of Franklin, North Carolina, was, as always, ready to help, as was my dear friend Dale "Fish" Fishel of Olympia, Washington, whose hands-on assistance was as vital to the development of this book as it was to my previous two publications.

Jack Dickinson, curator of the Rosanna A. Blake Library of Confederate History at Marshall University was, as always, a dependable source of information and assistance. Thanks as well to Jessica Ray, a student at Marshall who assisted me with research, and to her business professor, Dr. Ben Eng, who is mentoring her to a doubtless bright future.

To Jim Huffman, a retired schoolteacher from Picayune, Mississippi, I offer special thanks for his research on former Confederates who became law enforcement officers after the war and died in the line of duty.

David Connon, author of *Iowa Confederates in the Civil War* (2019), also contributed material to the book.

Finally, thanks to my high school English teacher at the Kentucky Military Institute, Russell "Cappy" Gagnon, now of South Bend, Indiana, whose combination of knowledge and wit kept me and my fellow cadets alert and engaged in his classroom.

Introduction

No more will the war cry sever,
Or the inland rivers run red.
We have buried our anger forever,
In the sacred graves of the dead.

Under the sod and the dew,
Awaiting the Judgment Day.
Love and tears for the blue!
Tears and love for the gray!

— Thomas Hughes, 1895

After all wars, reconciliation is difficult at first, but as monarchs and politicians responsible for the conflict age and die, the young combatants who survived the suffering and carnage remain and, in time, rightly become the most prominent influencers of the memory of the events. More often than not the men who attempted to kill each other eventually forgive their former foes. Anger and vengeance are replaced with respect for the trials and tribulations shared by the former adversaries. Most important, they respect the trait most admired by all soldiers: a former foe's answer to the call of duty.

Speaking in 1902 at a memorial service honoring Confederate soldiers who died at the Camp Chase prisoner-of-war camp in Columbus, Ohio, Union Army veteran and Grand Army of the Republic state commander Judge David Pugh said of Robert E. Lee's defeated soldiers, "I pity the American who cannot be proud of their valor and endurance."

Theodore Roosevelt, whose two beloved uncles served the Confederate cause in the Civil War, addressed a gathering in Roswell, Georgia on October 20, 1905. "It has been my very great good fortune to have the right to claim my blood is half Southern and half Northern," the young president said, "and I would deny the right of any man here to feel a greater pride in the deeds of every Southerner than I feel." Roosevelt concluded his remarks by proclaiming,

> I have the ancestral right to claim a proud kinship with those who showed their devotion to duty as they saw the duty, whether they wore the grey or whether they wore the blue. All Americans who are worthy of the name feel an equal pride in the valor of those who fought on one side or the other, provided only that each did with all his strength and soul and mind, his duty as he saw his duty.[1]

Similarly, noted author and Union veteran Ambrose Bierce wrote of unknown Confederate dead:

> They were honest and courageous foemen, having little in common with the political madmen who persuaded them to their doom and the literary bearers of false witness in the after time. They did not live through the period of honorable strife into the period of vilification—did not pass from the iron age to the brazen—from the era of the sword to that of the tongue and pen. Among them is no member of the Southern Historical Society. Their valor was not the fury of the non-combatant; they have no voice in the thunder of the civilians and the shouting. Not by them are impaired the dignity and infinite pathos of the Lost Cause. Give them, these blameless gentlemen, their rightful part in all the pomp that fills the circuit of the summer hills.

> — Ambrose Bierce, "A Bivouac of the Dead," 1905

In the decades after the war the survivors of the continent's bloodiest-ever conflict gradually reconciled and, for many, simple forgiveness morphed into a brotherly bond. One incident illustrative of the wave of late-life reconciliation between former enemies occurred in the unlikely setting of Martha's Vineyard, Massachusetts, involving Charles Strahan, a former Confederate private in the 21st Virginia Infantry Regiment, and the local Union Army veterans of the Civil War.

After the war Strahan moved to the town of Oak Bluffs on the island of Martha's Vineyard, purchased the local newspaper, and, over the years, prospered.

---

1 For information on Teddy Roosevelt's relatives, see: https://opinionator.blogs.nytimes.com/2014/06/25/teddy-roosevelts-confederate-uncles/

Not surprisingly, Strahan was the only Confederate veteran on the island, and he observed with admiration and respect the comradery of the local chapter of the Grand Army of the Republic (GAR), the fraternal organization of former Union soldiers of the Civil War. In 1891, using his own personal funds, Strahan erected a statue in the town square honoring the Union soldiers of the war; shortly before Strahan's death in 1925, in a gesture of admiration and respect, the GAR chapter attached a plaque onto the statue's pedestal that read,

"THE CHASM IS CLOSED"

IN MEMORY OF THE RESTORED UNION
THIS TABLET IS DEDICATED BY
UNION VETERANS OF THE CIVIL WAR
AND PATRIOTIC CITIZENS OF MARTHA'S VINEYARD
IN HONOR OF THE CONFEDERATE SOLDIERS[2]

The chasm referenced on the plaque had been largely closed twenty-seven years earlier in the Spanish-American War, the first military test for postwar America, when many Southerners were eager to prove their patriotism, if necessary, with their own blood. A former Confederate soldier wrote,

When the Spanish-American War came on, the men of the blue and the men of the gray stood shoulder to shoulder, the sons of the men who wore the blue and the gray in 1861-65 marched step with step, and won the victory that made us proud that we were Americans. Our country was thus cemented together as never before, and prejudices gave way to an era of good feeling throughout this Union.[3]

While the nation was still basking in the glow of the decisive victory over the Spanish empire, Congress acknowledged the vital part played by Southerners in the brief but momentous war. On January 26, 1903, a bill was introduced in the U.S. Senate by Senator Joseph Foraker of Ohio requesting $100,000 for headstones for Confederate soldiers who had died in Northern prisoner-of-war camps. The bill passed *unanimously* and is often cited as the genesis of the official reconciliation that had already permeated American society.

2 This statue, "The Soldiers Memorial Fountain," is located in Ocean Park in Oak Bluffs.

3 Marcus B. Toney, *The Privations of a Private: Campaigning with the First Tennessee, C.S.A., and Life Thereafter* (Fire Ant Books, 1905), 123.

Reconciliation, forgiveness, and expressions of mutual respect became common after the turn of the century. A postwar exchange of letters between a former Union soldier and a Confederate commander regarding the May 3-4, 1863, Battle of Salem Church (Virginia) vividly illustrates the personal affection shared by the former enemies, as well as the public's desire to permanently honor the dedication and sacrifice of all Civil War soldiers.

A monument had been erected near the Salem Church battlefield, with two plaques (one honoring Union soldiers, including those of the 23rd New Jersey Infantry Regiment), and one for Confederate soldiers (among them members of the 8th Alabama Infantry Regiment including Lieutenant Colonel Hilary A. Herbert, who thirty years earlier served as secretary of the U.S. Navy in the Grover Cleveland administration). The plaques are inscribed:

TO THE MEMORY OF OUR HEROIC COMRADES
WHO GAVE THEIR LIVES FOR THEIR COUNTRY'S
UNITY ON THE BATTLEFIELD THIS TABLET IS DEDICATED

TO THE BRAVE ALABAMA BOYS,
OUR OPPONENTS ON THIS FIELD OF BATTLE
WHOSE MEMORY WE HONOR THIS TABLET IS DEDICATED

On May 18, 1907, Herbert wrote to Edmund Burd Grubb, a former soldier in the 23rd New Jersey:

Dear Sir:

A recent number of the Montgomery Ala. *Advertiser* copies an account from the *Fredericksburg Star* of May 3rd, of the erection of a "Monument to Commemorate the Services of the 23rd New Jersey Volunteer Infantry in the Battle of Salem Church, Virginia, May 3rd, 1863," and I have noted with unmixed pleasure that . . . on one of the plates upon the monument are inscribed the words: To the memory of our heroic comrades who gave their lives for their country's unity on the battlefield, this tablet is dedicated.

Upon another plate is this inscription: To the brave Alabama boys, our opponents on this field of battle, whose memory we honor, this tablet is dedicated.

I was with my regiment, the 8th Alabama, and was its Lieutenant Colonel in the bloody fight which you and your brave soldiers have so fittingly commemorated. Indeed, the 8th Alabama was on the south side of the plank road, and therefore almost immediately confronted your gallant regiment. Being the oldest surviving field officer of the five Alabama regiments that participated in the memorable struggle, I feel that I may appropriately assume, on behalf of the Alabama boys whose memory you and your brave soldiers so chivalrously extol, to extend to you and the other survivors of the 23rd New Jersey, as I do hereby, the heartfelt thanks of the living Alabamians who participated in that battle.

. . . The brave soldiers of the 23rd New Jersey are not the first, either federal or Confederate, that have done honor to those who were their opponents in the civil war. Many an orator, thank God, both Northern and Southern, has delighted his audience by patriotic sentiments along this line. But as far as I know, the gallant regiment which you had the honor to command at Salem Church, is the first to inscribe upon an enduring monument erected to the memory of its own dead so noble a special tribute to those who were its antagonists in the particular field marked by the monument.

In conclusion, permit me to personally testify, as I well may, to the superb courage of the gallant boys whom you so nobly led in that bloody battle at Salem Church. Expressing the hope that at some time in the future I may have the gratification of meeting you in person, I am, sir, with the sincerest admiration and respect,

Yours very truly

Hilary A. Herbert
last Colonel 8th Ala Vols

Grubb replied two weeks later, acknowledging that Colonel Herbert, his wartime adversary, had served the reunited country as President Cleveland's navy secretary three decades earlier:

Dear Colonel Herbert,

It has surely fallen to the lot of but very few men in this world, ever to have received, from a brave and gallant foeman, forty-four years after a battle, such a splendid letter as I have the honor to acknowledge from you, and moreover, to have received it unaware from one, who after the war was over, served a re-united country in one of its highest offices with such signal ability and distinction.

I beg, sir, on behalf of myself, and my comrades, the survivors of the Twenty-third New Jersey Volunteers, their descendants, relations, and friends, whose name is legion in this State, to tender our most sincere thanks for your letter, to reciprocate most heartily all the noble sentiments contained therein, and to assure you that we congratulate ourselves, that by good fortune, we happened to be the first to mark in enduring bronze, the sentiments which we are sure are uppermost in the hearts of every Northern soldier, for the men who evinced the courage of their convictions by such heroic bravery in the days gone by.

I may add that while we knew that Gen Cadmus Wilcox had noted in his report of the Battle of Salem Church how gallantly Lieut. Colonel Hilary A. Herbert had rallied and fought the 8th Alabama after a disabling wound to Colonel Royston, we certainly did not know that our country was indebted for distinguished services as Secretary of the Navy to the officer whose final line of battle we could not break through.

I hope, sir, I may have the pleasure of meeting you personally, and I shall have the honor of calling upon you when I am in your vicinity.

With great respect, I am,

Very sincerely yours,

E. Burd Grubb[4]

As Civil War veterans aged, reunions often became demonstrations of respect among patriotic countrymen—the former Billy Yanks and Johnny Rebs. One such reunion occurred in Memphis, Tennessee, on June 10, 1909, as reported in the monthly periodical of the United Confederate Veterans, the Southern fraternal counterpart to the Union veterans' Grand Army of the Republic:

> Tears welled in 20,000 Southern eyes, and 10,000 tongues shouted their approval when General Fred Dent Grant, son of General U. S. Grant, clasped the hand of General Clement A. Evans, commander-in-chief of the United Confederate Veterans, during the greatest Veterans' parade ever witnessed in the South to-day.
>
> A moment later scores of grizzled Veterans broke from their ranks and extended their hands to grasp in friendship the hand of the son of the man they had fought against nearly half a century ago. General Grant was presented to General Evans by Mayor Malone, one of the party occupying the box in the grand stand on the Main Street side of Court Square with General Grant.
>
> Following the example of their leader, scarce a man in the line of march clasped General Grant's hand and in several instances, old men bearing the battle torn banners they fought under, stopped in front of General Grant's seat and grasped his hand while the tattered folds of the flag they bore rested across their shoulders.
>
> Probably no Northern man, excepting a president, has ever been the recipient of such a tremendous ovation as was accorded the son of the Northern leader to-day. Not a commanding officer in the line but what rode his mount close enough to shake hands with General Grant, and many openly shed tears at the sight.

4   *New York Times,* July 13, 1913.

At one point in the parade, laughter and cheers were aroused by the action of a regiment of Veterans. Their leader, on catching sight of General Grant, shouted to the other aged soldiers under his command, "Come on kids. Here's General Grant now!" With a yell the Veterans ran to shake his hand, for the time throwing the parade into confusion.

One of the most touching incidents of the morning around the reviewing stand was when the few surviving members of the immortal 600, who suffered during the war as federal prisoners, reached the General's box.[5] The old men were tired by their march beneath the burning sun. At sight of General Grant their leader proposed "Three cheers for General Grant." They were given with a gusto that would have done credit to a band of college boys.[6]

No doubt Fred Dent Grant, the son of the great Union general and U.S. president, recalled former Confederate generals Joseph E. Johnston and Simon Bolivar Buckner, pallbearers along with former Union generals Philip Sheridan and William T. Sherman at the funeral of his father on August 8, 1885. Indeed in 1909, national reconciliation and forgiveness was in its second generation.

Loyalty to the United States was codified by the official organization of Confederate veterans on the eve of America's entry into World War I, when on May 16, 1916, the United Confederate Veterans of Alabama passed a motion that was sent to President Woodrow Wilson:

To the President and Congress of the United States: We, the United Confederate Veterans in Reunion assembled at Birmingham, Ala., this the 16th day of May, 1916, do hereby again renew and declare our unfaltering allegiance to the government of the United States in this its hour of great international difficulties.

We took up arms against the government, not as rebels, but to protect our homes and firesides, to preserve and maintain the principle of States' rights; and although the arbitrament of arms was against us, we lost neither our courage, our manhood, nor our patriotism.

To-day the remnant of the armies of the Confederate States of America does hereby offer itself, its sons, and its property upon the altar of a reunited country which we love and seek to serve, protect, and defend.

---

5 The Immortal Six-hundred were 600 Confederate officers who were prisoners of war and refused to take the oath of allegiance to the United States. They were subjected to intentionally harsh treatment by their Union captors and became a symbol of sacrifice and resolve in the South, both during and after the war.

6 https://archive.org/stream/minutesucv190910unit/minutesucv190910unit_djvu.txt, accessed August 14, 2019; page 15 of the minutes of the nineteenth meeting of the United Confederate Veterans, Memphis, TN, June 8-10, 1909.

We recommend that every male citizen over sixteen years of age residing in the United States and its territories be required to report immediately to the probate judge of his county or other like officer under penalty of the law and there swear allegiance to this government, pledging him loyally to support the government against any and all foes, whether internal or foreign, that may attempt to hinder or destroy the rights, property, or liberty of its people.[7]

Reconciliation and memorialization of the former combatants continued into the latter part of the twentieth century, and as late as 1977 a monument was erected near Selma, Alabama, to honor Union soldiers killed more than a century earlier. The Alabama chapter of the United Daughters of the Confederacy, an organization of female descendants of Confederate veterans, erected a monument to honor twelve Union soldiers killed in the April 1, 1865, Battle of Ebenezer Church.

*   *   *

Many descendants of Confederate veterans demonstrated their patriotism by service to the reunited nation, while some proved their loyalty by giving their own lives.

Lieutenant General Simon Bolivar Buckner Jr., son of Confederate Major General Simon Bolivar Buckner, died on Okinawa in World War II on June 18, 1945, the highest-ranking U.S. military officer to be killed in action in the war. The great-grandson of Confederate Lieutenant General Thomas J. "Stonewall" Jackson, Colonel Thomas Jonathan Jackson Christian of the U. S. Army Air Corps was killed in action over northern France on August 12, 1944. Likewise, U.S. Army Brigadier General Nathan Bedford Forrest III, great grandson of the famous Confederate cavalryman, was killed in action leading a bombing raid on a German submarine base on June 14, 1943. At the time of his death, Forrest was chief of staff of the U.S. Second Air Force.

Legendary United States Marine Corps Lieutenant General Lewis "Chesty" Puller was a descendent of Confederates, as was former Commandant of the Marine Corps, Lieutenant General John Archer Lejeune, namesake of Camp Lejeune, North Carolina. John Archer Lejeune's father Ovide Lejeune was a Confederate officer. The legendary World War II General George Patton was a grandson of Confederate Colonel George Smith Patton of the 22nd Virginia

---

7 *Confederate Veteran*, 40 vols. (May 1916), vol. 24, 243.

Infantry Regiment, who was mortally wounded at the Third Battle of Winchester (Virginia) on September 19, 1864.

Other famous Americans purported to have Confederate ancestors include Presidents Bill Clinton and Harry Truman, Senator John McCain, Governor Rick Perry of Texas, and Supreme Court Justice Sandra Day O'Connor. Celebrities Anderson Cooper, Robin Williams, Larry Hagman, Will Rogers, Muppets creator Jim Henson, and iconic Hollywood director Cecil B. Demille are said to be descendants of Confederates. Performers Elvis Presley, Trace Adkins, Hank Williams, Hank Williams Jr., and Charlie Daniels ostensibly descend from Confederate soldiers.

The founder and first president of the Girl Scouts of America, Juliette "Daisy" Gordon Low was the daughter of Confederate Captain William Washington Gordon. The Reverend Billy Graham and his son Franklin Graham descend from Private William Cook Graham of the 11th South Carolina Infantry Regiment. Helen Keller was the granddaughter of a Confederate colonel, and Audie Murphy, the most decorated American soldier in World War II, is also said to have descended from Confederates, as was Nobel Prize winning author William Faulkner, whose great grandfather was Colonel William Clark Falkner [sic] of the 2nd Mississippi Infantry Regiment.

*   *   *

In early 2020 it remains to be seen if monuments honoring the men who fought in the American Civil War will survive the ever-changing standards of worthiness. Many Confederate monuments and landmarks are being removed, and even memorials to some Union commanders have fallen prey to fluid values.

The strict reconsideration of characters and events doesn't only befall those related to the Civil War. In April 2019 the state of Maine renamed Columbus Day as Indigenous People's Day, following Alaska, Vermont, and South Dakota in no longer honoring the Spanish-Italian explorer Christopher Columbus as the symbolic discoverer of the Western Hemisphere in 1492. Also in 2019, George Washington High School in San Francisco decided to destroy a seventy-year old mural depicting the school's namesake George Washington, once universally considered by American school children as "The Father of our Country." Similarly, the same year the City of Charlottesville, Virginia, decided to no longer celebrate the birthday of Washington's fellow Founding Father Thomas Jefferson, the principal author of the Declaration of Independence and the third president of the United States and founder of the University of Virginia. The city instead will celebrate the day the Union army entered and occupied Charlottesville in the waning days of the Civil War.

In August 2017, a statue of Revolutionary War hero Colonel William Crawford was decapitated in Bucyrus, Ohio. Crawford had served under George Washington in the Continental Army in New York and New Jersey and later commanded colonial troops in battles against Native Americans in northern Ohio. In 1782 he was captured by Delaware Indians, tortured, and burned alive. Also in August 2017 a statue of "the Great Emancipator" Abraham Lincoln was vandalized in Chicago, perhaps because his 1863 Emancipation Proclamation freed only some, but not all, of the slaves.

The presence of the tomb of Ulysses S. Grant in New York City has been targeted for reconsideration by the city, due, supposedly, to his anti-Semitism. A statue of early twentieth century president William McKinley was removed by the city government of Arcata, California, in 2018 because of McKinley's imperialistic views. Similarly, in 2009 Alaska's Mt. McKinley, North America's highest mountain, was renamed Denali. Even a statue of famous World War II-era patriotic singer Kate Smith was removed from a public location in Philadelphia because she had recorded songs in the 1930s with racially insensitive lyrics. Smith's iconic rendition of God Bless America, a staple at New York Yankees' home games since the terrorist attacks of September 11, 2001, was silenced in 2018 because of those songs she had recorded so long ago.

Honors and recognition bestowed upon all historic American figures are currently under pressure the entirety of their lives, and their contributions to humanity seemingly soiled by their imperfections as judged by standards 200 years hence.

*   *   *

The Fuller Story is a program instituted in the historic city of Franklin, Tennessee, in 2017, in response to the then-accelerating nationwide movement of reassessing national and local historic monuments.

On November 30, 1864, Franklin was the site of one of the bloodiest battles in American military history when Confederate General John Bell Hood's 20,000-strong Army of Tennessee attacked an equal number of entrenched defenders under the command of Union General John McCallister Schofield. In just five hours of intense combat, nearly 10,000 Union and Confederate soldiers were killed or wounded—casualties that rivaled in intensity the more famous World War II battles of Normandy and Iwo Jima.

In 1899, the United Daughters of the Confederacy erected a statue in the Franklin town center honoring the personal sacrifices made by Confederate soldiers. In 2017, local activists called for a reassessment of the appropriateness of the statue's presence. After much reasoned debate and consideration, representatives of the Fuller Story movement, the local history and preservation community, and the City of Franklin realized that removing the statue would effectively erase history, resulting in a "lesser story." Instead, it was realized that a fuller story would best tell Franklin's remarkable history.

Recognizing the wisdom and utility of Franklin, Tennessee's "Fuller Story" concept, the former Confederates featured in the following pages likewise have stories fuller than their lives in the four years of the American Civil War.

Part 1

United States Presidential Administrations

After the American Civil War, ten United States presidents appointed former Confederates to positions within the federal government.[1] In many cases, especially in the years immediately following the end of hostilities known as Reconstruction, the selections were made as part of the reintegration of Southerners into the federal government, and thus into American society.[2] After the first few presidential postwar administrations Southerners were assigned to important and influential positions, less for reasons of reintegration than because they were considered—to the extent that political appointments are supposed to be—worthy of holding the positions because of their own merit.

1 An eleventh president, Calvin Coolidge, retained a former Confederate in the U.S. diplomat corps.

2 The Reconstruction Era was a tumultuous political and cultural period after the Civil War—generally identified as the years between 1865 and 1877. During that time, the federal government and military authorities implemented control over conquered areas of the eleven states that had seceded to eventually form the Confederacy. Reconstruction included the formal abolition of slavery, the rebuilding and restoration of the local and state political structure of the Southern states, and the attempted transformation of the South from a slavery-based society to one of full civil rights and suffrage for freed slaves.

Ulysses S. Grant Administration

The restoration of Southerners into the federal government began during the administration of Ulysses S. Grant, the former commanding general of the United States Army and the man credited with organizing and leading the defeat of the South that brought an end to the Civil War in the spring of 1865. Hiram Ulysses Grant was born on April 27, 1822, in the Ohio River Valley hamlet of Point Pleasant, Ohio, and raised in nearby Georgetown.[3] The son of a tanner, Grant reluctantly enrolled at the U.S. Military Academy at West Point in 1839 and graduated in 1843 in the middle of his class—21st of 39 cadets.

He served in the U.S. Army during the Mexican War (1846-48) under General Zachary Taylor and alongside many officers who would later become generals in the Confederate Army, including Robert E. Lee, Thomas J. "Stonewall" Jackson, James Longstreet, Pierre Gustave Toutant Beauregard, Braxton Bragg, Joseph E. Johnston, Edmund Kirby Smith, Albert Sidney Johnston, and others. Although a quartermaster, Grant was twice promoted for "Gallant and Meritorious Conduct."

In 1848 Grant married Julia Dent, whose prominent slaveholding family

owned a large plantation in eastern Missouri. Julia's brother Frederick was a classmate of Grant's at West Point. After the Mexican War Grant served at Fort Humboldt, California, but resigned from the army in 1854 and returned to Missouri. After unsuccessful insurance and farming ventures he and Julia and their four children moved in 1860 to Galena, Illinois, where he worked for his father in a tannery and leather goods store.

At the outbreak of the Civil War, Grant returned to military service and in June

Ulysses S. Grant

LOC

---

3 Upon enrolling at West Point, Grant's name was mistakenly recorded as "Ulysses S. Grant," a name that he retained for the rest of his life. The initial "S" stands for no specific name.

1861 was appointed colonel of the 21st Illinois Infantry. His effective training techniques quickly organized the group of raucous recruits and by September Grant was a brigadier general of volunteers. In February 1862 he was promoted to major general and commanded Union forces at Forts Henry and Donelson, Shiloh, Corinth, and after several failed efforts, led in 1863 the bold and ultimately successful operation that captured Vicksburg and helped open the Mississippi River. Later that year Grant assumed command of federal forces partially besieged in Chattanooga, Tennessee, and scored victories there at Lookout Mountain and Missionary Ridge that drove the Confederate army back into North Georgia.

President Abraham Lincoln promoted Grant to the rank of lieutenant general in March 1864 and appointed him general in chief of the U.S. Army. Grant delegated command of Union forces in the Western Theater to his friend and former direct subordinate Major General William Tecumseh Sherman, who led the spring campaign into Georgia that eventually captured Atlanta in September. Sherman launched his March to the Sea two months later and captured Savannah, Georgia, and then moved north into the Carolinas, where he would accept the surrender of Joseph E. Johnston in late April 1865. Grant, meanwhile, accompanied George Meade's Army of the Potomac into the field in May of 1864 in its campaign against General Robert E. Lee's Army of Northern Virginia. A bloody series of battles collectively known as the Overland Campaign followed that carried Northern forces south to around Richmond and Petersburg. A nine-month siege followed. Both major cities fell in early April 1864, and Lee's exhausted army was pursued and overtaken at Appomattox, Virginia, where Lee surrendered on April 9. Although other Southern armies remained in the field, Lee's capitulation effectively ended Confederate hopes for independence. Grant's magnanimous terms of surrender offered various protections for the defeated Confederates and was widely recognized at the time as the beginning of postwar reconciliation.

President Lincoln was assassinated in Washington on April 14, 1865, and was succeeded by his vice president Andrew Johnson, a Southern Democrat from Tennessee. Late in Johnson's administration, Grant quarreled with the president and soon found himself aligned with the Radical Republicans.[4] As a national hero

---

4 The Radical Republicans were a powerful faction within the Republican Party from the mid-1850s until the end of the Reconstruction era. Before the Civil War, the Radical Republicans supported an immediate and complete abolition of slavery without compensation to slaveholders. During the war they demanded aggressive military force against the seceded states. After the war they pushed heavy-handed measures and urged complete control over the Southern political establishment and full civil rights and suffrage for freed slaves.

symbolic of the Union victory in the Civil War, Grant was nominated by the Republican Party and elected president in 1868. He was reelected in 1872.

The political, social, and cultural chaos of Reconstruction began under Andrew Johnson. Grant inherited the turmoil. When he was elected, the American people hoped for an end to the lingering troubles. Grant, however, was a military man and not a politician or bureaucrat. He struggled in his new role and often looked to Congress for help. Grant presided over the government much like he had commanded the army, and even brough with him to the White House part of his army staff. His friends in the Republican Party came to be known as "the Old Guard."

As is common with military men and women, Grant respected soldiers who served honorably, whether as former comrades or former foes. In fact, two of Grant's pallbearers were former Confederate generals Joseph E. Johnston and Simon Bolivar Buckner—the latter of whom had unconditionally surrendered to Grant at Fort Donelson, Tennessee, on February 16, 1862.

Grant entrusted former Confederates with important positions in his government, most prominently Amos Tappan Akerman as U.S. district attorney for Georgia in 1869, and in 1870 as U.S. attorney general. Akerman, a native of Portsmouth, New Hampshire, lived in Illinois and North Carolina after his graduation from Dartmouth College, and eventually settled in Elberton, Georgia. Although Akerman opposed secession, he enlisted in the Confederate Army at the start of hostilities and rose to the rank of colonel while serving under Brigadier General Robert Toombs.

Akerman assumed office on February 21, 1870, making him the first attorney general of the newly created United States Department of Justice. He was the first attorney general to hire full-time law enforcement officers, and he established an investigative unit that would, in 1908, become the Federal Bureau of Investigation.

Akerman had not been politically active before the Civil War but joined the Republican Party in 1866. Two years later he served as a delegate to the Georgia constitutional convention that guaranteed—in law, if not always in practice—equal political rights for former slaves.

As attorney general, Akerman drew the ire of railroad robber barons when he refused to grant federal land subsidy guarantees to the railroad companies until they had fulfilled their commitments. Akerman's most pressing problem, however, was the Ku Klux Klan's efforts to deny the newly granted civil rights of former slaves. He resented how casually some Southerners disobeyed new federal laws guaranteeing equal civil and political rights to blacks and whites, and as attorney general aggressively investigated and prosecuted members of the Klan. U. S. Grant

Amos Tappan Akerman

LOC

biographer William S. McFeely wrote of Akerman, "No attorney general since . . . has been more vigorous in the prosecution of cases designed to protect the lives and rights of black Americans." Akerman resigned his federal office in December 1871 and returned to Georgia, where he practiced law until his death on December 21, 1880.[5]

In addition to Akerman, Grant's Department of Justice appointed other former Confederates, including a former lieutenant in the 21st North Carolina Infantry named Thomas Settle, who in 1877 was appointed judge of the U.S. District Court for the Northern District of Florida. In 1875, Major General James Fleming Fagan was appointed as a U.S. marshal and, two years later, as receiver for the U.S. Department of the Interior's General Land Office (now known as the Bureau of Land Management). A native of Arkansas, Fagan had commanded Confederate brigades against Grant at the Battle of Shiloh and during the siege of Corinth.

Grant also appointed a former lieutenant in the 3rd Missouri Artillery Battalion named Thomas Benton Catron as territorial attorney general for New Mexico from 1869 to 1872. Grant later promoted Catron to U.S. district attorney for New Mexico. Catron was later elected mayor of Santa Fe, New Mexico, and represented the state in the U.S. House of Representatives and in the U.S. Senate.

* * *

---

5 Parker, David B. "Amos T. Akerman (1821-1880)," *New Georgia Encyclopedia*, October 28, 2019.

Grant was the first of several presidents to appoint or retain former Confederates as United States diplomats in his Department of State, where three of them would serve.

Before becoming a federal judge, Thomas Settle served as the U.S. ambassador to Peru in 1871. Darwin Ponton Fenner, a former Confederate surgeon in Eldridge's Louisiana Light Artillery Battery, served as the U.S. consul to Guatemala during Grant's administration. James Lawrence Orr, a prewar speaker of the U.S. House of Representatives and former colonel of the 1st South Carolina Rifles, was appointed as Grant's U.S. ambassador to Russia.

Another former Confederate who served the U.S. government after the war was President Jefferson Davis's private secretary Burton Norvell Harrison. Born in New Orleans in 1838, Harrison graduated from the University of Mississippi and from Yale University, where he was a member of the legendary Skull and Bones Society. After his graduation from Yale in 1859, Harrison taught mathematics at the University of Mississippi, and in 1862 joined the Washington (Louisiana) Artillery before being sent to the Confederate White House in Richmond to become Davis's personal secretary. Harrison was with Davis and his wife when they were captured by Union forces near Irwinville, Georgia, on May 10, 1865. Harrison was imprisoned at Fort Delaware, and after his release in 1866 moved to New York City and began practicing law. In 1872, he was appointed by President Grant as the U.S. envoy to the Dominican Republic. After his return, Harrison was named secretary and general counsel of the New York Rapid Transit Commission and became involved in national Democratic Party politics. Harrison was offered appointments as assistant U.S. secretary of state and U.S. ambassador to Italy by President Cleveland in 1893, but declined both positions. He died in Washington, D.C., in 1904.

Another former Confederate served as a diplomat—but not for the U.S. government. Lieutenant Colonel Paul Francis de Gournay was a French citizen who had spent his early adulthood as a manager of his family's sugar plantations in Cuba. In 1851, de Gournay fled the island nation during its bloody revolution and settled in New Orleans. At the outbreak of the Civil War, the dashing young Frenchman enlisted in the Confederate Army and quickly became a skilled artillerist. He rose in rank and responsibility to eventually command artillery batteries during the siege of Port Hudson in Louisiana, whose garrison finally surrendered to Union forces in July 1863 after Vicksburg had fallen. De Gournay remained a captive nearly a year and a half until December of 1864. After the war, de Gournay returned to France but was back in the United States by 1867, this time as French vice consul in Baltimore, Maryland. He served in that position until 1874.[6]

Rutherford B. Hayes Administration

Like his predecessor Ulysses S. Grant, the nineteenth president of the United States, Rutherford Birchard Hayes, was a former Union general and native Ohioan. Hayes ended Reconstruction and continued Grant's efforts toward national reconciliation and unity. He also instituted civil service reforms intended to end political patronage appointments in favor of qualified and experienced applicants.

Hayes was born in Delaware, Ohio, in 1822, was educated at Kenyon College, and studied law at Harvard University, where he received his degree in 1845. He practiced in Lower Sandusky, Ohio, until 1849 and moved to Cincinnati, where his law practice flourished. Hayes, who opposed slavery, was active in the Whig Party, which was the predecessor of the Republican Party.

Influenced by the deep religious convictions and abolitionist sentiments of his wife, the former Lucy Webb, Hayes volunteered for the Union Army at the outbreak of the war, was commissioned as a major, and placed in command of the 23rd Ohio Infantry Regiment. Hayes saw significant action during the war and was seriously wounded on September 14, 1862, at the Battle of South Mountain. In 1864, Republicans in Cincinnati nominated Hayes for the U.S. House of Representatives. Despite his refusal to campaign, he won the election while still serving in the field and refused to take his seat in Congress until the war ended. "Any officer fit for duty who at this crisis would abandon his post . . . ought to be scalped," scoffed Hayes. When he eventually entered Congress in December 1865, he expressed concern over "Rebel influences . . . ruling the White House" of President Andrew Johnson, Lincoln's successor.[7]

Hayes served two terms in Congress and three terms as governor of Ohio before gaining the Republican nomination for president in 1876 after proclaiming that, if elected, he would serve only one term. The Democratic Party nominated Governor Samuel J. Tilden of New York, and even though an array of famous

6 Joslyn, Mauriel, "Well-born Lt. Col. Paul Francois de Gournay was the South's adopted 'marquis in gray'", *America's Civil War*, September 1995, p. 8, 85-88.

7 Rutherford B. Hayes. (n.d.). Retrieved from http://ohiohistorycentral.org/w/Rutherford_B_Hayes.

Rutherford B. Hayes

LOC

Republicans—including Mark Twain—campaigned for Hayes, he was not expected to win. The election was extremely close, with Tilden leading by a comfortable majority of the popular vote. After four months of uncertainty and the appointment of a special electoral commission made up of eight Republicans and six Democrats, Hayes was declared the victor with 185 electoral votes to Tilden's 184. The tension surrounding the election was so high that Hayes secretly took the oath of office on March 3, 1877, inside the White House.

Hayes brought honesty and integrity to the presidency, but during the campaign and contentious post-election period, Northern Republicans had promised Southern Democrats federal infrastructure subsidies, the withdrawal of federal troops Grant had sent into Louisiana and South Carolina to quell civil unrest, and a cabinet post for a Southerner. Hayes wrote in his diary on February 17, 1877, "I should like to get support from good men of the South, late Rebels. How to do it is the question. I have the best disposition towards the Southern people, Rebels and all."[8]

Hayes based his appointments on merit rather than political favoritism. He selected men of high character and ability for his cabinet, but he angered many Republicans by appointing ex-Confederates to high government positions.

Hayes also advocated for African-American rights in the South while seeking the restoration of "wise, honest, and peaceful local self-government" in the former Confederate states. He withdrew troops from those states and hoped conciliatory policies would help establish a "new Republican party" in the South, winning the support of white businessmen and conservatives.[9]

8 Ibid.

9 Ibid.

Some Southern leaders embraced conservative Republican economic policies, but in return faced rejection at the polls if they joined the widely despised party of Reconstruction. Notwithstanding Hayes's efforts, the Democrats retained their domination over Southern government offices and institutions throughout his presidential term. As promised, after his single term in office Hayes retired and returned to his home in Fremont, Ohio, where he died in 1893.

During his presidency Hayes fulfilled a campaign commitment by appointing Greeneville, Tennessee, native David McKendree Key as U.S. postmaster general. Hayes explained in his diary: "I could appoint a Southern Democrat in the Cabinet. But who would take it among the capable and influential good men of those States? General Joseph E. Johnston occurs to me." Hayes briefly considered the popular former Confederate general for secretary of war, and more seriously for secretary of the interior. "General Johnston's [postwar] character and conduct was patriotic and upright, but that some of his associations and connections were such that it might be embarrassing to him and to me to offer him a place." Anticipating opposition from fellow Republicans if Johnston joined his cabinet, Hayes instead chose Key, a less prominent Confederate.[10]

Key had actively opposed secession but remained loyal to his state once it joined the Confederacy. In 1861 he was commissioned an officer in the 43rd Tennessee Infantry and eventually reached the rank of lieutenant colonel.

After the war Key advocated reconciliation and worked to heal sectional strife. He served as postmaster general from 1877 to 1880, when he was appointed by Hayes as judge of the U.S. District Court for the Middle District of Tennessee and the U.S. District Court for the Eastern District of Tennessee, where he served until his retirement in 1894.

David McKendree Key

LOC

10 Ibid.

On the domestic front, in 1879 the Hayes administration created the Mississippi River Commission as a division of the U.S. Department of War. The commission was tasked with managing the Mississippi River watersheds for the purpose of enhancing navigation and controlling flooding. One of the members of the first Board of United States Engineers for that commission was Paul Octave Hebert, a former Confederate brigadier general. Hebert was a prominent postwar civil engineer in New Orleans and a member of the Louisiana Board of State Engineers. He served only one year in the new federal position before dying in 1880.

James Longstreet was the highest-profile former Confederate to become part of the Hayes administration. The native of South Carolina and ex-lieutenant general and corps commander in Robert E. Lee's Army of Northern Virginia was appointed to the important position of U.S. ambassador to the Ottoman Empire. At its height in the sixteenth and seventeenth centuries the empire encompassed much of northern Africa, the Middle East, the Arabian Peninsula, and southeastern Europe. Although significantly reduced in size by the second half of the nineteenth century, it still included present-day Turkey, Iraq, Syria, Kuwait, Lebanon, Jordan, Israel, and Palestinian-administered territories, as well as portions of the Arabian peninsula. After a year of service as a diplomat Longstreet returned to the United States and was appointed a U.S. Marshal from 1881 until 1883. After several years of semi-retirement Longstreet returned to public service in 1898 as the United

States commissioner of railroads in William McKinley's administration.

Another renowned Confederate appointed by Hayes was Colonel John Singleton Mosby, a Virginia native and former leader of one of the most famous Confederate military units: the 43rd Battalion Virginia Cavalry. Better known as Mosby's Rangers, the battalion was a partisan cavalry regiment that operated in northern Virginia, independent of the central Confederate Army command. Mosby received his postwar pardon

James Longstreet

John Singleton Mosby

LOC

personally from President Grant, who wrote of Mosby in his memoirs, "Since the close of the war, I have come to know Colonel Mosby personally and somewhat intimately. He is a different man entirely from what I supposed . . . He is able and thoroughly honest and truthful."[11]

"War loses a great deal of its romance after a soldier has seen his first battle," wrote Mosby in 1887. "I have a more vivid recollection of the first than the last one I was in. It is a classical maxim that it is sweet and becoming to die for one's country; but whoever has seen the horrors of the battlefield feels that it is far sweeter to live for it."[12]

And live for his country he did. In addition to winning Grant's personal respect, Mosby earned the confidence of succeeding presidents Hayes, Garfield, and Arthur by serving in the important position of consul to Hong Kong, where Mosby exposed corruption and advocated and protected United States interests on the other side of the globe. After his service in China, Mosby served in a number of federal government positions under presidents McKinley and Theodore Roosevelt by representing the interests of the Department of the Interior and Department of Justice, mainly in the western United States.

Joining Longstreet and Mosby as former Confederates in the United States diplomatic corps was North Carolina native Henry Washington Hilliard, former colonel and commander of Hilliard's Alabama Legion. Hilliard organized a five-battalion, 3,000-man infantry and cavalry corps in Montgomery, Alabama, in June 1862. The cavalry battalion later became part of the 10th Tennessee Cavalry

---

11 Ulysses S. Grant Quotes (Author of Personal Memoirs) (page 4 of 6). (n.d.). Retrieved from https://www.goodreads.com/author/quotes/6926.Ulysses_S_Grant?page=4.

12 John S. Mosby Quotes (Author of The Memoirs of Colonel John S. Mosby). (n.d.). Retrieved from https://www.goodreads.com/author/quotes/7324186.John_S_Mosby.

Regiment. After the war Hilliard practiced law in Georgia and in 1877 was appointed by Hayes as U.S. ambassador to Brazil.

Edwin Harvie Smith was yet another former Confederate appointed by Hayes as U.S. consul, this time to Naples, Italy. A lifelong resident of Virginia, Smith was a surgeon at Chimborazo Hospital in Richmond from 1861 until the end of the war, attaining the position of surgeon in charge of Chimborazo Hospital Number Three.

Former Confederate foreign agent Jose Agustin Quintero served as a diplomat during the Hayes administration, but not as a representative of the United States. Instead, Quintero served on behalf of Belgium and Costa Rica as consul to New Orleans. The former agent was born in Havana, Cuba, became a lawyer, and as an opponent of Spanish colonial rule was condemned to death and escaped to the United States. At the outbreak of the Civil War he enlisted in the Quitman Rifles of Austin, Texas, but was soon sent to Mexico by President Davis to spy and establish covert supply routes via Mexico on behalf of the Confederacy.

Arguably, Hayes's most important (and enduring) appointment was that of Stanford Emerson Chaille, the surgeon general of Louisiana in 1862 and medical director of the Confederate Army of Mississippi. Known as the "Father of Hygiene and Health Education," Chaille was appointed by Hayes as chairman of the Havana Yellow Fever Commission, created to study the disease following the deadly 1878 yellow fever epidemic in the lower Mississippi Valley and New Orleans. Chaille's bacterial studies of the blood of yellow fever victims led to the eventual discovery of the *Aedes aegypti* mosquito as the carrier of the plague-like disease.

Chaille advocated for the establishment of community sanitary and sewage drainage systems, water purification, and mosquito control, and was instrumental in the creation of the National Board of Health, which later became the U.S. Department of Health, Education, and Welfare.

Another Hayes appointee who served in the Confederate Army was Colonel William Henry Hunt of the 1st Louisiana Militia. Hayes appointed Hunt to a relatively obscure position as a judge of the United States Court of Claims in May 1878, a move that enhanced Hunt's visibility such that he was tapped by President Garfield to serve as the ambassador to Russia and as secretary of the U. S. Navy.

James A. Garfield Administration

The last of the seven plebeian "log cabin presidents," James Abram Garfield was the twentieth president of the United States. He was elected in 1880 after serving nine terms as a member of the House of Representatives from Ohio. His brief but influential presidency was cut short when he was struck down by an assassin's bullet only 120 days into his term. He died on September 19, 1881.

Garfield was born in Cuyahoga County, Ohio, in 1831. The fatherless youth worked on the Erie Canal and earned enough money for a formal education. He graduated from Williams College in Massachusetts in 1856 and returned to Ohio, where he taught classical languages at Western Reserve Eclectic Institute (later Hiram College). Within a year he was the president of the institution.

Although Garfield studied law and was an ordained minister, he decided politics was his calling. In 1859 he was elected to the Ohio state senate as a Republican. He opposed the expansion of slavery and during the secession crisis argued for coercing the seceding states back into the Union.

With the outbreak of the Civil War, Garfield helped recruit the 42nd Ohio Infantry and became its commander with the rank of lieutenant colonel. The staunch abolitionist was an early advocate of the same harsh warfare against the Southern homeland later infamously waged by Union generals William T. Sherman and Philip Sheridan. After serving as a brigade commander at the Battle of Middle Creek, Kentucky, in January 1862, Garfield was promoted to brigadier general and commanded a brigade at the Battle of Shiloh in April 1862. He served as General William Rosecrans' chief of staff, and after the disastrous Battle of Chickamauga in September 1863 was ordered to report to Washington, D.C. He eventually was promoted to the rank of major general.

In October 1862, Ohioans had elected Garfield to the U.S. House of Representatives while he was still serving in the army. President Lincoln sought aggressive and effective Republicans for Congress and persuaded Garfield to resign his commission. In December 1863 he was seated as the representative of Ohio's 19th District. Garfield was reelected several times and served for 18 years, during which he became one of the leading Republicans in the House of Representatives.

James Abram Garfield

LOC

Garfield worked unsuccessfully to secure the presidential nomination for John Sherman at the 1880 Republican convention, and eventually Garfield himself became the party's nominee on the 36th ballot. He defeated Democratic nominee and fellow Union war hero General Winfield Scott in the general election by a margin of only 10,000 popular votes, and was inaugurated president on March 4, 1881. As president, Garfield fought political corruption and rampant political patronage. During his short presidency his administration won back much of the prestige the office had lost during the Reconstruction era.

Garfield was en route to deliver a speech at his alma mater Williams College on July 2, 1881, when he was shot in a railroad station in Washington, D.C. by Charles Guiteau, a deranged lawyer who had unsuccessfully sought a consular position in Paris, France. The mortally wounded Garfield lingered for several weeks. He was treated by inventor Alexander Graham Bell, who tried but failed to locate the bullet with an electrical detection device of his own design. Garfield was taken to the New Jersey seaside in the late summer and seemed to be improving. He took a turn for the worse and died from an infection and internal hemorrhage on September 19.

Among Garfield's appointees was self-described Southern unionist William Henry Hunt, a former Hayes appointment as judge of the U.S. Court of Claims. Hunt became U.S. secretary of the navy on March 5, 1881, and served into the Chester A. Arthur administration until April 7, 1882, at which time he was appointed U.S. ambassador to Russia.

Hunt was born in Charleston, South Carolina, on June 12, 1823. His father, Thomas Hunt, died in 1832, after which his mother moved with her seven children to New Haven, Connecticut. In 1839, the Hunt family moved to New Orleans, but William remained in New Haven and enrolled at Yale University. In his third year he was forced to withdraw from school due because of a lack of finances, but he eventually completed his studies and entered Yale's law school. Financial burdens again interrupted his education and he rejoined his family in New Orleans. William's brothers were prominent young attorneys in the Crescent City and he resumed his law studies with them. He was admitted to the Louisiana bar in 1874 and successfully practiced law in New Orleans until May 15, 1878, when he was appointed by President Hayes as an associate judge, a position he held until he was appointed secretary of the navy by Garfield in 1881. Hunt was serving as ambassador in Russia when he died in St. Petersburg in 1884.

After his election Garfield retained former Confederate Colonel John Singleton Mosby as U.S. consul to Hong Kong, and appointed former Confederate General George Earl Maney to a diplomatic post.

William Henry Hunt

LOC

Maney was born in Franklin, Tennessee, and served as a brigadier general in the Army of Tennessee. After the war he returned to his home state and served for nine years as president of the Tennessee and Pacific Railroad. Unlike most former Confederates, Maney joined the Republican Party and was active in Tennessee politics during Reconstruction. He is credited with having nurtured reconciliation and improving relations between former enemies.

Maney's aptitude in cultivating reconciliation between former enemies earned him the respect of federal authorities. He was appointed by presidents Garfield, Arthur, Cleveland, and Harrison to diplomatic posts, including ambassador to Colombia (1881-82), ambassador and consul general to Bolivia (1882-83), and ambassador to Uruguay and Paraguay (1884-88).

Chester A. Arthur Administration

Vice President Chester Arthur became America's twenty-first president when James Garfield died, serving from 1881 to 1885. He was born in Fairfield, Vermont, in 1829, the son of an Irish-born Baptist minister. Arthur graduated from Union College in 1848, taught school, and, after gaining admission to the New York bar, opened a successful law practice in New York City. Arthur was a U.S. Army veteran, but had served in quartermaster and administrative positions in New York and elsewhere, far away from the front.

Arthur's father was a staunch abolitionist, but in 1859 Chester married Ellen Lewis Herndon, the daughter of a prominent Virginia slave- owning family. Ellen's father, Commander William Lewis Herndon, was a naval captain best known for heroically saving 150 women and children from his doomed ship S.S. *Central America*. He was unable to save himself, however, and died with 400 passengers when the ship sank in a storm near Cape Hatteras, North Carolina. (The *Central America*, which went down with 30,000 pounds of gold coins and ingots, was located in 1988 and has been the subject of salvage lawsuits ever since. Its sinking helped trigger the Panic of 1857.) Herndon was a relative of famed scientist Captain Matthew Fontaine Maury, known as the Father of Modern Oceanography and Naval Meteorology who served in the U.S. Navy before resigning and joining the Confederate Navy at the outbreak of the Civil War.

Although Arthur's predecessor James Garfield had appointed a former Confederate Army officer as secretary of the navy, and his successor Grover Cleveland named several former Confederates to federal positions, Arthur appointed or retained only a few of his former enemies. Garfield's navy secretary, ex-Confederate Colonel William H. Hunt, served only briefly in the Arthur administration before resigning to become the U.S. ambassador to Russia in April 1882. John Singleton Mosby, who as earlier noted had been U.S. consul to Hong Kong in the Hayes and Garfield administrations and remained in the diplomat corps of the Arthur administration, was offered the more important consulship in Shanghai by Arthur. Mosby declined, preferring instead to remain in Hong Kong. Another prior appointee, George Earl Maney, retained his position as ambassador to Columbia and later was appointed by Arthur as ambassador and consul general to Bolivia in 1883.

George Washington Carter, former colonel of the 21st Texas Cavalry Regiment, was appointed by Arthur as ambassador to Venezuela in 1881. Before his diplomatic career, Carter had been speaker of the Louisiana House of Representatives.

Arthur appointed former Brigadier General Francis "Frank" Crawford Armstrong as U.S. Indian inspector in 1885. The ex-Confederate cavalry commander would later serve as U.S. assistant U.S. Commissioner of Indian affairs in the Benjamin Harrison administration. Armstrong's interesting military life began in the Choctaw Agency of present-day Oklahoma as the son of a U.S. Army officer stationed there. Armstrong enlisted in the army and eventually achieved the rank of captain. He led a Union cavalry company at First Bull Run (First Manassas) before resigning his commission and joining the Confederate Army. He served as a staff officer for Confederate generals Benjamin McCulloch and James McIntosh before their deaths at the Battle of Pea Ridge, Arkansas, in March 1862. In 1863, Armstrong was promoted to brigadier general and was transferred from the Trans-Mississippi Department to the Army of Tennessee, where he served at Chickamauga, in the Atlanta Campaign, and in Hood's Tennessee Campaign. Armstrong was captured at Selma, Alabama, shortly before the end of the war.

Former Confederate Colonel Alexander Robinson Boteler, who had served on the staffs of generals Robert E. Lee, Thomas J. "Stonewall" Jackson, and J.E.B Stuart, was appointed by President Arthur to serve on the U.S. Tariff Commission. In 1871 Boteler had co-founded Shepherd College (later Shepherd University) in Shepherdstown, West Virginia.

Grover Cleveland Administrations

Stephen Grover Cleveland was a man of firsts: he was the first Democrat elected president of the United States after the Civil War, the first presidential candidate to win the popular vote three times, and the first and only president to serve two non-concurrent terms in office. Cleveland won the presidency in the 1884 and 1892 elections to become the twenty-second and twenty-fourth president of the United States.

Cleveland was born in New Jersey in 1837 and was raised in upstate New York. His father, Richard Falley Cleveland, was a Presbyterian minister and the great grandson of a Revolutionary War veteran. Grover Cleveland did not attend college. Instead, he studied law as a clerk in a firm in Buffalo, New York, and passed the New York bar exam in 1859.

Cleveland was assistant district attorney of Erie County, New York, in 1863 when Congress passed the Conscription Act, which required all able-bodied men of a certain age to either enlist in the army or provide a substitute in their stead. Cleveland chose the latter course and paid a recent Polish immigrant to serve in his stead—a relatively common practice in the North during the Civil War. Cleveland carved out a successful career as a lawyer and soon entered politics. He was elected sheriff of Erie County, mayor of Buffalo, and in 1882, governor of New York.

Cleveland won the presidency in 1884 and immediately adopted a policy of making political appointments and granting civil service positions based on merit rather than favoritism. In fact, when he took office Cleveland—a Democrat— announced that all Republicans working for the federal government would be retained provided they were performing their jobs well, and that no Democrat would be hired or appointed solely on the basis of party affiliation. Cleveland, a fiercely independent fiscal conservative, vigorously opposed favors to special interest groups including the powerful Grand Army of the Republic and its push to expand pension availability to Civil War veterans for disabilities not related to military service.[13] One notable instance in which Cleveland boldly used his veto power involved a bill to provide federal aid to drought-stricken Texas farmers. "Federal aid in such cases encourages the expectation of paternal care on the part of the Government," complained Cleveland, "and weakens the sturdiness of our national character."[14]

Cleveland also demonstrated his independence when he signed the Interstate Commerce Act in 1887, the first law to attempt federal regulation of the railroads—a move that angered the powerful owners of the lines. When cautioned during the presidential campaign of 1888 that he was making politically unwise decisions, Cleveland shot back, "What is the use of being elected or reelected unless you stand for something?"[15] He was defeated in his bid for reelection but won the popular vote. He returned to the White House by winning the presidency once more in 1892.

Cleveland faced the challenges of a deep economic depression during his second term, but still retained his independent streak. When striking railroad workers in Chicago violated a court injunction, Cleveland sent in federal troops, proclaiming, "If it takes the entire army and navy of the United States to deliver a post card in Chicago, that card will be delivered."[16]

Neither Cleveland nor his wife had ancestral connections to the South, but he nonetheless appointed more former Confederates to his administrations than any of the other ten U.S. presidents who did so. He was the first Democrat elected to the presidency after the Civil War, and that doubtless was the major factor in his appointment of Southern Democrats. According to his biographer Allan Nevins, the Southerners who were strong candidates for Cleveland's cabinet were limited to Lucius Q. C. Lamar of Mississippi, North Carolinian Matt W. Ransom, Joseph E. Brown of Georgia, South Carolinian Wade Hampton, Isham G. Harris of Tennessee, Arkansan Augustus H. Garland, and George Vest of Missouri. All of them were U.S. senators, and because the Democratic Party could not afford to risk

13 The Grand Army of the Republic, founded in 1866, was a fraternal organization of Union veterans of the Civil War. It was the counterpart to the United Confederate Veterans.

14 Dems and the 2nd Amendment: Why Repeal What You Already Ignore? (n.d.). Retrieved from www.americanthinker.com/articles/2018/03/dems_and_the_2nd_amendment_why_repeal_what_you_already_ignore.html.

15 Ibid.

16 Ibid.

Lucius Quintus Cincinnatus Lamar II

LOC

losing so many Senate seats, only Lamar and Garland were named to Cleveland's initial cabinet.

The most prominent Confederate appointed by Cleveland was the nobly named Lucius Quintus Cincinnatus Lamar II. A nephew of Mirabeau Buonaparte Lamar, the second president of the Republic of Texas, Lamar was born in Putnam County, Georgia, in 1825, graduated from Emory College (later Emory University) in 1845, and after studying law for two years in Macon, Georgia, was admitted to the Georgia bar in 1847. Lamar moved to Oxford, Mississippi, in 1849 to practice law, and briefly taught mathematics at the University of Mississippi. In 1852 he returned to Georgia, where he practiced law in the city of Covington until 1855, at which time he returned to Mississippi, which he then made his permanent home.

Lamar's remarkable political career began with his election to the U.S. House of Representatives from Mississippi in 1856, where he served until his resignation in December 1860 to become a delegate to the Mississippi Secession Convention. Lamar authored the state's Ordinance of Secession. After Mississippi joined the new Confederacy on January 9, 1861, he proclaimed, "Thank God we have a country at last; to live for, to pray for, and if need be, to die for."[17]

With his law partner Christopher H. Mott, Lamar raised and funded the 19th Mississippi Infantry and was commissioned its lieutenant colonel. In the spring of 1862 Lamar was stricken with vertigo and resigned his commission, but later served briefly with the Confederate Army as a judge advocate and a staff member of his wife's cousin, Lieutenant General James Longstreet. In late 1862 Lamar was

17 *The Civil War*, a film by Ken Burns, narrated by David McCullough, PBS DVD Gold edition DVD, Warner Home Video, 2002.

appointed by the Confederate government as ambassador to Russia and special envoy to France and Great Britain.

After the war Lamar returned to the University of Mississippi and taught metaphysics, social science, and law. With his United States citizenship and civil rights restored, Lamar resumed his robust political and public service career, serving two terms each in the U.S. House of Representatives and the U.S. Senate. His second Senate term was cut short by his appointment as U.S. secretary of the interior by Cleveland on March 6, 1885. When Lamar moved to Washington, D.C., to administer the Interior Department, he took with him former Confederate Major Sidney Alroy Jonas to serve as clerk. Jonas, a Jewish Confederate, served on the staff of Confederate Lieutenant General Stephen D. Lee.

Appointed to the Interior Department with Lamar was another former Confederate named Henry Lowndes Muldrow, who had been colonel of the 11th Mississippi Cavalry Regiment. Muldrow was a member of the U.S. House of Representatives from Mississippi and was appointed to serve with Lamar as first assistant secretary of the interior.

Lamar's tenure as secretary of the interior ended on December 6, 1887, when he was chosen by Cleveland to be an associate justice of the Supreme Court of the United States. Lamar was confirmed by the Senate on January 6, 1888, and became the first Supreme Court justice from a former Confederate state. He served on the high court until his death five years later.

Lamar was featured in John F. Kennedy's 1957 Pulitzer Prize-winning book *Profiles in Courage*, which examined Lamar's unpopular vote against the Bland-Allison Act of 1878.[18] Lamar's service as secretary of the interior was honored when the East Fork of the Yellowstone River in Yellowstone National Park was named the Lamar River, and a portion of the park itself was named Lamar Valley.

President Cleveland also appointed former Confederate John Carmichael as inspector of surveyors-general for the United States Land Office. In May 1898, Carmichael was commissioned a captain of U. S. Volunteers in the buildup to the Spanish-American War. The native of Augusta, Georgia, was a cadet at the Virginia Military Institute (VMI) during the Civil War. To his everlasting regret, he was assigned to guard duty on May 15, 1864, and missed the Battle of New Market,

---

18 The Bland-Allison Act of 1878 was a law that required the U.S. Treasury Department to purchase silver and place a certain amount of silver dollars into circulation.

Edward Douglass White

LOC

where VMI cadets earned everlasting fame. In late 1864 Carmichael returned to Georgia and was commissioned a lieutenant of a state militia regiment.[19]

During his second term, Cleveland named another former Confederate to the Supreme Court when on February 19, 1894 he appointed Edward Douglass White as an associate justice. White would be elevated to chief justice in 1910 by President Taft.

White was born near Thibodaux, Louisiana, on November 3, 1845, and was educated at the Jesuit School in New Orleans before attending Mount St. Mary's College in Emmitsburg, Maryland, and Georgetown College (later Georgetown University) in Washington, D.C. At the outbreak of the Civil War White withdrew from Georgetown and enlisted in the 9th Louisiana Cavalry Regiment with the rank of lieutenant. He served throughout the war, saw significant action, and was captured on March 12, 1865 shortly before the end of hostilities.

After the war White studied law at the University of Louisiana (now Tulane University Law School) and began a law practice in New Orleans in 1868. He served in the Louisiana State Senate and on the Louisiana Supreme Court before his selection to the U.S. Senate in 1891. Justice White served on the high court until his death on May 19, 1921.

---

19 The VMI cadet corps marched off campus three times during the Civil War, but only once entered battle as a unit. On May 15, 1864, in the Confederate victory at New Market, Virginia, where ten cadets were killed and 47 were wounded. One month later the campus was evacuated and the cadets joined Lt. Gen. Jubal Early's army in Lynchburg. Thereafter the cadets were transferred to Richmond, where they participated in the defense of the city until its surrender during the closing days of the war. For more on the role of the cadets at New Market, see Charles R. Knight, *Valley Thunder: The Battle of New Market and the Opening of the Shenandoah Valley Campaign, May 15, 1864* (Savas Beatie, 2018).

Hilary Abner Herbert

LOC

Cleveland called upon yet another former Confederate, Hilary Abner Herbert, to serve as secretary of the navy in 1893. Herbert, a native of Laurens, South Carolina, was colonel of the 8th Alabama Infantry before being discharged as a result of a serious wound sustained at the Battle of the Wilderness in early May of 1864.

After the war Herbert practiced law in Montgomery, Alabama, and was elected to the U.S. House of Representatives in 1877, where he served eight consecutive terms. During his tenure he was a member of the Ways and Means Committee and chaired the Committee on Naval Affairs for six years. He was largely responsible for the increased appropriations that modernized and expanded the U.S. Navy. After his appointment as navy secretary in 1893 Herbert persuaded a reluctant Congress to fund the expansion despite the Panic of 1893 and a severe economic depression that lasted from 1893 to 1897, which spanned Herbert's entire term.

Herbert returned to private life in 1897 and practiced law in Washington until his death on March 6, 1919. The USS *Herbert* (DD-160), a Wickes class destroyer that saw extensive duty during World War II, was named in his honor.

Augustus Hill Garland was another former Confederate appointed by Cleveland as attorney general of the United States, one of the most powerful positions in the U.S. government, on March 9, 1885. His journey to that esteemed post was a long one.

Garland was born in Covington, Tennessee, on June 11, 1832. He attended St. Mary's College in Lebanon, Tennessee, graduated from St. Joseph's College in Bardstown, Kentucky, and studied law in Washington, Arkansas. He began his legal career in 1853 as an attorney in Little Rock. As the sectional crisis unfolded Garland made it clear that he opposed secession and argued in favor of Arkansas' continued allegiance to the United States. However, after Abraham Lincoln called for 75,000 volunteers to suppress the Southern rebellion, Garland changed his position and supported secession.

Augustus Hill Garland

LOC

Garland's reluctant backing of secession may have contributed to his decision not to enter the Confederate military. Instead, he followed a political path and served in the Confederate House of Representatives, and in late 1864 was elected to the Confederate Senate. Anticipating the imminent fall of the Confederacy, he returned to Arkansas in February 1865 to help guide the state through the defeat and prepare it to rejoin the Union.

Garland's political career did not end with the war. He served as governor of Arkansas from 1874 to 1877 and was a strong supporter of education, especially for former slaves and for the blind and the deaf. His pressure on the Arkansas legislature earned him recognition as a founder of the Branch Normal College (now the University of Arkansas at Pine Bluff), an institution established so that African-Americans had access to higher education.

In 1876 Garland was elected to the U.S. Senate and served in that office until 1885, when he accepted the position as Cleveland's attorney general. When Cleveland lost the 1888 election Garland returned to the practice of law. He suffered a stroke and died while arguing a case before the Supreme Court on January 26, 1899.

Two other former Confederates held one of the highest positions in the U.S. Department of Justice. The important yet obscure office of solicitor general was once held by ex-Rebels John Goode and Holmes Conrad. "The task of the Office of the Solicitor General," explains the Department of Justice's website,

> is to supervise and conduct government litigation in the United States Supreme Court. Virtually all such litigation is channeled through the Office of the Solicitor General and is actively conducted by the Office. The United States is involved in approximately two thirds of all the cases the U.S. Supreme Court decides on the merits each year.
>
> The Solicitor General determines the cases in which Supreme Court review will be sought by the government and the positions the government will take before the Court . . .

The Solicitor General conducts the oral arguments before the Supreme Court. Those cases not argued by the Solicitor General personally are assigned either to an Assistant to the Solicitor General or to another government attorney. The vast majority of government cases are argued by the Solicitor General or one of the office attorneys.

Another responsibility of the Office is to review all cases decided adversely to the government in the lower courts to determine whether they should be appealed and, if so, what position should be taken. Moreover, the Solicitor General determines whether the government will participate or intervene, in cases in any appellate court.

Later solicitors general included future president William Howard Taft and Supreme Court justices Thurgood Marshall and Elena Kagan (who sits on the court as of this writing).

John Goode was the third U.S. solicitor general. He had served two terms in the Confederate Congress and as an aide on the staff of General Jubal Early. A native Virginian, Goode graduated from Emory and Henry College in 1848 and was admitted to the Virginia state bar in 1851. After the war ended Goode lived in Norfolk, Virginia, and practiced law in Washington, D.C. He was elected to the U.S. House of Representatives and served from 1875 until 1881, and was appointed solicitor general in May of 1885. He remained in that office until August 1886.

Confederate veteran Holmes Conrad was appointed by President Cleveland as

assistant attorney general of the United States in 1893. Two years later Conrad, who had served as a staff officer with the rank of major for Confederate Brig. Gen. Thomas L. Rosser, became solicitor general.

Conrad was born in Winchester, Virginia, and attended VMI and the University of Virginia before enlisting as a private in the 1st Virginia Cavalry at the outbreak of the Civil War. He quickly rose in rank to major and assistant inspector

John Goode

LOC

general of Rosser's cavalry division and served until the end of the war.

In 1865 Conrad began to study law and was admitted to the Virginia bar in 1866. Twelve years later he was elected to the Virginia legislature and over the next several years became a leader in the Virginia Democratic Party.

After leaving the office of solicitor general, Conrad was retained by President William McKinley in 1897 to represent the federal government in litigation, and he was again retained as a prosecutor in 1904 by the Theodore Roosevelt administration to handle major postal fraud cases.

Cleveland selected another former Confederate as United States postmaster general. William Lyne Wilson, who served as a priviate in the 12th Virginia Cavalry, was appointed to the position in 1895 and served until 1897, at which time he accepted the presidency of Washington and Lee University. Wilson also served briefly as president of West Virginia University (1882 to 1883) and was elected to five consecutive terms as a member of the U.S. House of Representatives from West Virginia. Wilson also was a member of the board of regents of the Smithsonian Institution. The well-traveled Wilson was born in Charles Town, Virginia (now West Virginia), in 1843 and studied at Columbian University (now George Washington University) in Washington, D.C., as well as the University of Virginia.

Erskine Mayo Ross, another former Southern soldier called upon by Cleveland to serve in the U.S. Department of Justice, was named judge for the Southern District of California in 1887. In 1895, Cleveland selected Ross as judge for the newly created U.S. Court of Appeals for the Ninth Circuit, where he served until 1925. Before his federal judicial appointments Ross sat as a justice on the California Supreme Court.

Ross, a native of Culpeper County, Virginia, had been a cadet sergeant at VMI, served in Richmond and at the Battle of Cedar Mountain on August 9, 1862, and took part in the Confederate victory at New Market. After the war Ross moved to

Erskine Mayo Ross

LOC

California, practiced law in Los Angeles, and was elected a circuit judge. According to a published account, during an anti-Chinese riot in Los Angeles on October 24, 1871, Judge Ross, "[w]ith drawn revolver . . . quelled a murderous and incendiary mob." Ross was the nephew of former Confederate soldier Cameron Erskine Thom, who was mayor of Los Angeles from 1884 to 1886.

Another ex-Confederate appointed by Cleveland was Hamilton Chamberlain Jones Jr., formerly colonel of the 57th North Carolina Infantry. Jones became U.S. district attorney for the Western District of North Carolina in 1885.

In 1887, Cleveland appointed Charles Henry Simonton, a former colonel of the 25th South Carolina Infantry, as a U.S. district judge in Charleston, South Carolina. Six years later Cleveland elevated Simonton to the U.S. Court of Appeals for the Fourth District, where he served until his retirement in 1904.

The same year Simonton was made a district judge Cleveland appointed Harry Theophilus Toulmin as a U.S. district judge for the Southern District of Alabama. Toulmin had been a member of the 22nd Alabama Infantry during the Civil War and had achieved the rank of colonel.

The Cleveland administration's Department of State welcomed its first former Confederate with the appointment of James Davis Porter as assistant U.S. secretary of state in 1885. Porter was born in Paris, Tennessee, in 1828, graduated from the University of Nashville (later incorporated into Vanderbilt University) in 1846, studied law, and was admitted to the Tennessee bar five years later. After Tennessee seceded from the Union, Porter organized Confederate troops, received a commission as a lieutenant colonel and served as Major General Benjamin F. Cheatham's chief of staff until the end of the war.

After the war Porter resumed his law practice and was elected to various local and state offices, including two terms as Tennessee's governor. From 1880 to 1884 he served as president of the Nashville, Chattanooga, and St. Louis Railroad before accepting President Cleveland's appointment as assistant secretary of state. During Cleveland's second administration Porter was called upon once again and accepted the position as ambassador to Chile in 1893.

Samuel D. Shannon, a native of South Carolina and a captain on the staff of General Robert H. Anderson was appointed by Cleveland as secretary of state of the Wyoming Territory, and served in that capacity from 1887 to 1889.

Former Confederates were entrusted with several ambassadorships and consulships during Cleveland's two administrations. Confederate Major Thomas B. Ferguson of Ferguson's Battery, South Carolina Light Artillery, served in the Department of State as U.S. ambassador to Norway-Sweden from 1894 to 1898. Ferguson, a cadet at the Citadel, was serving as an artillerist in the Morris Island battery when the USS *Star of the West* tried to reach Fort Sumter in Charleston Harbor on January 9, 1861. The ship was attempting to deliver supplies to the Union garrison when Southern guns opened fire. Some consider the shots as the first fired in the Civil War. In fact, the attack on the *Star of the West* predated the formation of the Confederate States of America, whose provisional constitution was not adopted until February 8, 1861. It was, however, a prelude of the more famous bombardment of Fort Sumter on April 12, 1861.

In 1897 Cleveland called upon Edward Porter Alexander to act as a special envoy in an effort to resolve a border dispute between the Central American nations of Costa Rica and Nicaragua. It was an important matter that involved the preplanning of a proposed trans-isthmus waterway that would eventually become the Panama Canal. Alexander was an engineer by training and a superb artillerist for most of the Civil War. He saw action during the first summer of the war in 1861 at First Manassas and served all the way through to General Lee's surrender at Appomattox in 1865, having attained the rank of brigadier general. Before being called upon by Cleveland to serve in his state department, Alexander had been a professor of civil and military engineering and mathematics at the University of South Carolina.[20]

Alexander and Grover Cleveland became close friends, and the president visited the former Confederate's South Carolina home to hunt and fish. The ex-artillerist was a strong and outspoken postwar advocate of reconciliation and delivered the Confederate veterans' speech at the U.S. Military Academy at West Point on Alumni Day 1902. President Theodore Roosevelt was in attendance.

After the war North Carolinian Edward Joseph Hale, a former major in James Lane's North Carolina Brigade, served the United States government as a consul and ambassador. Hale was a newspaper publisher in Fayetteville, North Carolina (and briefly in New York City), and in 1885 was appointed by Cleveland as U.S. consul to Manchester, England, where he was invited to join the British Association for the Advancement of Science. Hale also was named vice president of the International Congress on Internal Navigation and, after spending 1891 in New York, he returned to North Carolina. During his second term, Cleveland offered Hale the ambassadorships to the Ottoman Empire and Russia, but he declined both positions.

---

20 It was not realized until fairly recently that Alexander began writing his very personal memoirs during his downtime in Nicaragua. They were edited and published as Edward P. Alexander, *Fighting for the Confederacy: The Personal Recollections of General Edward Porter Alexander*, edited by Gary W. Gallagher (UNC Press, 1989).

In connection with his interest in inland water transportation, Hale served as director of the National Rivers and Harbors Congress and as president of the Upper Cape Fear (North Carolina) Improvement Association. In 1913, he reentered public service when he was appointed the U.S. ambassador to Costa Rica by President Woodrow Wilson, a position he held until 1917.

Matt Whitaker Ransom, a former Confederate brigadier general in Robert E. Lee's Army of Northern Virginia, was a postwar senator from North Carolina from 1871 to 1895; he served briefly as president pro tem of the Senate during the 53rd Congress. In 1895 Ransom was appointed by Cleveland as ambassador to Mexico, a position he held until 1897.

Another former North Carolina brigadier general in Lee's Virginia army was appointed by Cleveland to a diplomatic post in Canada. William Paul Roberts was a postwar North Carolina legislator and state auditor before being named by Cleveland as U.S. consul to Victoria, British Columbia, in 1889.

On April 18, 1885, Cleveland appointed William Dunnington Bloxham as ambassador and consul general to Bolivia. Bloxham, the former commander of the Leon County (Florida) Militia, took the ministerial oath of office but was appointed U.S. surveyor general of Florida before he could report to Bolivia. He served in that capacity until 1889. Bloxham was elected governor of Florida twice; he served one term beginning in 1881 prior to his tenure as surveyor general, and was governor a second time from 1897 to 1901.

William Harwar Parker had been a captain in the Confederate Navy and superintendent of the Confederate States Naval Academy on the James River. He had previously served in the U.S. Navy, where he had participated in blockading the port of Veracruz during the Mexican War. Parker served as president of the University of Maryland from 1875 to 1882, and Cleveland named him U.S. ambassador to Korea in 1886.

Alfred Cumming was a professional soldier in the U. S. Army before going on to fight through most of the Civil War as a Confederate brigadier general in the Army of Tennessee. He saw extensive combat and was wounded twice and captured once. President Cleveland called upon him to serve on the United States Military Commission to Korea in 1888. The native Georgian was a West Point graduate and the nephew of Alfred Cumming, a prewar governor of the Utah Territory.

In 1885 Cleveland appointed as envoy and ambassador to Spain former Confederate Colonel Jabez Lamar Monroe Curry, a staff officer for Generals Joseph E. Johnston and Joseph Wheeler. In addition to his diplomatic service, Curry was a prominent postwar educator who taught at the University of

Jabez Lamar Monroe Curry

LOC

Richmond and served as president of Howard College (now Samford University, in Alabama). He was instrumental in the founding of both the Southern Education Foundation and the University of North Carolina at Greensboro. The Curry School of Education at the University of Virginia is named in his honor, as is Curry Hall at Longwood University, and the Curry Building on the campus of the University of North Carolina at Greensboro.

The Spanish government rewarded Curry with the Royal and Distinguished Spanish Order of Charles III, an award established by Spain's King Carlos III in 1771 to recognize individuals for their actions in benefit to Spain and the Spanish Crown. Since its creation, it has remained Spain's most distinguished civil award.

James Biddle Eustis, a lieutenant and judge advocate in the Confederate Army of Tennessee, was appointed ambassador to France by Cleveland in 1893 and served in that important diplomatic position until 1897. Eustis was a native of Louisiana and an 1854 graduate of Harvard Law School. He was heavily involved in Louisiana state politics both before and after the war, and from 1873 to 1891 served two non-consecutive terms as a U.S. senator before resuming his law practice in New Orleans and Washington, D.C. After he retired in 1897 Eustis lived in New York City. He died in Newport, Rhode Island in 1899.

Another distinguished former Rebel called upon to serve in the United States diplomatic corps following the Civil War was John Williams Walker Fearn. The native of Huntsville, Alabama, had extensive diplomatic experience before the sectional conflict erupted into open warfare. Fearn graduated from Yale University in 1851 with "distinguished honors," and went on to earn a degree from the College de France in Paris before practicing law in Mobile, Alabama. In 1854, Fearn was appointed U.S. charge d'affaires to Belgium, Spain, and Mexico but resigned at the onset of the Civil War. He achieved the rank of lieutenant colonel during the war and served on the staff of several generals including Joe Johnston, William Preston, and E. Kirby Smith. Returning to a more peaceful existence, Fearn resumed the practice of law in New Orleans and taught Italian and Spanish at Tulane University until 1885, when Cleveland reached out and appointed him ambassador to Greece, Romania, and Serbia. In 1892 Fearn was chosen as the United States' representative judge on the Court of First Instance, International Tribunal, in Cairo, Egypt—the judicial body that ruled on international disputes pertaining to the Suez Canal.

Another important appointment by Grover Cleveland was that of native Georgian Richard Bennett Hubbard as the U.S. ambassador to Japan from 1885 to 1889. During this time Japan was emerging from a centuries-old feudal society into a more modern form of government and culture. In 1899, Hubbard published a book on his diplomatic experiences entitled *The United States in the Far East.*

Hubbard was the colonel of the 22nd Texas Infantry and served during the entire Civil War. Before the war he graduated from Mercer University in Macon, Georgia, and briefly attended the University of Virginia before transferring to Harvard, where he graduated in 1853. Afterward, Hubbard and his family moved to Texas, where he practiced law and became involved in politics. President James Buchanan appointed Hubbard as U.S. Attorney for the Western District of Texas in 1856. After the war Hubbard resumed his involvement in politics and was elected lieutenant governor and governor of Texas before heeding Cleveland's call for diplomatic service in Japan.

Cleveland also tapped Henry Rootes Jackson, a native of Athens, Georgia, who attained the rank of brigadier general in the Army of Tennessee, for foreign service. Born in 1820, Jackson went north to Yale University and graduated there in 1839. He returned home to practice law in Georgia before volunteering for service in the U.S. Army. As a colonel he commanded the 1st Georgia Volunteer Infantry in the Mexican War. After the war, President Franklin Pierce appointed Jackson as U.S. charge d' affaires to the Austrian Empire in 1853, and as minister to the Austrian Empire from 1854 to 1858.

After the Civil War Jackson returned to Georgia, practiced law, and became involved in politics. In 1885 Cleveland named him ambassador to Mexico, and after two years as a diplomat Jackson returned to Georgia to work as a railroad executive, banker, and president of the Georgia Historical Society. He died in 1898.

Cleveland also appointed Thomas Jordan Jarvis to the diplomatic corps. The native North Carolinian seemed destined for a long and varied life. He worked hard as a youth and earned a master's degree from Randolph-Macon College in Virginia in 1861, enlisted early in the Civil War, and rose to captain in the 8th North

Carolina Infantry. Jarvis was captured and exchanged early in the war, and severely wounded and permanently disabled at the Battle of Drewry's Bluff, part of the Bermuda Hundred Campaign, on May 5, 1864. After the war he worked as an educator and politician and, in 1885, was appointed U.S. ambassador to Brazil.

Jarvis was elected as lieutenant governor and governor of North Carolina, during which time he was heavily involved in the establishment of mental health facilities and reforms in public education, including the establishment of systems of publicly elected boards of education, county school superintendents, teacher certifications, and a method of recommending textbooks. Jarvis also was instrumental in the founding of what is now East Carolina University.

After his gubernatorial term and his diplomatic service in Brazil, Jarvis returned to North Carolina and served in the U.S. Senate. He resumed his law practice in 1912 and died in 1915.

Another Southerner to serve in the Cleveland administration as a diplomat was Alexander Caldwell Jones, a native of Moundsville, Virginia (now West Virginia) and former colonel of the 44th Virginia Infantry Regiment. Jones graduated from VMI in 1850, after which he moved to Minnesota to practice law. He was appointed adjutant general of Minnesota in 1858, but resigned and returned to Virginia at the outbreak of the Civil War. Jones was wounded in June 1862 and later was transferred to the Trans-Mississippi Department. He was recommended for promotion to brigadier general in March 1865 by General E. Kirby Smith, but the war ended before Richmond could confirm the rank. After the war Jones served in the Mexican army before returning to West Virginia in 1867. In 1880 Cleveland appointed Jones as consul to Nagasaki, Japan, and in 1886 he was transferred to the U.S. embassy in Chungking, China, where he died in 1898.

Another influential Confederate to serve as a diplomat in the Cleveland administration was Alexander Robert Lawton. A native of Beaufort, South Carolina, Lawton graduated from the U.S. Military Academy at West Point in 1839 and from Harvard Law School three years later. He moved to Savannah, Georgia, where he practiced law and became involved in politics.

At the outbreak of the Civil War, Lawton was commissioned colonel of the 1st Georgia Volunteers. His was a promising career and he made brigadier general, but a severe wound at Sharpsburg (Antietam) on September 17, 1862, ended his field service. After a lengthy recovery Lawton was appointed quartermaster general of the Confederate States.

Lawton returned to his law practice in Savannah after the war and in 1882 was elected president of the American Bar Association. In 1887 he was appointed U.S.

Dabney Herndon Maury

LOC

ambassador to Austria-Hungary and served for two years in that important diplomatic post.

Another diplomat in the Cleveland administration was former Confederate Major General Dabney Herndon Maury, who was U.S. ambassador to Colombia from 1887 to 1889. Maury was a native of Virginia. His father died when he was two years old and he was adopted by his uncle, the famous United States and Confederate States mariner Matthew Fontaine Maury, who was known as the "Father of Modern Oceanography and Naval Meteorology."

Dabney Maury graduated from West Point and served in the Mexican War. At the outbreak of the Civil War he resigned from the U.S. Army to throw his lot in with the South. He received a commission as a colonel and was soon promoted to brigadier general. Maury held several important positions during the war, including as chief of staff for General Earl Van Dorn, and he eventually attained the rank of major general. Maury played a prominent role in the late-war siege of Mobile. When the war ended he founded an academy in Fredericksburg, Virginia, to teach classical literature and mathematics, endured a business failure in New Orleans, and returned to Virginia. In 1868 Maury began working on his greatest gift to posterity by organizing the Southern Historical Society in Richmond. He spent two decades working for the society which eventually published the *Southern Historical Society Papers*, a 52-volume study of the Civil War and related Southern history that continues to be widely utilized today. In addition to his diplomatic service in Colombia under Cleveland, Maury was involved in the original organization of the U.S. Army National Guard and served on its executive committee.

In 1893, Cleveland appointed Alexander Watkins Terrell as U.S. ambassador to the Ottoman Empire, where he served until 1897. Terrell was a native of Virginia, attended the University of Missouri, and moved to Austin, Texas, in 1852, where he practiced law and served as a judge. When the Civil War began, Terrell was commissioned a colonel and commanded the 1st Texas Cavalry Regiment, also known as "Terrell's Texas Cavalry." After the war he served briefly in the Mexican army but soon returned to Texas to practice law. He was heavily involved in state politics and in the growth of the University of Texas, where he served on the school's Board of Regents.

One of the more interesting former ex-Confederates to serve in the Cleveland administration was Danish-born Julius Gabriel Tucker, who by the war's end was the colonel and commander of Tucker's Confederate Regiment. Tucker was Jewish, and his last name was actually Tachau. He emigrated from Denmark to Memphis, Tennessee, and moved later to Virginia, where he enlisted in the 10th Virginia Cavalry at the beginning of the war. He served as an aide-de-camp to General Fitzhugh Lee during the Gettysburg Campaign, and in October 1864 recruited foreign-born federal prisoners being held in Florence, South Carolina, Salisbury, North Carolina, and Richmond to serve in the Confederate Army. He organized the volunteers into the 1st Confederate Foreign Legion (later named Tucker's Confederate Regiment). After the war he settled in Brownsville, Texas, his place of residence when President Cleveland appointed him U.S. commissioner for the Rio Grande Valley. In 1897, Tucker was named U.S. consul to Martinique.

Cleveland also appointed former Confederate Colonel Charlton Hines Way as U.S. consul to St. Petersburg, Russia. Way was a native Georgian, a graduate of the Georgia Military Institute, and was elected colonel of the 54th Georgia Infantry in 1862. After long hard service the war ended and Way worked as a commission merchant and real estate developer in Savannah, Georgia.

Robert Enoch Withers served in the Cleveland administration as U.S. consul to Hong Kong. The resident of Lynchburg, Virginia, enlisted as a private in the 18th Virginia Infantry in 1861 and eventually rose to the rank of colonel. After suffering multiple disabling wounds, Withers was assigned to administrative posts in the Confederate government until the close of the war. Thereafter, Withers established a newspaper and became involved in politics. He was elected as Virginia's lieutenant governor in 1873 and as a U.S. senator from 1875 to 1881, serving as chairman of the Committee on Pensions. He was appointed consul to Hong Kong in 1885, and held that post until 1889 before retiring to Wytheville, Virginia.

Charles Lewis Scott was appointed U.S. consul general to Caracas and ambassador to Venezuela in 1885. Scott, a native of Richmond, Virginia, graduated from the College of William and Mary in 1846 and practiced law in his hometown in 1847. Like so many others, Scott moved to California during the 1849 gold rush. He worked for a short time without striking it rich, and resumed the practice of law in Sonora, California. In 1856 Scott was elected to the U.S. House of Representatives from California and served three terms. While a member of Congress he met and married a woman from Mobile, Alabama. In 1861 he resigned his congressional seat and enlisted in the Confederate Army, eventually attaining the rank of major in the 4th Alabama Infantry. His military career was cut short by a disabling leg wound at First Manassas (Bull Run) in July 1861, and he was forced to resign the following spring. After his postwar diplomatic service in Venezuela Scott returned to Alabama, where he died in 1899.

The aforementioned George Earl Maney was appointed by Cleveland as U.S. ambassador to Uruguay and Paraguay. Maney, a native Tennessean, had previously served as ambassador to Colombia in the Garfield administration, and as consul general and ambassador to Bolivia under President Chester Arthur. After Cleveland's reelection defeat in 1888, Maney was retained in his diplomatic post by President Benjamin Harrison.

Another former soldier was William Carrington Mayo. The Virginian was a graduate of Yale and served in the ranks of the 12th Virginia Infantry. He was serverely wounded at Spotsylvania in May 1864 but survived the war. Mayo, a renowned linguist fluent in a dozen languages, worked for the U.S. Department of State in the Cleveland administration, where his fluency in Russian was employed during the Bering Sea Tribunal of Arbitration in Paris in 1893.

In 1886 Cleveland appointed Hugh Smith Thompson as assistant secretary of the treasury. Thompson was the former leader of The Citadel Battalion of Cadets and was in command of the battery that fired on the *Star of the West* in Charleston Harbor in January 1861. Thompson later served on the U.S. Civil Service Commission in the Benjamin Harrison administration. In the private sector, he served as comptroller of the New York Life Insurance Company.

Also serving in the Cleveland administration was William Alfred Freret, Jr., a noted postwar architect and engineer who had been a lieutenant in the 5th Company, Washington (Louisiana) Artillery. Freret was appointed in 1884 to head the Office of the Supervising Architect, which at the time was an agency of the U.S. Treasury Department, and served there until 1888. During his tenure Freret and his staff designed post offices across the United States, usually in a Romanesque architectural style.

Cleveland also named former Confederate Colonel James Q. Chenoweth of the 1st Kentucky Cavalry as auditor of the U.S. Department of the Treasury in 1885. Chenoweth acted in that capacity until Cleveland was defeated in his reelection bid in 1888. He returned home to Bonham, Texas, where he served three terms as a county judge.

George Doherty Johnston, yet another former brigadier general in the Confederate Army of Tennessee, was appointed by Cleveland to the U.S. Civil Service Commission, the predecessor of the federal government's Office of Personnel Management.

President Cleveland appointed at least four former Confederates to positions in the Bureau of Indian Affairs, an agency within the U.S. Department of Justice. Beal Gaither, a former colonel of the 27th Arkansas Infantry, was appointed as U.S. Indian agent for the Confederated Tribes of Siletz Indians, a league of Native American tribes in northern California, Oregon, and Washington.

In 1885, former Confederate Brigadier General George Washington Gordon was named as a special Indian agent in Nevada and the Arizona Territory. Gordon served in this capacity for four years before returning to his home in Tennessee, where he was the superintendent of Memphis schools from 1889 until 1907. Prior to his tenure in the Cleveland administration, Gordon had served three terms in the U.S. House of Representatives from Tennessee.

Another U.S. Indian agent was former Confederate Brigadier General Daniel C. Govan, who had like Gordon served in the Army of Tennessee. Govan was appointed in 1894 as the agent for the Tulalip Tribes confederation in the Puget Sound area of the state of Washington. Joining Govan was fellow Confederate veteran William Levin Powell, who had been a captain on the staff of General John B. Gordon. Powell served as an Indian agent in Neah Bay, Washington.

Benjamin Harrison Administration

Benjamin Harrison, the twenty-third president of the United States, served from 1889 to 1893, sandwiched between the two non-consecutive terms of Grover Cleveland.

Harrison was born in 1833 on a farm on the banks of the Ohio River near Cincinnati. He attended Miami University in Oxford, Ohio, and studied law in Cincinnati. While a student in Oxford, Harrison met and in 1853 married Caroline Lavinia Scott, the daughter of a local Presbyterian minister. Caroline was a music teacher with a deep interest in history and preservation. In 1890 as the First Lady of the United States, Caroline would help found the Daughters of the American Revolution and she served as its first president.

After studying law, Harrison and his wife moved to Indianapolis, Indiana, where in 1854 he opened a law practice and became involved in local and state Republican politics. In 1862 he answered President Lincoln's call for more troops

Benjamin Harrison

LOC

and helped recruit a regiment of volunteers from northern Indiana. He was offered command of the new 70th Indiana Infantry but declined because of his lack of military experience. He agreed instead to command a company in the regiment and accepted a commission as a captain. That July he was promoted to colonel and assumed command of the 70th Indiana. Harrison's regiment spent most of 1862 and 1863 on reconnaissance and guard duty in Kentucky and Tennessee, but in January 1864 he was given a brigade and was transferred to Major General William T. Sherman's army assembling around Chattanooga in anticipation of invading northern Georgia that spring. Harrison spent much of the next year on the war's front lines, participating in the long and bloody Atlanta Campaign and the battles around the city, and later confronting Confederate Lieutenant General John Bell Hood's invasion of Tennessee in late 1864. On February 14, 1865, Harrison was promoted to brigadier general and mustered out of the army on June 8, 1865.

After the Civil War Harrison returned to his law practice in Indiana. In 1880 he was elected to the U.S. Senate and served until 1887. He was the Republican nominee for president in 1888, and although he received fewer popular votes than did Grover Cleveland, Harrison won the Electoral College by a comfortable margin. During his four years in office Harrison conducted an aggressive foreign policy. The first Pan American Congress met in Washington, D.C., in 1889 and established an organization of Western Hemisphere nations that would later become the Pan American Union.

In 1892 Harrison lost his reelection bid to Cleveland, who he had defeated just four years earlier. He returned to Indianapolis and spent the next decade as an attorney and a lecturer at universities and national organizations until his death from influenza in 1901.

Benjamin Harrison's most prominent appointment of a former Confederate was Howell Edmunds Jackson, who succeeded Lucius Q. C. Lamar as an associate

Howell Edmunds Jackson

LOC

justice on the U.S. Supreme Court in 1893. Born in 1832 in Paris, Tennessee, Jackson studied at West Tennessee College, graduated from the University of Virginia in 1849, and earned a law degree in 1856 from Cumberland University in Lebanon, Tennessee. He practiced law in Jackson, Tennessee, before moving to Memphis in 1859. When that city fell to Union forces in early 1862 he moved to LaGrange, where he served the Confederate government as a civil servant until the end of the war. Jackson's younger brother William Hicks "Red" Jackson was a brigadier general in the Confederate Army and commanded a cavalry brigade in several campaigns and battles.

After the war Howell Jackson returned to Jackson, where he served as a judge and became involved in politics. He was a member of the Tennessee House of Representatives and was elected to the U.S. Senate in 1880. Six years later he resigned from the Senate to accept an appointment as a federal judge.

Howell's younger brother William had returned to Tennessee after the war and became a renowned breeder of thoroughbred horses at Belle Meade, his famous Nashville-area plantation that eventually would be added to the National Register of Historic Places. Belle Meade, of which Howell Jackson was part owner, was a popular destination for celebrity visitors during the 1880s and '90s. Guests included President and Mrs. Grover Cleveland, Abraham Lincoln's son Robert Todd Lincoln, Ulysses S. Grant, and William T. Sherman (who at the time was commander of the Army of the United States). Developing acquaintances with prominent federal government officials doubtless contributed to Howell Jackson's high profile.

The elder Jackson held his federal judgeship until 1893, when he was appointed associate justice of the U.S. Supreme Court by President Harrison. Jackson would serve only two years on the high court before his death at his West

Meade home on August 8, 1895. His funeral was held at nearby Belle Meade plantation.

Another of President Harrison's high-level appointments was former Confederate judge advocate general William Arden Maury. A postwar lawyer and educator, Maury served as U.S. assistant attorney general from 1889 to 1893. He also was a member of the federal government's Spanish Treaty Claims Commission, a professor of law at the University of Richmond, and a professor at Columbian University (later George Washington University) in Washington, D.C.

In 1892 Harrison appointed former Confederate cavalryman John Benjamin Rector, a private in the famous 8th Texas Cavalry (better known as "Terry's Texas Rangers"), as judge of the U.S. District Court for the Northern District of Texas. Rector served until his death in 1898.

The Harrison administration also employed William Edward Sims, who in 1890 was appointed U.S. consul to Panama. Sims was a native of Sligo, Mississippi, who graduated from Yale University in 1861 before returning home and enlisting as a private in the 21st Mississippi Infantry. Sims served the entire war in the Army of Northern Virginia, and he made Virginia his home after the war. He practiced law in Chatham, Virginia, and was involved in state politics. Around 1880 he switched his party affiliation from Democrat to Republican and ran unsuccessfully for the Virginia Senate, the U.S. House of Representatives, and the U.S. Senate. He moved to Washington, D.C., in 1884 and was employed as a bookkeeper for the U.S. Senate. Although nearly deaf, Harrison appointed Sims to the consular post in Panama, which he held until his death on July 26, 1891.

In 1889 Harrison named Hugh Smith Thompson, former Rebel artillerist, to the U.S. Civil Service Commission. Thompson had served as assistant U.S. secretary of the treasury in the Cleveland administration.

Another ex-Confederate general, cavalryman Francis "Frank" Crawford Armstrong, was appointed by Harrison as assistant commissioner of Indian affairs in 1893. Armstrong had previously served in the Cleveland administration as an Indian inspector from 1885 to 1889.

John Cecil Legare, a surgeon in the 5th Company, Washington (Louisiana) Artillery, had been chosen by President Cleveland to be U.S. consul to Tampico, Mexico, in 1886 but declined the position. On May 1, 1891, he accepted the appointment of President Harrison to be the melter and refiner of the U.S. Mint in New Orleans.

William McKinley Administration

William McKinley Jr., the twenty-fifth president of the United States, was elected in November 1896, reelected in 1900, and served until his death by assassination on September 14, 1901, only six months into his second term. McKinley oversaw the swift American victory in the Spanish-American War in 1898.

McKinley was born in Niles, Ohio, in 1843, and briefly attended Allegheny College in Meadville, Pennsylvania. When the Civil War began McKinley enlisted as a private in the 23rd Ohio Infantry. His first commander was Major Rutherford B. Hayes. The two future presidents would maintain a friendship until Hayes's death in 1893. McKinley served the entire war and was a major when discharged.

After the war, McKinley attended law school in New York, and in 1867 opened a law office in Canton, Ohio. His law practice flourished, and, like many prominent attorneys, McKinley became involved in politics. He won election to the U.S. House of Representatives and served three terms, including one as chairman of the Ways and Means Committee. In 1891 McKinley was elected governor of Ohio, and after one term ran successfully for president.

McKinley's four and one-half year presidency was dominated by foreign affairs, including the Spanish-American War and the nation's expansion in the Far East and the Pacific. McKinley retained a few of Grover Cleveland's appointees who were former Confederates and named another to an international commission. He also appointed eight former Rebel Army officers to generalships in the U.S. Army in the buildup to the Spanish-American War.

McKinley had few nonmilitary appointees. One, James Longstreet, had served in the Hayes administration as a U.S. diplomat and U.S. marshal, and after several years of retirement returned to public service in 1898 to be McKinley's commissioner of railroads.

William McKinley, Jr.

LOC

Another McKinley appointee was Charles James Faulkner, a U.S. senator from West Virginia who was named as the American representative to the International Joint High Commission of the United States and Great Britain. The commission was tasked with resolving territorial and other disputes between the United States and Canada that had existed for several decades.

Born near Martinsburg, Virginia (now West Virginia), in 1847, Faulkner's father was U.S. ambassador to France. The younger Faulkner accompanied his father to Europe and attended schools in Paris and Switzerland before returning to the United States in 1861 to enroll at VMI, where as a cadet he fought at the Battle of New Market in May 1864.

After the war Faulkner enrolled at the University of Virginia and earned a law degree in 1868. He opened a practice in Martinsburg and was elected to two terms as a U.S. Senator, in 1887 and 1893. While a senator he was chairman of the Committee on Territories. Faulkner retired from public life in 1899 and devoted his time to his law practice in Martinsburg and Washington, D.C., until his death in 1929.

Theodore Roosevelt Administration

With the assassination of William McKinley, Theodore Roosevelt became the twenty-sixth president of the United States and, at age 42, the youngest to hold that office. Roosevelt's youth and energy made him an independent and active chief executive. Like his predecessors, he appointed former Confederates to important—although less conspicuous—positions in the federal government. Roosevelt was uninhibited in both foreign policy and domestic governance, and in his memoirs admitted, "I did not usurp power, but I did greatly broaden the use of executive power."[21]

Unlike most of his predecessors, Roosevelt was born in New York City to wealth and privilege instead of in a frontier cabin or a small Midwestern town. He struggled with ill health early in life, but led an active lifestyle in adulthood . Born in 1858, Roosevelt was too young to understand or remember the Civil War with any clarity, but he later became familiar with the causes of the war and those who fought it. Roosevelt was just six when he watched Abraham Lincoln's funeral

---

21 Theodore Roosevelt, William Howard Taft, and Woodrow Wilson on the Presidency, www1.cmc.edu/pages/faculty/JPitney/Roosevelt-Taft-Wilson.html.

procession from a window in the family's house near Union Square in New York City. As he grew older, he came to admire and respect the grit and determination of Confederate soldiers and sailors.

Roosevelt's father's family were serious-natured establishment Yankee merchants and bankers—fixtures of New York society and respected philanthropists. Theodore's mother, Martha "Mittie" Bulloch, was a native of Connecticut who had been raised in Roswell, Georgia. She was the ideal of a Southern belle and she raised Teddy on romanticized stories of the antebellum South, stately plantations tended by contented slaves, beautiful and sophisticated women, and dashing and chivalrous gentlemen. In contrast to the staid, business-oriented Roosevelts, Mittie's was a family of soldiers, sailors, and adventurers. Of his Southern ancestors Roosevelt later wrote, "I felt a great admiration for men who were fearless and who could hold their own in the world," and, he admitted, as a child "I had a great desire to be like them."[22] The Bullochs were indeed daring, and during the Civil War nearly all of their men fought for the Confederacy; all of the Roosevelts, meanwhile, remained safely in New York.

Two of Mittie's most prominent military kin were her brothers Irvine and James Bulloch. At the outbreak of the war, Irvine was a student at the University of Pennsylvania, but withdrew to volunteer for the Confederate Navy. His older half-brother James, a 15-year veteran of the U.S. Navy, resigned to join the Confederate Navy and initially serving as the captain of a blockade runner. He was later sent to England, where he ran covert operations and acquired ships and supplies on behalf of the Confederate government.

None of the daring exploits of Roosevelt's uncles was more profound than the career of the legendary Confederate raider CSS *Alabama*. James had secretly commissioned the construction of the cruiser (ostensibly a merchant ship) by a Liverpool shipbuilder. Eventually the true nature of the ship of war and her owner—the Confederate Navy—became known, and the United States government petitioned British authorities to impound the vessel. While the petition was being processed through the British bureaucracy, on July 29, 1862, Irvine, a young midshipman, cleverly sailed the unfinished ship out of the harbor under the guise of a seaworthiness test; but the *Alabama* journeyed on to the Azores, where her construction was completed and she was outfitted for war. For two years the *Alabama*, with Irvine as an officer, wreaked havoc on Union shipping before she was sunk off Cherbourg, France, in August 1864 by the USS *Kearsarge*.

---

22 Ibid.

Irvine and James Bulloch

LOC

Both uncles, Irvine and James, Bulloch, survived the war, but both were denied general amnesty because of their covert actions. They decided to remain in England and lived and prospered in Liverpool. Despite living overseas, they became close with their nephew Teddy, with whom they corresponded and, on a few occasions, met with personally.

On a visit to Mittie's old home in Roswell, Georgia, during his presidential term in 1905, Roosevelt gave a speech and said of his Southern ancestry: "Men and women, don't you think I have the ancestral right to claim a proud kinship with those who showed their devotion to duty as they saw that duty, whether they wore the gray or whether they wore the blue?"[23]

Roosevelt graduated magna cum laude from Harvard University in 1880, and attended Columbia University Law School before entering politics. He was elected to the New York State Assembly and served as minority leader in 1883 and in 1895 worked as president of the New York City Board of Police Commissioners. In 1897 Roosevelt accepted President McKinley's appointment as assistant secretary of the U.S. Navy. In his 1882 book *The Naval War of 1812*, Roosevelt acknowledged his uncle James as one of his mentors in naval tactics. In 1898 Roosevelt was elected governor of New York, and two years later joined the McKinley ticket and was elected vice president. Only six months after taking office Roosevelt was elevated to the presidency when McKinley was killed. He served the remaining three-and-a-half years of McKinley's term, and then four more years when he was elected on his own behalf in 1904.

Earlier, at the outbreak of the Spanish-American War in 1898, Roosevelt had resigned his position as assistant secretary of the navy and volunteered for the

---

23 Theodore Roosevelt: The Plunger, www.american-presidents.Org/ 2007/09/theodore-roosevelt-plunger.html.

army. Along with his friend Colonel Leonard Wood, he formed the 1st United States Volunteer Cavalry Regiment, which later earned fame as the Rough Riders. Roosevelt had been a member of the New York National Guard, and he and Wood quickly transformed the volunteer cavalrymen into a highly efficient fighting unit.

After arriving in Cuba, Roosevelt, now a commissioned lieutenant colonel of volunteers, led the Rough Riders in the decisive July 1, 1898, Battle of San Juan Hill. "On the day of the big fight," he penned in his memoirs,

> I had to ask my men to do a deed that European military writers consider utterly impossible of performance, that is, to attack over open ground an unshaken infantry armed with the best modern repeating rifles behind a formidable system of entrenchments. The only way to get them to do it in the way it had to be done was to lead them myself.[24]

Roosevelt's Rough Riders were a part of a division commanded by former Confederate major general Joseph "Fighting Joe" Wheeler, who had been commissioned a major general of volunteers in the U.S. Army. Wheeler was one of eight former Confederates to serve as U.S. Army generals during the Spanish-American War. After returning from Cuba in August 1898, Roosevelt rode his popularity as a war hero to the governorship of New York, opening the door to his national political aspirations.

Roosevelt's presidency proved very influential in both foreign and domestic matters, but international affairs were of paramount interest to the well-traveled and naturally aggressive Republican. On the domestic front, Roosevelt appointed former Confederate brigadier general Francis Marion Cockrell to the Interstate Commerce Commission in 1905, and in 1911 chose him as special federal commissioner to negotiate the establishment of the border between Texas and the New Mexico Territory, which was preparing to enter the Union as the forty-seventh state. Cockrell had returned to Missouri after the Civil War and was elected to the U.S. Senate in 1875, serving until his retirement in 1905. While a senator Cockrell served as chairman of the Appropriations Committee.

During the war Cockrell commanded the Missouri Brigade in the Army of Tennessee, which is routinely recognized as one of the finest fighting brigades of the entire war on either side. A prewar lawyer, Cockrell volunteered for the Missouri State Guard in 1861 and was commissioned captain, and in 1862

24 McClarey, D. R. (2015, February 16). Theodore Roosevelt: A Force of Nature, www.the-american-catholic.com/2015/02/16/theodore-roosevelt-a-force-of-nature/.

Francis Marion Cockrell

LOC

mustered into the Confederate Army as a colonel in command of the 2nd Missouri Infantry. He was promoted to brigadier general on July 18, 1863, and commanded his namesake brigade in the Army of Tennessee during Sherman's Atlanta Campaign and Hood's ill-fated 1864 Tennessee Campaign. Late in the war Cockrell commanded a division in the defense of Fort Blakely, near Mobile, Alabama, and surrendered on April 9, 1865.

In 1901 Roosevelt appointed Thomas Goode Jones as U.S. district judge for the Northern and Middle District of Alabama. Jones, a former Confederate lieutenant and postwar governor of Alabama, served on the staff of General John Brown Gordon during the war. The Thomas Goode Jones School of Law at Faulkner University in Montgomery, Alabama, is named in his honor.

Another former Confederate who served in the Roosevelt administration was Benjamin Azariah Colonna, who, as a VMI cadet captain, served in the 21st and 36th Virginia Infantry regiments and fought in the Confederate victory at New Market. After graduating in June 1864, Colonna served as a captain on the staffs of several Confederate generals until he surrendered with the Army of Tennessee in North Carolina on April 26, 1865.

After the war Colonna taught school in the Eastern Shore region of Virginia, and in 1870, he joined the United States Coast and Geodetic Survey, where he would work for 25 years. In 1884, while surveying the Strait of Juan de Fuca in Washington state, he was severely injured in an avalanche that left him partially paralyzed. He transferred to the department's headquarters in Washington, D.C., where he worked until 1895. Colonna later served as an adviser to the U.S. Senate Committee on Naval Affairs, and was appointed assistant secretary of the navy by Roosevelt.

As president, Roosevelt had a keen interest in the strategic and economic need for a shortcut between the Atlantic and Pacific oceans, and he strongly advocated for the construction of the Panama Canal. France had begun construction on the canal in 1881 but abandoned the project in 1894 because of engineering difficulties and high worker mortality from illnesses attributable to the tropical climate. Roosevelt revived the project in 1905 and it was completed in 1914 during the Woodrow Wilson administration. In addition to engineering and health challenges, construction of the canal proved to be a complex diplomatic task. France had an established interest in the canal, and at that time the proposed route of the waterway was part of the South American nation of Colombia, whose inhabitants were seeking independence.

Panama declared independence from Colombia in 1903, and the following year the United States recognized the new nation, declared it a protectorate, and created the Isthmian Canal Commission (ICC) to oversee construction of the canal. The ICC would go through various incarnations over the next 75 years, and it became the Panama Canal Commission in 1979. Among Roosevelt's first appointments to the important ICC was former Confederate Benjamin Morgan Harrod, who would be the only member of the first ICC retained to serve on the second commission.

Born in New Orleans in 1837, Harrod earned two degrees from Harvard University: a bachelor of arts in 1856 and a master's from Harvard's Lawrence Scientific School in 1859. In 1861 he enlisted in the Louisiana Crescent Rregiment as a lieutenant and was captured at Vicksburg in July 1863. After his parole he joined the Second Regiment of Engineers at Petersburg, Virginia, and served as an engineering officer on Robert E. Lee's staff. Harrod surrendered with the Army of Northern Virginia at Appomattox on April 9, 1865.

After the war, Harrod put his experience to good use by opening an engineering practice in New Orleans. From 1877 to 1902 he served as chief engineer for the state of Louisiana, New Orleans city engineer, chief engineer in charge of construction of New Orleans's water and sewer systems, and as a member of the Louisiana River Commission. Harrod's private engineering firm planned and designed historic Metairie Cemetery on property that was formerly used as a horse racing track in suburban New Orleans, and also designed many of the buildings at Tulane University. Harrod was president of the American Society of Civil Engineers in 1897 and 1898.

Roosevelt called upon another former Southern soldier, Joseph Clay Stiles Blackburn, to serve as governor of the Panama Canal Zone in 1907. A native of Kentucky, Blackburn was an 1857 graduate of Centre College in Danville, Kentucky, studied law in Lexington, and after being admitted to the bar entered law practice in Chicago.

Blackburn returned to Kentucky in 1861 and enlisted in the Confederate Army as a private. He became a judge advocate and rose to the rank of lieutenant colonel. When the war ended, Blackburn was in command of an independent cavalry regiment in Mississippi.

After the war Blackburn lived briefly in Arkansas before returning to Kentucky in 1868 to open a law office. He entered politics and served in the Kentucky legislature from 1871 to 1875. He was elected to the U.S. House of Representatives in 1874, where he served for ten years; duringhis tenure, Blackburn was chairman of the Committee on the District of Columbia, and was a member of the Committee on Military Expenditures and the Rules Committee. He was elected to the U.S. Senate in 1884 and served three terms. Blackburn's final political post was as governor of the Panama Canal Zone. He served two years and returned to his home in Woodford County, Kentucky. In 1885, Lieutenant Henry Tureman Allen, an engineer with the U.S. Army (and later a major general) named a mountain in Alaska—the fifth tallest in the entire United States—"Mt. Blackburn" in honor of Joseph C. S. Blackburn.

Another former Confederate entrusted with an important American diplomatic matter was Uriah Milton Rose, a Little Rock, Arkansas, attorney and judge appointed by Roosevelt as the U.S. representative to the Second Hague Peace Conference in 1907. The conference, which had been called by Roosevelt, was tasked with several subjects of international interest, including the immunity of civilian property on the high seas. The conference also dealt with international debt collections in private contracts, an arbitration process, and the establishment of international arbitration courts.

Uriah Rose, who was born in 1834 in Kentucky, earned a law degree in 1853 from Transylvania University in Lexington, Kentucky, and moved to Arkansas to open a law practice. Rose was opposed to secession, but at the outbreak of the Civil War he remained loyal to his home state. He was physically unable to serve in the military, so he volunteered for administrative duties at the Confederate capital in Richmond. He returned to Arkansas before the end of the war and was appointed a county judge. After the war, Rose resumed his law practice and became a prominent and respected attorney. The law firm he founded is fairly well known today as the Rose Law Firm, one of the largest law practices in Arkansas.[25]

---

25 Former First Lady and presidential candidate Hillary Clinton was a partner in the Rose Law Firm in the late 1970s.

During his 40-year career, Rose co-founded the Arkansas Bar Association and served as its first president, and in 1878 was one of the 75 founding members of the American Bar Association, of which he twice served as president (1891-92, and 1901-02).

In 1917, the state of Arkansas designated Uriah Rose as one of its two statues in the U.S. capitol's Statuary Hall Collection. In 2019, Arkansas replaced the state's two statues with those of singer Johnny Cash and civil rights activist Daisy Bates.

William Howard Taft Administration

Serving from 1909 to 1913, William Howard Taft was the twenty-seventh president of the United States and the sixth from Ohio. Although Taft achieved the highest office in the land, his life's ambition was to be chief justice on the U.S. Supreme Court—a goal he achieved *after* leaving the presidency. During his single term in office Taft appointed one former Confederate as an associate justice of the court and another as chief justice.

Taft was born in 1857, the son of Alphonso Taft, a distinguished judge, diplomat, and U.S. attorney general under Ulysses S. Grant. The younger Taft graduated from Yale University and returned to his hometown to earn a law degree from the University of Cincinnati Law School. Taft preferred law to politics but then as now, the two disciplines were tightly intertwined.

Taft's reluctant political career began in 1880 when he became an assistant prosecutor in Hamilton County, Ohio. Seven years later he was appointed by Ohio's governor to a judgeship on the Superior Court of Cincinnati, where he served for five years. In 1889, Taft actively sought appointment to a vacant U.S. Supreme Court seat, but President Harrison chose another to serve and instead appointed Taft as U.S. solicitor general. In 1892 Harrison appointed Taft judge of the newly created U.S. District Court in Cincinnati. A dozen years later Taft, still hoping for a Supreme Court seat, sought to ingratiate himself to President Roosevelt by accepting the position of secretary of war. He was offered vacant seats as an associate justice on the high court in 1905, and again in 1906, but Taft declined both times.

Roosevelt served the remaining three and one-half years of McKinley's term and a full four-year term of his own, and fulfilled a pledge not to run for what would effectively have been a third term in 1908. He groomed his chosen successor: William Taft. Although he was reluctant to run and had a strong dislike for campaigning, Roosevelt's coattails delivered the presidency to Taft and he assumed office on March 4, 1909. Taft's and Roosevelt's relationship soured over the next four years, however, and they were open political enemies by the time of the 1912 election.

Taft's presidency was largely conservative. Roosevelt—a boistrous progressive—was displeased with Taft and ran as a third-party candidate for president in 1912 under the newly formed and short-lived Bull Moose Party. Because of his concern that the next president would revert to progressivism, Taft once more (and reluctantly) ran for reelection. His detest for campaigning convinced him to do very little of it, and he was soundly defeated, winning only eight electoral votes to Roosevelt's 88 and Woodrow Wilson's 435.

Taft's defeat was, and remains, one of the most lopsided in American history, but he eventually achieved his lifelong dream when President Warren Harding appointed him chief justice of the U.S. Supreme Court on June 30, 1921. Taft is the only person in American history to serve as president and as a Supreme Court justice. He served on the high court until his death in 1930.

During his four years as president, Taft appointed six Supreme Court justices, the first of which was a former Confederate cavalryman Horace Harmon Lurton. Lurton was born in 1844 in Newport, Kentucky, just across the Ohio River from Taft's hometown of Cincinnati. Lurton, who spent much of his childhood in Tennessee, was a student at the University of Chicago in 1860 when the impending Civil War compelled him to withdraw and enlist in the Confederate Army. Lurton first served in the 5th Tennessee Infantry and later as a sergeant major in the 3rd Kentucky Cavalry. He was twice captured and was paroled near the end of the war.

After the war Lurton resumed his studies and graduated from Cumberland College in 1867. He began practicing law in Clarksville, Tennessee and was appointed to a Tennessee judgeship in 1875. He returned to his law practice three years later. Lurton was elected to the Tennessee Supreme Court in 1886, and in 1893 was appointed by Grover Cleveland as judge for the U.S. Court of Appeals for the Sixth Circuit, where he served for sixteen years before being appointed to the Supreme Court by President Taft. Lurton was 66 years old when he joined the high court, and served only four years before dying on January 12, 1914.

In 1910 Taft made another Supreme Court appointment from the former Confederate ranks when he named Edward Douglass White as chief justice. White had served as a lieutenant in the 9th Louisiana Cavalry and had been appointed as an associate justice to the high court by Grover Cleveland in 1894. With his appointment, White became the first and only ex-Confederate to serve as chief justice of the U.S. Supreme Court. He held that distinguished position until his death on May 19, 1921.

Horace Harmon Lurton

LOC

Woodrow Wilson Administration

Thomas Woodrow Wilson served as the twenty-eighth president of the United States, winning election in 1912 and again in 1916. A leader of the progressives, he inserted the United States into World War I to, in his words, "make the world safe for democracy."

Wilson was the first president elected from a former Confederate state and the first Southerner since Zachary Taylor was elected in 1848. Wilson was born into a slaveholding family in Staunton, Virginia, in 1856. During the war he lived in Augusta, Georgia, and afterward among the charred remains of Columbia, South Carolina. His first wife, Ellen, was a Southerner from Rome, Georgia, who had, for a time, lived in Savannah.

Wilson attended Davidson College in North Carolina for two years before transferring and graduating from Princeton in 1879. He entered the University of Virginia Law School but withdrew due to ill health and moved to Wilmington, North Carolina, where he studied law on his own. He eventually passed the Georgia bar exam and established a law practice in Atlanta in 1882. Wilson found the study of law a tedious endeavor and decided to resume his study of political science and history. In 1883 he enrolled at Johns Hopkins University in Baltimore, earned his doctorate in 1886, and began a career in education, first at Bryn Mawr College in Philadelphia and in 1888 at Wesleyan University in Middletown, Connecticut. After two years at Wesleyan, Wilson accepted a professorship at Princeton, and two years later was appointed the university's president.

By 1910 Wilson had drawn the interest of the New Jersey Democratic Party and was nominated as its candidate for governor. Although ostensibly a conservative democrat, in the general election he ran as a progressive and campaigned on a platform of independence from the party establishment that had nominated him. He won and pursued liberal policies during his brief two-year tenure as governor.

Wilson's victory drew the attention of the national Democratic party, which recognized the broad appeal of a transplanted Southerner who was governor of a populous Northern state. He was nominated as the Democratic presidential candidate in 1912, and although he won only a plurality of the popular vote in a three-way contest, his electoral vote majority was overwhelming. Wilson defeated two former presidents—incumbent William Howard Taft and former president Theodore Roosevelt. He carried forty of the forty-eight states, including all eleven of the former Confederate states.

Wilson openly eschewed many aspects of the Constitution and was reelected to a second term in 1916, but by a much narrower margin. Soon after taking the oath of office he concluded the United States could no longer remain neutral in World War I. On April 2, 1917, he asked Congress to declare war on Germany. In January 1918 Wilson presented to Congress the American war goals—the "Fourteen Points" that would establish a "general association of nations . . . affording mutual guarantees of political independence and territorial integrity to great and small states alike." The enormous American intervention made an immediate impact on the war in Europe and the Middle East, and by November 1918 the western Allies had defeated the coalition of Germany, Austria-Hungary, the Ottoman Empire, and Bulgaria, commonly referred to as the Central Powers.

After the war and against the advice of his doctors, Wilson made an exhaustive tour of the country to generate public support in order to pressure the Senate into ratifying the Treaty of Versailles, which would have included the United States joining the newly created League of Nations. Wilson suffered a stroke in October 1919 and was incapacitated for the remainder of his presidency, which ended in 1921.

As noted in more detail earlier, former Confederate Francis Cockrell was appointed to a federal government position by Wilson, and in 1913 became a member of the U.S. Department of War's Board of Ordnance and Fortifications. Cockrell, a former U.S. senator from Missouri, had previously served on the Interstate Commerce Commission in the Theodore Roosevelt administration.

Wilson appointed two former Confederates to diplomatic posts. Edward J. Hale, a former major in Lane's North Carolina Brigade, had served during the Cleveland administration as the U.S. consul to Manchester, England, and had been offered but declined ambassadorial appointments to Russia and the Ottoman Empire. Hale reentered public life in 1913 when Wilson appointed him ambassador to Costa Rica, a position he held until 1917.

Otis Allan Glazebrook

LOC

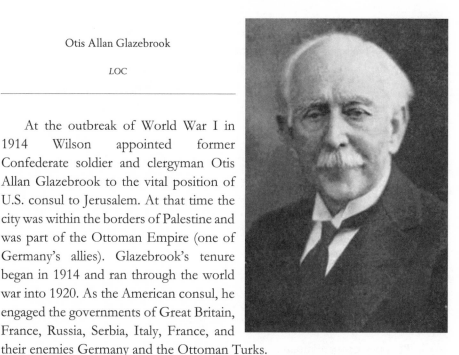

At the outbreak of World War I in 1914 Wilson appointed former Confederate soldier and clergyman Otis Allan Glazebrook to the vital position of U.S. consul to Jerusalem. At that time the city was within the borders of Palestine and was part of the Ottoman Empire (one of Germany's allies). Glazebrook's tenure began in 1914 and ran through the world war into 1920. As the American consul, he engaged the governments of Great Britain, France, Russia, Serbia, Italy, France, and their enemies Germany and the Ottoman Turks.

Glazebrook was born in Richmond, Virginia, in October 1845. He began his studies at Randolph-Macon College, but transferred to VMI at the outbreak of the Civil War. Glazebrook, an artillerist, fought in the Southern victory at New Market and later served with the cadet corps during the siege of Richmond and Petersburg. After the war he resumed his studies at VMI. On September 11, 1865, Glazebrook and fellow cadets Erskine Mayo Ross and Alfred Marshall founded the Alpha Tau Omega fraternity, a Christian society that advocated postwar reconciliation. "Alpha Tau Omega began as an idea in the mind of a young Civil War veteran who wanted peace and reconciliation," explains the history of the fraternity. "His name was Otis Allan Glazebrook. His people were defeated, it continues,

> many of their cities burned, much of their countryside ravaged. But Glazebrook, who had helped bury the dead of both sides, believed in a better future. He saw the bitterness and hatred that followed the silencing of the guns and knew that a true peace would come not from force of law, but rather from with the hearts of men who were willing to work to rekindle a spirit of brotherly love.[26]

26 ATO History Alpha Tau Omega America's Leadership Development Fraternity. (n.d.). Retrieved from https://ato.org/home/ato-history/.

After graduating from VMI Glazebrook enrolled at the Virginia Theological Seminary and 1869 was ordained a priest in the Episcopal Church. He served as a clergyman until his retirement in the spring of 1913, at which time he answered the call of Woodrow Wilson and entered the diplomatic service of the U.S. Department of State.

In November 1914 the Ottoman Turks entered World War I as an ally of Germany, and the Middle East became a sprawling secondary battleground between the Allies and the Central Powers. British forces from Egypt engaged Turkish, German, and Austrian forces in ferocious fighting for control of Palestine, whose capital city of Jerusalem was revered by both sides as a holy site. Most of the November-December 1917 Battle of Jerusalem occurred in the surrounding areas, thus sparing the city from any significant damage.

Glazebrook's diplomatic skills during such tenuous times were admired by both sides. Walter Hines Page, the U.S. ambassador to Great Britain during World War I, said of Glazebrook, "He founded a new diplomacy in the East and raised a consulate to the dignity of an embassy." Even the Turkish military commander of Jerusalem praised Glazebrook: "He is not only a consul by man's appointment, but of God's, a perfect gentleman and the ideal diplomat."[27]

After six highly successful years in the stressful position of consul to Jerusalem in 1920 Glazebrook was rewarded by Wilson with a transfer to the American consulate in Nice, France, then considered the choicest post in the U.S. diplomatic service. Glazebrook was retained in that position by President Calvin Coolidge, and retired in 1929.

Another VMI cadet who played a prominent role during the Wilson presidency was Virginia senator Thomas Staples Martin, coauthor of the Declaration of War against Germany in April 1917. Although Martin was ill and did not participate in the Battle of New Market in May 1864, as a cadet corps member he served in other actions, including the defense of Richmond and Petersburg in 1865.

Martin was born in Scottsville, Virginia, in 1847 and attended VMI in 1864 and 1865 before transferring to the University of Virginia. A lawyer by profession after the war, Martin became involved in politics and rose to become one of the most powerful U.S. senators. He was first elected in 1894, and in 1913 became Senate majority leader and president pro tem. In addition to authoring the Declaration of

27 Kamins, T. L., Friedman, G., Wineburg, R., And Wiener, J. (1931, May 12). Death of U. S. Consul in Jerusalem Who Distributed Jewish Relief Funds During War. Retrieved from https://www.jta.org/1931/05/12/archive/death-of-u-s-consul-in-jerusalem-who-distributed-jewish-relief-funds-during-war.

Thomas Staples Martin

LOC

War against Germany, during the war years Martin was chairman of the Senate Appropriations Committee.

Before his death in 1919, Martin served on the Board of Visitors of the U.S. Naval Academy and at the University of Virginia. At the time of his death he was the penultimate former Confederate soldier to serve in the U.S. Senate, survived only by Senator Charles Spalding Thomas of Colorado.

Woodrow Wilson's Declaration of War speech to Congress in 1917. *National Archives*

Part 2

United States Congress

The election of United States senators and members of the House of Representatives during the Reconstruction era was a complex process. Federal military rule immediately after the war, and the ratification of the Fourteenth Amendment on July 9, 1868, forbade many former Confederates from holding federal and state office. The Amnesty Act of 1872 restored the voting rights of most, but not all, former Confederates, and soon thereafter control of state governments was effectively returned to the former Confederate states.

Before the ratification of the Seventeenth Amendment to the Constitution in 1913, United States senators were elected by the legislatures of the individual states. This was deemed important by the Founders because it tied the senators to their states and made them answer to the state legislatures. The Seventeenth Amendment mandated that senators be elected by popular vote, which changed that key balancing act forever and shifted the centralizing power from the state capital to Washington, D.C. With the exception of Charles Spalding Thomas of Colorado, all former Confederates who had served in the U.S. Senate prior to that amendment were elected by their state legislatures.

Many former Confederates were elected to the U.S. Senate and House of Representatives from the eleven seceded states, but ex-Confederates were also elected to Congress from New York, Colorado, Kansas, New Mexico, from the "border states" of Kentucky and Missouri, and from West Virginia, which was

Isidor Straus

LOC

born in 1863 when its western counties seceded from Virginia and joined the Union. All of those states except Colorado also sent popularly elected former Rebels to the House of Representatives.

Perhaps the most intriguing former Confederate to serve in the U.S. Congress was Isidor Straus, a member of the House of Representatives from New York in 1894 and 1895.

Straus was born into a Jewish family in Bavaria (Germany) in 1845 and immigrated to Talbotton, Georgia, in 1854. Just before the outbreak of the Civil War Straus planned to attend the U.S. Military Academy at West Point, but after Fort Sumter he instead volunteered to serve with a Georgia infantry regiment. He was rejected because of his youth. When he turned eighteen in 1863 Straus was sent by the Confederate government to Europe as a commissioner to procure war supplies and blockade runners.

After the war Straus moved to New York, became a prosperous merchant, and along with his brother Nathan purchased the R. H. Macy and Company department store in 1896. Straus was a prominent member of the New York Board of Trade and was vice president of the New York City Chamber of Commerce. In 1905 he was awarded an honorary doctorate degree from Washington and Lee University.

William Alexander Harris

Kansas Historical Society

Charles Spalding Thomas

Kansas Historical Society

Straus was a business partner of, among others, the legendary financiers and philanthropists William Rockefeller and Cornelius Vanderbilt. Isidor and his wife Rosalie Ida were returning home in 1912 after wintering in southern France, and died aboard RMS *Titanic*. His body was recovered and interred in New York, but his wife was never found.

Kansas, a Union state during the Civil War and the scene of bloody guerrilla warfare prior to it, elected former Confederate William Alexander Harris as senator in 1897. Harris was a former VMI cadet and a captain and ordnance officer on the staff of Major General Robert E. Rodes. He also served as a member of the U.S. House of Representatives from Kansas.

In Colorado, a U.S. Territory from 1861 until gaining statehood in 1876, voters sent ex-Confederate and former governor Charles Spalding Thomas to the U.S. Senate, where he served from 1913 to 1921. According to the *Biographical Directory of the United States Congress*, Thomas was the last Confederate veteran to serve in the U.S. Senate. While a senator Thomas was both chairman of the Committee on Women's Suffrage and chairman of the Committee on Coastal Defenses.

West Virginia, created during the height of the war in 1863 when a group of Unionist counties seceded from Virginia, sent three former Confederates to the U.S. Senate. Allen Taylor Caperton, who had served in the Confederate Senate, was West Virginia's U.S. senator in 1875 and 1876. Charles James Faulkner, a former VMI cadet and combatant at New Market, was West Virginia's senator from 1887 to 1899. Faulkner also was the U.S. representative to the International Joint High Commission of the United States and Great Britain in 1898. The third former Confederate to represent West Virginia in the Senate was John Edward Kenna, a former private in the 23rd Battalion Virginia Infantry, who served from 1883 to 1893.

Former Southern soldiers who served in the U.S. House of Representatives from West Virginia included Eustace Gibson, a captain in the 49th Virginia Infantry, and Alpheus Haymond, a major on the staff of Brigadier General John Pegram. Haymond also was a justice on the West Virginia Supreme Court.

Border states Kentucky and Missouri sent several former Rebels to Washington, D.C. Representing Kentucky in the senate was the previously mentioned Joseph C. S. Blackburn, who served from 1885 to 1897 and again from 1901 to 1907. He also was a member of the House of Representatives and later was named governor of the Panama Canal Zone.

James Bennett McCreary, Kentucky's senator from 1903 to 1909, was a former colonel in the 11th Kentucky Cavalry. He also served in the U.S. House of Representatives, and was governor of Kentucky from 1912 to 1916. McCreary was appointed by President Benjamin Harrison as the U.S. delegate to the International Monetary Conference in Brussels, Belgium, in 1892.

Also serving as senators from Kentucky were William Lindsay of the 7th Kentucky Mounted Infantry; Willis Benson Machen, a former member of the Confederate House of Representatives; and former Brigadier General John Stuart Williams, who also was a cofounder of the city of Naples, Florida.

Kentucky's ex-Confederates who became members of the U.S. House of Representatives included William Breckinridge, a colonel in the 9th Kentucky Cavalry; John Caldwell, former colonel in the 9th Kentucky Infantry; Edward Crossland, an officer in the 1st Kentucky Infantry and 7th Kentucky Mounted Infantry; and Brigadier General Joseph H. Lewis, who also was chief justice of the Kentucky Supreme Court.

Two former Confederates represented Missouri in the U.S. Senate. Francis Marion Cockrell, who was written about earlier, was a senator from 1875 to 1905. Cockrell was joined in the Senate by George G. Vest, a former judge advocate and member of the Confederate House of Representatives.

In the New Mexico Territory, Thomas B. Catron served as U.S. senator from 1912 to 1917, as well as territorial U.S. representative from 1895-1897. Catron, a former lieutenant in the 3rd Missouri Artillery Battalion, also was the attorney general for the New Mexico Territory, U.S. district attorney for New Mexico, and the mayor of Santa Fe.

(See the Appendix for a complete list of senators and house members.)

Part 3

United States Military

"When the Spanish-American War came on, the men of the blue and the men of the gray stood shoulder to shoulder, the sons of the men who wore the blue and the gray in 1861-65 marched step with step, and won the victory that made us proud that we were Americans. Our country was thus cemented together as never before, and prejudices gave way to an era of good feeling throughout this Union."

— Marcus B. Toney, former Confederate private, 1st Tennessee Infantry

The Spanish-American War was a brief but momentous conflict between Spain and the United States that ended 400 years of Spanish colonialism in the Western Hemisphere. It also resulted in the United States acquiring Puerto Rico and Spanish-held territories in the Far East and western Pacific.

The struggle for Cuban independence began in earnest in 1868 when an armed rebellion was instigated by Carlos Manuel de Cespedes. The Ten Year War, as it is known, ended in failure for the Cuban nationalists. A second war for Cuban independence began in February 1895. Spain's brutal repression of the second rebellion was sensationalized by American newspapers, sparking outrage and public sympathy for the Cuban freedom fighters.

On January 24, 1898, in response to anti-Spanish violence in Havana, President William McKinley sent the battleship USS *Maine* into Havana's harbor to protect American citizens and property. On February 15, an explosion destroyed the *Maine* and the lives of 260 American sailors. Spain denied involvement in the tragedy, but the American public was enraged. Fearing United States involvement in the war with the Cuban rebels, Spain—in an effort to defuse tensions—announced on April 9 that Cuba would be granted limited autonomy. The U.S. Congress was unmoved and demanded that Cuba be granted full independence and that all Spanish armed forces be withdrawn from the island. Spain responded by declaring war on the United States on April 24, and the next day the United States answered by declaring war on Spain.

The U.S. Army had been greatly reduced during the three decades since the Civil War. Although the American navy was sizable, relatively modern, and growing, the Regular Army in April 1898 numbered only 2,100 officers and 26,000 enlisted personnel; it had approximately 13,000 infantry, 6,000 cavalry, 4,000 artillerymen, and 3,000 administrative and support personnel. After the declaration of war, President McKinley called for volunteers, hoping to recruit about 50,000 men. Between May 30 and August 24, however, 220,000 answered the call by volunteering and via the mobilization of state national guard units. In fact, 100,000 volunteers stepped forward on February 15, 1898, the day *after* the explosion and sinking of the USS *Maine*. Ultimately, only 72,000 troops were deployed to Cuba, with a smaller number sent to the Philippines.

The ensuing war was very brief, but it proved exceedingly costly for the Spanish. On May 1, 1898, the entire Spanish fleet stationed in the colony of the Philippines was destroyed or captured in Manila Bay by a single U.S. naval squadron. By that August, American troops had occupied Manila. Meanwhile, the Spanish Caribbean fleet was destroyed by United States naval forces between July 3 and July 17 while attempting to escape the harbor at Santiago, Cuba. U.S. ground forces and Cuban rebels encircled the city of Santiago, and Spanish forces there surrendered on July 17, effectively ending the war after less than three months. The Treaty of Paris, signed on December 10, 1898, granted independence to Cuba, and ceded Puerto Rico, Guam, and the Philippines to the United States.

In the buildup leading to the invasion of Cuba, the McKinley administration sought experienced and successful army and cavalry commanders. Many Confederate veterans—with their citizenship having been fully restored decades earlier—volunteered for service. Presidents Garfield and Cleveland had both appointed former Confederate officers William Hunt and Hilary Herbert as secretaries of the U.S. Navy in 1881 and 1893, respectively, and in 1898 McKinley would also call upon former Rebels to serve the reunited country.

The most high-profile of McKinley's former Confederate military appointees was Fitzhugh "Fitz" Lee, the nephew iconic General Robert E. Lee. Fitz Lee's military pedigree was further enhanced because his grandfather was none other

Fitzhugh "Fitz" Lee

LOC

than Henry "Light Horse Harry" Lee III, the commander of George Washington's cavalry during the Revolutionary War and later a governor of Virginia. Fitz Lee's great-great uncle was George Mason, a Founding Father and one of the authors of the Bill of Rights.

Fitzhugh Lee was born in Virginia in 1835. He graduated from West Point in 1856 and was assigned as a second lieutenant to the 2nd Cavalry Regiment. His uncle, Robert E. Lee, was the regiment's lieutenant colonel, and Colonel Albert Sidney Johnston was its commander. Fitz was wounded fighting Comanche Indians in 1859 in the Oklahoma Territory. When Virginia seceded in 1861, Lee resigned his position as instructor of cavalry at West Point and joined the Confederate Army. He initially served as a staff officer but was soon assigned to General J. E. B. Stuart's cavalry, rising to the rank of colonel, in command of the 1st Virginia Cavalry. Lee was promoted to brigadier general in July of 1862. Fitz Lee fought in most of the major campaigns in the Eastern Theater and held the rank of major general when he and the Army of Northern Virginia surrendered at Appomattox on April 9, 1865.

Renowned for his joviality and friendliness, Lee refused to allow sectional affiliation to affect his prewar relationships. During and after the war he retained cordial friendships with Confederate and Union officers alike, and during the postwar years he was a champion of national unity and reconciliation.

At the end of hostilities Lee returned to Virginia and took up farming and other business interests. He married in 1871 and had five children, two of whom became cavalry officers in the U.S. Army. In 1875 he delivered an address at the Battle of Bunker Hill centennial celebration in Boston, and in 1885 joined the governing board of West Point.

Lee became involved in politics and served as governor of Virginia from 1886 to 1890, and in 1896 was appointed consul general to Havana by President Grover Cleveland. With increasing tensions between Spain and the United States, Lee's consular duties expanded to include wider diplomatic and military matters. At the end of Cleveland's term, Lee was retained in his post by President McKinley. The sinking of the USS *Maine* and the declarations of war between Spain and the United States prompted Lee rejoined the U.S. Army. He became one of eight former Confederates to become general officers in the American army—four were commissioned major generals and four were brigadier generals of U.S. Volunteers. Lee was placed in command of the 7th Army Corps but at sixty-two years of age took no part in combat operations in Cuba. When Spain capitulated, however, he was assigned as military governor of Havana and the inland city of Pinar del Rio. Lee retired from the U.S. Army with the rank of brigadier general.

Joseph Wheeler

Encyclopedia of Alabama

Another renowned ex-Confederate general and cavalry corps commander to once again don a blue uniform was Joseph Wheeler, who, at age sixty-one, volunteered for duty during the Spanish-American War. President McKinley commissioned the aging Wheeler a major general of volunteers and he led a cavalry division that included future president Theodore Roosevelt and his famed "Rough Riders." Wheeler was in command at the decisive Battle of San Juan Hill on July 1, 1898.

Wheeler, a native of Georgia, had been raised in Derby, Connecticut, and New York City, and graduated from West Point in 1859. After brief service in the U.S. Army, Wheeler resigned his commission and volunteered for the Confederate Army. He quickly rose in rank to colonel and commanded the 19th Alabama Infantry. In the fall of 1862 Wheeler was promoted to brigadier general and made chief of cavalry of the Army of Tennessee with the rank of major general, a position he held for the remainder of the war with varying degrees of success.

After hostilities ended Wheeler briefly lived in New Orleans before moving to Alabama to become a planter and lawyer. He was a strong advocate of reunification and reconciliation between the North and South, and served in the U.S. House of

Joseph Wheeler and his subordinate commanders during the Spanish-American War.
Colonel Theodore Roosevelt is standing on the far right.

Encyclopedia of Alabama

Representatives from 1885 to 1900, where he was chairman of the Committee on Expenditures.

In 1897, Wheeler began advocating for American intervention in the Cuban revolution, proclaiming the United States had a duty to support "freedom, Christianity, and civilization." After the victory over Spain he was commissioned a brigadier general in the U.S. Army and commanded the 1st Brigade of the 2nd Division in the Philippine-American War. The division commander was General Arthur MacArthur, a former Union colonel in William T. Sherman's army who had opposed Wheeler in the 1864 Atlanta Campaign. He was also the father of Douglas MacArthur (1880-1964), future general of World War II and Korean War fame.

Thomas Lafayette Rosser

LOC

Wheeler retired from the U.S. Army in September 1900 and moved to New York City, where he died in 1906. He is one of the few Confederate officers buried at Arlington National Cemetery.

Another former Confederate general, Thomas Lafayette Rosser. The native Virginian attended West Point but resigned two weeks before graduation when his adopted state of Texas seceded from the Union. He volunteered for the Confederate Army and commanded a battery of the Washington (Louisiana) Artillery at First Manassas. He was promoted to captain and was seriously wounded during the Seven Days' Battles at Mechanicsville (Beaver Dam Creek) on June 26, 1862. Rosser later returned to service as colonel of the 5th Virginia Cavalry Regiment.

As part of General J. E. B. Stuart's command, Rosser participated in most of the Army of Northern Virginia's major battles in 1862 and early 1863 until he was wounded a second time at Kelly's Ford, Virginia, on March 17, 1863. He returned to duty in time to participate in Gettysburg Campaign, after which he was promoted to brigadier general. Rosser was wounded a third time at Trevilian Station, Virginia in June 1864—one of the largest cavalry battles of the war. Once more he recovered and returned to duty. He was promoted to major general in November 1864 and participated in the siege of Petersburg and Robert E. Lee's retreat to Appomattox. Rosser's command escaped the Union encirclement of Lee's army at Appomattox and refused to formally surrender. The war ended for Rosser when he was finally captured on May 4, 1865, near Staunton, Virginia.

After the war Rosser became a superintendent and engineering executive for three railroad companies, and was involved in new rail construction in the American and Canadian West. In 1886 he resigned and purchased land near Charlottesville, Virginia, where he took up farming. In 1898, on the eve of the Spanish-American War, Rosser returned to military service, this time with the U.S. Army. He was commissioned a brigadier general of volunteers by President

McKinley on June 10, 1898, and was tasked with training cavalry recruits in northern Georgia near the old Chickamauga battlefield. The old (and often ornery) officer did not see any action during the Spanish-American War and was honorably discharged on October 21, 1898. After the war he retired to his Charlottesville farm, where he died in 1910.

Several landmarks are named for Rosser in recognition of his service as a railroad executive: Rosser Avenue in Brandon, Manitoba, Canada; the village of Rosser near the Canadian city of Winnipeg; and Rosser Avenue in Bismarck, North Dakota. Rosser Avenue in Waynesboro, Virginia, and Rosser Lane in Charlottesville are named in honor of Rosser's Confederate military service.

Another former Confederate to wear the blue of the United States Army during the Spanish-American War was Matthew Calbraith Butler, a native of Greenville, South Carolina. Butler came from a family of soldiers and politicians. He was the nephew of U.S. Navy Commodore Oliver Hazard Perry, a hero of the War of 1812, and one of his first cousins, James Bonham, was killed at the Alamo in 1836. One of Butler's uncles, Andrew Butler, was a U.S. senator from South Carolina, and another uncle, Pierce Mason Butler, was a governor of the same state.

Matthew Butler graduated from the University of South Carolina in 1856, began practicing law in 1857, and enlisted in the Confederate Army in 1861. During the war he served as a cavalry commander in the Army of Northern Virginia, and lost a foot when he was wounded at the Battle of Brandy Station on June 9, 1863.

After returning to duty he was promoted to brigadier general in February 1864. Late in the war Butler was transferred to North Carolina, where he led a cavalry division at the Battle of Bentonville. He surrendered with General Joseph E. Johnston's Army of Tennessee at Bennett Place, North Carolina, on April 26, 1865.

After the war Butler returned to his law practice in Edgefield, South Carolina. He was elected to the U.S. Senate in 1876 and served three terms. While a senator, Butler served on the Foreign Relations,

Matthew Calbraith Butler

LOC

Territories, Military Affairs, Naval Affairs, Interstate Commerce, and Civil Service committees. When Butler lost his reelection bid in 1896 to the popular Ggovernor Benjamin Tillman of South Carolina, he resumed the practice of law in Washington, D.C.

Two years later on the eve of the Spanish-American War, President McKinley appointed Butler a major general of U.S. Volunteers. The former Confederate cavalryman supervised the evacuation of defeated Spanish troops from Cuba and was honorably discharged from the army on April 15, 1899.

In addition to the four former Confederate general officers who achieved that rank in the U.S. Army during the Spanish-American War era, four other former Confederates were commissioned brigadier generals of volunteers: former Colonel William Calvin Oates, Colonel Henry Thompson Douglas, Major John B. Castleman, and Captain William Washington Gordon, Jr.

Oates had a colorful and controversial political career before and after the Civil War. He was mainly self-taught, and eventually worked as an instructor of English, Latin, and mathematics at a school in Lawrenceville, Alabama. Interested in politics and public affairs Oates studied law, earned admission to the Alabama bar, and opened a practice in Abbeville in 1859. He enlisted in the Confederate Army in 1861. He helped raise a company of infantry from Henry County. Oates and his company, the "Henry Pioneers," were sent to Virginia and became Company G of the 15th Alabama Infantry, a regiment Oates would later command in January

1863. He gained fame at Gettysburg when the 15th Alabama launched its repeated but unsuccessful assaults against that part of Little Round Top held by the 20th Maine Infantry and its now-celebrated colonel, Joshua L. Chamberlain.

Oates and his regiment traveled to North Georgia with the bulk of General Longstreet's First Corps that September to reinforce the Army of Tennessee and participated in the Confederate victory at Chickamauga, where Oates was seriously wounded. He returned to service in March

William Calvin Oates

Encyclopedia of Alabama

of 1864 and fought in the Overland Campaign in northern Virginia. That August he was transferred to command the 48th Alabama Infantry. Oates was wounded on August 16, 1864, near Petersburg, Virginia, and his right arm was amputated. The war ended while Oates was recuperating at his home in Abbeville, Alabama.

After the war Oates was elected to the U.S. House of Representatives in 1880 and reelected six times. He ran for Alabama governor in 1894 and was elected, but served only two years before resigning to conduct an ultimately unsuccessful campaign for the U.S. Senate. He returned to the practice of law and in 1898 volunteered for the U.S. Army; President McKinley commissioned Oates a brigadier general of volunteers. He served briefly at Camp Meade, Pennsylvania. His command was not deployed and he did not see combat. Oates died in Montgomery, Alabama, in 1910.

Henry Thompson Douglas was born in New Kent County, Virginia. His military service began in 1861 with his commission as lieutenant of engineers on General John Magruder's staff and was later named chief engineer of A. P. Hill's famous "Light" Division. Douglas was promoted to captain and major and was ordered by Robert E. Lee to design and construct the intermediate defensive line of fieldworks around Richmond. When he finished, Douglas was promoted to colonel and transferred to the Trans-Mississippi Department, where he served as chief engineer for E. Kirby Smith until the end of the war.

After the Civil War, Douglas worked as a civil engineer for several railroad companies in Mexico and the United States. He became chief engineer of the Baltimore and Ohio Railroad in 1883 and served in that position until 1896. The following year he was appointed engineering commissioner for the City of Baltimore. Two years later he volunteered for U.S. Army service and was commissioned brigadier general of U.S. Volunteers during the Spanish-American War. He was given command of the 4th Illinois Regiment. After the war with Spain, Douglas became the chief engineer of the New York Rapid Transit Railroad. He died on July 20, 1926, at the age of eighty-seven and is buried in Hollywood Cemetery in Richmond, Virginia.

Another Spanish-American War volunteer was former Confederate Major John B. Castleman of the 2nd Kentucky Cavalry Regiment. A postwar Kentucky lawyer and politician, Castleman became known as the Father of the Louisville Park System and also served as president of the American Saddlebred Horse Association in 1892. At the outbreak of the Spanish-American War, Castleman was commissioned colonel of the 1st Kentucky Regiment of U.S. Volunteers and was involved in the invasion and occupation of Puerto Rico. After Spain's capitulation,

John B. Castleman

Morgan's Men Association

Castleman was commissioned a brigadier general in the Regular Army and served as military governor of Puerto Rico.

The lowest-ranking Confederate officer to receive a general's commission in the U.S. Army during the Spanish-American War was William Washington Gordon Jr., a former captain in the Army of Tennessee. Gordon served on the staff of the Confederate General Robert H. Anderson and was wounded at Lovejoy's Station after the Battle of Jonesborough (Georgia) in early September 1864. At the onset of the Spanish-American War, Gordon was commissioned a brigadier general of U.S. Volunteers and served on the Military and Naval Commission of the Puerto Rico evacuation.

Gordon was from a prominent Savannah, Georgia, family, graduated from Yale University in 1854, and returned to Savannah to become a cotton and rice broker. At the outbreak of the Civil War he enlisted in the Georgia Hussars and was commissioned a lieutenant. The Hussars was a famous cavalry company formed in 1736 as a colonial militia unit and served in the Revolutionary War, the Indian Wars, the Mexican War, the Civil War, World War I, World War II, the Korean War, and the Vietnam War as part of the Georgia National Guard. In the Civil War the Hussars were incorporated into the 5th Georgia Cavalry and served in both the Army of Northern Virginia under General J. E. B. Stuart and in the Army of Tennessee as part of General Joseph Wheeler's cavalry corps.

After the war, Gordon returned to his family's plantation, became chairman of the Savannah Cotton Exchange, and entered the banking and railroad businesses. He was elected to the Georgia Assembly in 1884, and he served as commander of the Georgia State Militia before his brief service as a brigadier general in the U.S. Army in 1898.

While Gordon served in Puerto Rico and Cuba during the Spanish-American War, his wife Nellie and daughter Juliette "Daisy" Gordon Low volunteered as nurses in Miami, Florida, where they cared for wounded and sick American

William Washington Gordon Jr.

Wikipedia

soldiers. Daisy would later become the founder and first president of the Girl Scouts of America.

In addition to the eight former Confederate Army officers appointed to the rank of general of volunteers in the U.S. Army by McKinley—Lee, Wheeler, Rosser, Butler, Oates, Douglas, Castleman, and Gordon—many other former Confederates served in the United States armed forces.

Thomas Young Aby, for example, was born in Mississippi in 1840 and was a student at the University of Virginia in 1856-1857. In 1861 he enlisted as a private in the Washington Artillery and was a sergeant by January 1, 1863. Aby later passed the Confederate Army Board of Medicine examination and was appointed assistant surgeon of the Washington Artillery. Dr. Aby was slightly wounded at Gettysburg and remained behind to care for Confederate wounded. He was captured, imprisoned at Fort McHenry, Maryland, and escaped on October 10, 1863. He rejoined the Washington Artillery and surrendered with the Army of Northern Virginia in April 1865.

Aby returned to Louisiana and earned a medical degree from the University of Louisiana in 1866. He practiced medicine in Monroe, Louisiana, and was elected mayor of Monroe in 1885. In 1898 he volunteered for service in the U.S. Army and was appointed by McKinley as an assistant surgeon. He returned to his medical practice after the war, and died in 1905.

John S. Bransford was a VMI cadet and wounded at the Battle of New Market. In February 1865 he withdrew from school and enlisted in the 1st Company, Richmond Howitzers in the defense of Richmond. Bransford was with the Army of Northern Virginia when it surrendered at Appomattox on April 12, 1865.

After the war Bransford enrolled at the Medical College of Virginia, graduated in 1867, and in 1872 became the first known former Confederate to enlist in the U.S. Navy, doing so as an assistant surgeon. He was promoted to surgeon in 1885 and retired in 1890 after nineteen years of service. At the outbreak of the

Spanish-American War, Bransford returned to naval service as a surgeon aboard the USS *Gloucester*, a converted yacht owned by financier J. Pierpont Morgan. During the July 3, 1898, Battle of Santiago, Bransford (an experienced Civil War artillerist) was placed in command of a gun during the *Gloucester's* battle with the Spanish destroyers *Pluton* and *Furor*. After sinking the two Spanish destroyers, the *Gloucester* rescued the crews while Bransford tended to the wounds of the Spanish fleet commander, Admiral Pascual Cervera y Topete, and several other Spanish officers. Bransford was one of twenty-eight U.S. servicemen recognized for conspicuous gallantry after the Battle of Santiago. He retired once again from the U.S. Navy on March 12, 1901.

William Hyslop Sumner Burgwyn, a former captain on the staff of Confederate General Thomas Lanier Clingman, served in the U.S. Army during the Spanish-American War. Burgwyn was born in Boston, Massachusetts, in 1845 and spent his childhood in Northampton County, Virginia. He was educated at private schools in Baltimore and Oxford, North Carolina, and enrolled at the University of North Carolina at Chapel Hill in 1860. In late 1861 Burgwyn enlisted in the 35th North Carolina Infantry and served as a captain until January 1864, when he was assigned as assistant adjutant general of General Clingman's Brigade. He was wounded at the Battle of Cold Harbor on June 1, 1864, and after returning to duty was wounded again on September 30, 1864, and captured. Burgwyn spent the rest of the war at Fort Delaware prison.

After the war Burgwyn returned to civilian life, graduated from the University of North Carolina at Chapel Hill, and earned a law degree from Harvard University. He established a law practice in Baltimore, and entered Washington Medical University in Baltimore and earned a degree as a medical doctor. In addition to being an attorney and a doctor, Burgwyn was an accomplished soldier. In July 1877 he offered his services to the governor of Maryland during the Baltimore and Ohio Railroad riot. He was appointed lieutenant colonel of the 8th Maryland Regiment (National Guard,) and was later promoted to colonel of the 5th Maryland Regiment. At the outbreak of the Spanish-American War, Burgwyn volunteered for service and was appointed colonel of the 2nd North Carolina in May 1898. He died in Richmond in 1913 and was buried in the Confederate section of Raleigh (North Carolina) Cemetery beside his brother, 21-year-old Colonel Henry Burgwyn, who had been killed at Gettysburg on July 1, 1863, leading the 26th North Carolina Infantry.

Another former Confederate, Edwin Augustus Young Osborne, colonel of the 4th North Carolina Infantry Regiment, served in the Spanish-American War under Colonel Burgwyn, but as a chaplain rather than as a soldier.

Osborne was born in Lawrence County, Alabama. His father had fought with Andrew Jackson at the Battle of New Orleans in the War of 1812. At the start of the Civil War Osborne enlisted and was elected a captain in the 4th North Carolina. He fought in the 1862 Peninsula Campaign and was wounded at the Battle of Seven Pines. He returned to duty and was wounded again at Sharpsburg (Antietam) on September 17, 1862. Osborne returned to his regiment and was wounded a third time at the Battle of the Wilderness in early May 1864. He was recuperating at his home in North Carolina with the rank of colonel when his regiment surrendered at Appomattox in April 1865. After the war Osborne taught school and practiced law, but in 1877 decided to become a clergyman and was ordained a priest in the Episcopal Church in 1881. In 1886 he founded the Thompson Orphanage and Training Institution in Charlotte, North Carolina.

When war broke out with Spain, Osborne volunteered to serve as chaplain of the 2nd Regiment of North Carolina under Colonel Burgwyn. In May 1898 a training and mobilization facility was established at Camp Dan Russell near Raleigh, North Carolina. Problems plagued the 2nd North Carolina, including desertions, medical discharges brought about by the oppressive heat, insufficient weapons training, and low morale. By July half of the troops were sick and excused from duty and a typhoid fever outbreak killed seven men and hospitalized many more. The regiment was sent to Florida and Georgia to await deployment to Cuba, and by early August only one surgeon, a few attendants, and Chaplain Osborne remained at the Camp Russell hospital to care for twenty-seven patients.

The war ended before the 2nd North Carolina was deployed, and the men arrived back in Raleigh in September 1898. After the conflict Osborne returned to the priesthood, and served until his death in 1925 at the age of eighty-nine.

Another chaplain in the 1989 War with Spain who also saw service with the Southern army was Benjamin Franklin "Frank" Stringfellow, a former Virginia cavalryman and spy during the Civil War. At the outbreak of the war, Stringfellow enlisted and was commissioned a captain in the 4th Virginia Cavalry and served as a scout for General James Ewell Brown (Jeb) Stuart. Stringfellow also served as a confidential scout and spy for Robert E. Lee, and often traveled behind Union lines in Alexandria, Virginia, and Washington, D.C.

At the end of the war Stringfellow refused to take the loyalty oath and moved to Canada. In 1867 he returned to Virginia and enrolled at the Episcopal Seminary of Virginia (later named Virginia Theological Seminary) and was ordained an Episcopal priest. Stringfellow served in several Virginia parishes and was the first chaplain at the exclusive Woodberry Forest School for Boys when it was founded in 1889. When war with Spain was declared in 1898, Stringfellow volunteered as a chaplain for the U.S. Army.

Virgil Young Cook was a native of Graves County, Kentucky, who, as a 14-year-old in 1861, ran away from home to join his older brother in the 12th Kentucky Cavalry. The brothers were soon transferred to 7th Kentucky Mounted Infantry under General Nathan Bedford Forrest and survived the war, surrendering in Gainesville, Alabama, on May 16, 1865.

Cook moved to Arkansas and eventually became a successful merchant and plantation owner. At the outbreak of the Spanish-American War, Cook raised a company of volunteers named the V. Y. Cook Rifles, which was organized into the 2nd Regiment of Arkansas Volunteer Infantry. Cook, who had been commissioned a brigadier general in the Arkansas State Guard in 1897, was commissioned colonel of volunteers and placed in command of the 2nd Arkansas Infantry. The Arkansas troops were ordered to Camp Shipp in Anniston, Alabama, for equipping, training, and organization. At various times Cook commanded three different brigades of volunteers, and for a brief time was in command of all U.S. troops at Camp Shipp. Because of the short duration of the war, Cook and the 2nd Arkansas Infantry were not deployed, and were mustered out of service in February 1899.

After the war Cook returned to Arkansas and in 1908 moved to Batesville, Arkansas, where he built a large home now know as the Cook-Morrow House, which is on the National Register of Historic Places.

John Carmichael, a native of Augusta, Georgia, also served during the conflict with Spain. A VMI cadet, Carmichael withdrew from school in late 1864 to return to Georgia and was commissioned a lieutenant in the state militia. He returned to VMI after the war, graduated in 1870, and taught engineering at the school for one year before opening a private engineering practice.

Grover Cleveland appointed Carmichael as an engineer in the United States Land Office during hi first presidential administration, and during his second term appointed him inspector of surveyors-general of the U.S. Land Office. On May 18, 1898, Carmichael was commissioned a captain of U.S. Volunteers in the buildup to the Spanish-American War, but was not deployed overseas. He died in Lakeland, Florida, on August 17, 1898.

Hugh Haralson Colquitt enlisted as a private in the 2nd Battalion, Georgia Infantry early in the Civil War. He was commissioned a lieutenant and transferred to his older brother's brigade, where he served General Alfred H. Colquitt as an aide-de-camp and assistant adjutant general until he surrendered on May 24, 1865.

In the summer of 1898, Colquitt volunteered for the 3rd U.S. Volunteer Infantry in Macon, Georgia, and was commissioned a captain. The regiment

William Crawford Smith

Interestingamerica.com

departed for Cuba on August 13, 1898, and the next day Spain and the United States declared a cease fire, effectively ending the war. The 3rd U.S. Volunteers arrived in Cuba on August 17 and served as an occupation force until March 30, 1899. The regiment suffered no combat casualties, but forty enlisted men died of disease during their seven months of service.

One Confederate veteran who lost his life during the War with Spain was William Crawford Smith, who served as a sergeant and ensign in the 12th Virginia Infantry. Smith died on February 5, 1899, at the Battle of Manila during the Philippine Insurrection—a conflict related to the hostilities between Spain and the United States.

Smith was born in Petersburg, Virginia, in the 1837 and moved to Middle Tennessee in the 1850s. At the beginning of the Civil War he returned to Virginia and enlisted in the 12th Virginia on May 17, 1861. The next year Smith was wounded and captured at the South Mountain and exchanged. He was promoted to sergeant in August 1863 and was wounded again at the Battle of the Wilderness in 1864. He eventually returned to duty and surrendered with Lee's army at Appomattox.

After the war Smith returned to Tennessee and became a prominent Nashville building contractor and architect. He was involved in the construction of some of the early buildings erected at Vanderbilt University. He went on to designed and build the Parthenon in Centennial Park in Nashville, a full-scale replica of the ancient Parthenon in Athens, Greece that is now listed on the National Register of Historic Places. In 1887 Smith volunteered for service in the 1st Tennessee Militia and on May 19, 1898, was commissioned colonel in command of the regiment that would be named the 1st Tennessee Infantry Regiment of U.S. Volunteers.

In 1898 the 1st Tennessee was sent to Camp Merriam, at the Presidio in San Francisco, California, and deployed to the Philippines, where Smith led the 1,320-man regiment in combat against Filipino commander Emilio Aguinaldo's insurgent forces. Smith died while leading his men at the Battle of Manila on February 5, 1899, his death attributed to heat stroke. His body was returned to Nashville and, after a large state funeral on April 19, 1899, was buried in Mt. Olivet Cemetery.

Another former Confederate who served in the U.S. Army during the Spanish-American War era and led a rather remarkable life was Blair Dabney Taylor. Born in 1848 in Caroline County, Virginia, Taylor was also a cadet at VMI, fought at New Market, and served in the defense of Richmond. After the war Taylor earned a medical degree at the University of Virginia and entered New York University and graduated with another medical degree. In June 1875, Taylor was appointed assistant surgeon in the U.S. Army.

Taylor's notable U.S. Army career took him to the American West, where he accompanied Colonel George Custer's ill-fated expedition against the Sioux in 1876, as well as into the Dakota territories, Texas, the Indian territories, Minnesota, and Hawaii. By 1893 had earned promotions to major and surgeon. Taylor commanded the army hospital at Fort Oglethorpe, Georgia (next to the Chickamauga battlefield) during the Spanish-American War. From 1902 to 1906 he served as a lieutenant colonel in command of the Army and Navy General Hospital in Hot Springs, Arkansas, and from December 1906 to 1908 worked as chief surgeon of the U.S. Army during the Cuban Pacification. Taylor was promoted to colonel and assistant surgeon general of the U.S. Army in 1908, a position he held until his retirement in 1911. After he retired Taylor moved to Atlanta and died there in 1930 at age eighty-two.

William Alexander Montgomery, who would serve the Confederacy as an infantryman, cavalryman, and scout, was born in Winston County, Mississippi, in 1844. He was sixteen when he entered Confederate service in May of 1861 as a private in the 12th Mississippi Infantry. Montgomery developed a crippling condition in one of his knees while serving in Virginia and was discharged. He returned to Mississippi believing his military career was over.

In 1863, when General Ulysses S. Grant commenced what would be his final operation against Vicksburg, Montgomery offered his services as a scout to the Confederate commanders, who were happy to have a local resident who knew the area. After the May 12 Battle of Raymond, Montgomery served as a scout in Colonel Wirt Adams' Tennessee Cavalry. Adams's command eluded capture when Vicksburg surrendered and thereafter operated with General Joseph E. Johnston's small command in northern and central Mississippi. Montgomery continued to be an effective scout for Johnston and was commissioned a captain in March 1864 and ordered to raise a company of scouts to operate independently in the Natchez area.

The newly raised company eventually joined Adams's cavalry brigade in Alabama, and surrendered on May 12, 1865.

After the war Montgomery returned to Mississippi and became a lawyer, opening a practice in 1868. In 1875 he became a major in the Mississippi State Militia. At the outbreak of the Spanish-American War, Montgomery was commissioned a colonel and placed in command of the 2nd Mississippi Regiment of U.S. Volunteers. The unit was mustered into service in Jackson, Mississippi, in May 1898 and ordered to Jacksonville, Florida, on June 20. The 2nd Mississippi was never deployed and transferred to Lauderdale Springs, Mississippi, in September. It was mustered out of service on December 20, 1898.

Former Rebel officer William Mecklenburg Polk volunteered for the U.S. Army Reserve Medical Corps in 1917, received a commission as first lieutenant, and served until his death on June 23, 1918. Although his service was brief and he was not activated, Polk was the only known Confederate officer to have been a member of the United States Army during World War I.

Polk was born in Maury County, Tennessee, in 1844 and served as captain on the staff of his father, Confederate Lieutenant General Leonidas Polk, until the elder Polk was killed on June 14, 1864 north of Atlanta on Pine Mountain. After the war William attended the College of Physicians and Surgeons in New York City and taught medicine there at Bellevue Hospital Medical College (which later merged with the New York University School of Medicine), City College of New York (formerly the University of the City of New York). He eventually served as dean and professor of gynecology at the Cornell University Medical College. Polk was named president of the American Gynecological Society in 1896, and president of the New York Academy of Medicine in 1910.[1]

Patrick Henry Morgan, a VMI cadet veteran of the Battle of New Market, was a native North Carolinian who served as superintendent of the 7th District, U.S. Coast Guard (formerly the United States Life Saving Service) from 1896 to 1916. At that time, the district extended from Cape Henry, Virginia, to Little River in South Carolina.

Spier Whitaker, Jr. was born in North Carolina in 1841, and he and his family moved to Davenport, Iowa, in 1854. Three years later Whitaker enrolled at the University of North Carolina at Chapel Hill, but withdrew during his final year and enlisted as a private in the 1st North Carolina Infantry. He was captured in New Bern, North Carolina, on March 14, 1862, imprisoned for four months, exchanged,

---

1 See page 110 for more biographical information on Polk.

and joined the Army of Northern Virginia. Whitaker served the remainder of the war and attained the rank of lieutenant. He surrendered with Lee's army at Appomattox in April 1865.

Whitaker returned home to Iowa after the war, but in 1866 relocated to his native state of North Carolina, where he practiced law, served as a judge, and was elected to the state senate. When the Spanish-American War began, Whitaker was commissioned a major in the 6th Regiment of North Carolina Volunteers and was en route to Puerto Rico when the war ended.

Thomas Jordan, did not serve directly in the U.S. military after the Civil War, but he nonetheless furthered American regional interests in the postwar era. Jordan was a former brigadier general in the Confederate Army. Before the Civil War, Jordan had served in the U.S. Army in the Second Seminole War and the Mexican War. After the Civil War, Jordan returned to military duty and led the Cuban Liberation Army in 1869 and 1870, three decades before Cuban independence was won as a result of the Spanish-American War.

Jordan was a native of Virginia and graduated from West Point in 1840. He served in the U.S. Army until 1861, at which time he enlisted in the Confederate Army and received a commission as a captain. Jordan fought at First Manassas and later served on the staff of Generals P. G. T. Beauregard and Braxton Bragg. By the end of the war Jordan was a brigadier general in command of the Third Military District of South Carolina.

After the war Jordan lived in Tennessee and worked briefly as a newspaper editor. With the benefit of his lengthy military experience, he joined a Cuban insurgent army as chief of staff in 1869. On May 11, 1869, Jordan became general in chief of the Cuban Liberation Army and led a 300-man rebel invasion of Cuba in hopes of sparking a more widespread revolution. This first armed Cuban attempt for independence would become known as the Ten Years' War. In December 1869 Jordan took command of the Cuban "Mambi" army and defeated Spanish forces at Guaimaro in January 1870, but exhausted most of his ammunition and supplies doing so. Jordan resigned from the Cuban insurgency in February 1870, ending his extensive military career. He died in New York City in 1895, three years before Cuba would win its long-sought independence.

Part 4

Governors

should come as no surprise that many former Confederates were elected to governorships of the eleven seceded Southern states. Former rebels also became governors of the "border states" Missouri and Kentucky, the Union state of Colorado, and even West Virginia, which was comprised of counties that had seceded from Virginia in 1863 and joined the Union. Former Confederates also were appointed by American presidents to territorial governorships in Utah, New Mexico, Oklahoma, the Panama Canal Zone, and the United States possession of Alaska (later a territory).

In 1899, Coloradans elected Charles Spalding Thomas to a two-year term as governor. The native of Darien, Georgia, graduated from the University of Michigan and served the Confederate cause as a member of the Georgia State Militia near the end of the war. After his term as Colorado governor, Thomas represented the state in the U.S. Senate.

What a difference thirteen years can make. In 1876, the citizens of staunchly pro-Union West Virginia elected Henry Mason Mathews as their governor. The native of Greenbrier County, West Virginia (formerly Virginia) was a former major on the staff of Major General William Wing Loring. Mathews, who had served as the state's attorney general, became West Virginia's fifth governor.

The border state of Missouri elected former Confederate Major General John Sappington Marmaduke governor in 1884. Marmaduke was a native of the state

Simon Bolivar Buckner

Wikipedia

and the son of Meredith Miles Marmaduke, a former Missouri governor and veteran of the War of 1812. The younger Marmaduke attended Yale and Harvard before eventually graduating from the U.S. Military Academy at West Point in 1857. He served in the U.S. Army until the outbreak of the Civil War, at which time he resigned his commission to volunteer for Confederate service. Marmaduke gained fame as a high-ranking cavalry commander west of the Mississippi River and conducted numerous operations within his native state.

Another border state, Kentucky, elected two former Confederate officers to serve as governors. James Bennett McCreary was a lieutenant colonel of the 11th Kentucky Cavalry and a graduate of Centre College in Danville, Kentucky, and Cumberland University in Lebanon, Tennessee. McCreary, a native of the Bluegrass, was twice elected governor and served from 1875 to 1879, and again three decades later from 1911 to 1915. In addition to his two terms, McCreary represented Kentucky in the U.S. Senate and House of Representatives.

Kentuckians also elected Simon Bolivar Buckner governor in 1887. Buckner was born in Munfordville, Kentucky, in 1823, and graduated from West Point in 1844. He served in the U.S. Army, fought in the Mexican War, and played a prominent role in the Western Theater in many Civil War battles. He had the unfortunate luck of being trapped in Fort Donelson in February 1862 and forced by his superiors to surrender unconditionally to his prewar friend Maj. Gen. U. S. Grant. Bolivar's son, Simon Bolivar Buckner Jr., served as a lieutenant general in the U.S. Army during World War II and was killed in action on Okinawa on June 18, 1945—the highest-ranking American officer killed by direct enemy fire during the war.

William T. Thornton was New Mexico's former Confederate governor and he was also the first mayor of Santa Fe. He served as the state's fifteenth governor when he was appointed to a four-year term in 1893 by President Grover Cleveland.

Mottrom Dulany Ball

Unknown

Thornton was born in 1843 in Calhoun, Missouri, and volunteered for Confederate service in 1861 as a member of Wood's Battalion, Missouri Cavalry. He eventually gained the rank of sergeant, was captured in February of 1862, and spent a year as a prisoner in Alton, Illinois.

Former Confederate William Cary Renfro was appointed governor of the Oklahoma Territory by President Grover Cleveland on May 7, 1893. Renfro, a native North Carolinian, had served as a sergeant in the 50th North Carolina Infantry.

Another of President Cleveland's territorial governor appointments was former Confederate Sergeant Caleb Walton West of the 1st Kentucky Infantry. West served as governor of the Utah Territory from 1886 to 1889. He was appointed to a second term in 1893 and was its last territorial governor. Utah became the forty-fifth state on January 4, 1896.

Mottrom Dulany Ball, a veteran of the 11th Virginia Cavalry, was appointed by President Rutherford B. Hayes to a federal position in the United States' possession of Alaska in 1878. Ball is considered one of the state's founding fathers. Purchased from Russia in 1867, Alaska became a territory in 1912. During the intervening years, the United States government administered the area from the town of Sitka, where an office of the Department of the Treasury enforced customs regulations. Ball was the highest-ranking governmental official in Alaska (March 27, 1878 – June 13, 1879) and was recognized as the de facto governor.

Ball remained in Alaska after his tenure in Sitka ended with the change of presidential administrations. In 1881, he organized the Alaska Territorial Convention in the future state capital of Juneau. Ball was elected Alaska's unofficial representative and traveled to Washington, D.C., to lobby for Alaska to be granted territorial status. As a result of his efforts, in 1884 Congress authorized Alaska to have a governor, district court, district attorney, U.S. marshal, and other governmental offices. When Cleveland became president in 1885, Ball was appointed as the first U.S. district attorney for Alaska, a position he held for only two years until his death in 1887. Ball was the first publicly elected official in Alaska. The Ball Islets in Sitka Sound, southwest of Sitka National Park, are named in his honor.

Another possession of the United States—neither a territory nor a state—was the Panama Canal Zone, which at one time was governed by a former Confederate. After France abandoned its attempt to build a canal across the isthmus of Panama in the late nineteenth century, the United States joined with France and other nations to undertake another attempt in 1903. The U.S. led the massive undertaking and in 1907 President Theodore Roosevelt appointed former Confederate judge advocate Colonel Joseph C. S. Blackburn as the fourth governor of the Panama Canal Zone. Blackburn, a native Kentuckian, had previously served as U.S. senator from Kentucky, where he was chairman of the Senate Rules Committee, as well as in the House of Representatives, where he chaired the Committee on War Expenditures and the Rules Committee.

(See the Appendix for a complete list of governors.)

Part 5

City Founders and Mayors

$\mathcal{There}$ were numerous—indeed, too many to list—former Confederates elected mayors of cities and towns within the eleven seceded states. Some were elected in other states outside the old Confederacy. Former rebels also founded several cities in the South and elsewhere.

Among the most surprising locales that elected ex-Confederates were Los Angeles, California, Minneapolis, Minnesota, Ogden, Utah, and Santa Fe, New Mexico.

Mayors

Los Angeles, California

Cameron Erskine Thom was elected to a two-year term as mayor of Los Angeles on December 9, 1882, and in 1888 he was a member of the Board of Freeholders, the predecessor to the Los Angeles County Board of Supervisors.

Thom was born in Culpeper County, Virginia, in 1825, the son of a veteran of the War of 1812. The younger Thom earned a law degree from the University of Virginia, and in 1849 traveled to Sacramento, California, hoping to strike it rich in the gold fields. When that failed he moved to San Francisco in 1853 and later to Los Angeles, working in both cities as a U.S. Land Commission agent. He also served as

Cameron Erskine Thom

Los Angeles Public Library

Los Angeles city attorney from 1856 to 1858, Los Angeles county district attorney from 1854 to 1857, and in 1859 was elected to the California State Senate. When the Civil War began, he returned home to offer his services to the Confederacy.

Extensive records show Thom serving as a volunteer aide to generals J. E. B. Stuart and Gustavus W. Smith, and applications for an officer's commission were sent to the Confederate War Department and Adjutant General Samuel Cooper. Thom was wounded at Gettysburg in July 1863, recovered, and served in the Army of Northern Virginia through the Appomattox Campaign and its surrender on April 9, 1865.

After the war Thom returned to California and resumed his remarkable career as a public servant and entrepreneur. In 1869 he was reappointed to his previous position as Los Angeles County district attorney, a position he held until 1873, and again from 1877 to 1879. In 1887 Thom was one of the five individuals who founded Glendale, California. Heremained active in Los Angeles city and business affairs, including law and banking, until his death on February 2, 1915, at the age of eighty-nine.

Minneapolis, Minnesota

Philip Bickerton Winston left his home in Hanover Courthouse, Virginia, at the age of seventeen to enlist as a private in the 5th Virginia Cavalry. He eventually reached the rank of lieutenant and served most of the war on the staff of General Thomas L. Rosser. Winston saw extensive action at the battles of Brandy Station, Gettysburg, the Wilderness, Spotsylvania Court House, Cedar Creek, and Five Forks. He surrendered with Lee's army at Appomattox.

Philip Bickerton Winston

Wikipedia

Winston remained in Virginia until 1872, when he moved west with his younger brother Fendall to Minneapolis, Minnesota. Three years later the brothers founded a railroad construction company, and over the next twenty-five years worked on projects in Minnesota, Illinois, Indiana, Wisconsin, Iowa, Nebraska, and across the Dakotas. The popular and prosperous businessman was elected mayor of Minneapolis in 1891 and served in the House of Representatives of his adopted state from 1893 to 1895, and again from 1899 until his death in Chicago in 1901 at the age of fifty-six. He loved Minnesota, but was returned to Virginia for burial.

Ogden, Utah

Confederate veteran David Harold Peery was twice elected mayor of Ogden, Utah, serving from 1883 until 1887. Born on May 16, 1824, in Tazewell County, Virginia, Peery in early 1862 volunteered for Confederate service but because of his age was assigned to General Humphrey Marshall's staff. In December 1862 he was transferred to Kentucky, where he continued his staff duties for General John S. Williams.

David Harold Peery

Church of Jesus Christ of Latter Day Saints

At the end of his enlistment in 1864, Peery—a convert to the Mormon faith—moved his family to Ogden, where he took up farming and teaching. He established several businesses and prospered in banking, milling, and publishing. In 1875 he undertook missionary work in Texas, Tennessee, and Virginia. After returning to Utah, Peery was elected mayor of Ogden in 1883 and again in 1885. He also served on Utah's territorial council for many years and was a strong advocate of Utah statehood. Peery died on September 17, 1901.

Santa Fe, New Mexico

Citizens of the New Mexico Territory's capital of Santa Fe elected two former Confederate soldiers as mayors in the 1890s and early 1900s. As noted earlier, the first was former New Mexico governor William T. Thornton—mayor of Santa Fe from 1891 to 1893. The second was Thornton's early law partner Thomas Benton Catron, who held the office from 1906 to 1908.

Catron was born in Lafayette County, Missouri, in 1840 and graduated from the University of Missouri in 1860. He enlisted in the Confederate Army and served in the 3rd Missouri Artillery Battalion, earning the rank of lieutenant. He fought in the Trans-Mississippi Department before moving east to serve in campaigns in Mississippi, Alabama, and Tennessee. Catron surrendered in the spring of 1865 as part of Confederate General Richard Taylor's command.

In addition to serving as Santa Fe's mayor, Catron's extensive political career included six years as a member of the New Mexico Territorial Council, attorney general of the territory, one term as a delegate to the U.S. House of Representatives, and service as a U.S. district attorney. Catron was a driving force behind New Mexico statehood, and when it was admitted to the Union in 1912, Catron was rewarded by being elected as

Thomas Benton Catron

LOC

the new state's first U.S. senator. In that position he served as chairman of the Committee on Expenditures in the Interior Department. Catron also served as president of the New Mexico Bar Association. He died on May 15, 1916. Catron County, New Mexico, is named in his honor.

City Founders

Naples, Florida

The Florida city of Naples was co-founded in 1886 by former Confederate Brigadier General John Stuart Williams. A native of Mt. Sterling, Kentucky, Williams graduated from Miami University in Oxford, Ohio, in 1839, and served in the Mexican War as colonel of the 4th Regiment of Kentucky Volunteers.

Williams opened a law practice in Paris, Kentucky, in 1840 and served in the Kentucky House of Representatives from 1851 to 1853. At the outbreak of the Civil War he volunteered for the Confederate Army and was commissioned a colonel in command of the 5th Kentucky Infantry Regiment. In 1862 Williams was promoted to brigadier general and organized and commanded a brigade of cavalry. He fought in several battles in Kentucky and southwestern Virginia before joining General Joseph Wheeler's cavalry corps in Georgia in 1864. He served until the end of the war in the spring of 1865.

After the war Williams took up farming in Clark County, Kentucky. He returned to the Kentucky House of Representatives in 1873, and in 1879 was elected to a six-year term in the U.S. Senate. In the late 1880s Williams, along with Louisville businessman and newspaper publisher Walter N. Haldeman, became involved in land speculation and development in Florida, and in 1886 they founded the city of Naples. Williams died in 1898.

John Stuart Williams

Wikipedia

Abilene, Texas

The north-central Texas city of Abilene owes much of its existence to Claiborne Walker Merchant, a former captain in the 14th Texas Cavalry. Born in Nacogdoches County, Texas, in 1836, Merchant returned to the area after the war and became a cattle rancher and land speculator.

In 1880 a group of Taylor County ranchers and businessmen led by Merchant persuaded the Texas and Pacific Railroad to route a new rail line to an area where a new town would be established. In 1881 the town of Abilene—named after Abilene, Kansas—was created, and on January 2, 1883, residents voted to incorporate the city. According to the Texas State Historical Society, Merchant became known as the "Father of Abilene."

Merchant became a highly successful cattleman and banker and was a director of the Abilene Central Railroad. In 1891, Merchant was among a group of Abilene citizens who organized Hardin-Simmons University; the land for the school was donated by Merchant, who later served on the school's board of trustees. Merchant died on March 9, 1926.

Glendale, California

In addition to being mayor of Los Angeles in 1882 and 1883, Cameron Erskine Thom was a cofounder of the city of Glendale.

Land in Los Angeles County that was part of Rancho San Rafael was divided in 1871 in what was known as the "Great Partition." Thom was one of twenty-eight resultant landowners, and his 724 acres was one of the largest parcels. His land and that of three others evolved into Glendale. Thom, along with H. L. Crow, B. F. Patterson, B. T. Byram, and Thom's nephew and fellow Confederate veteran Erskine Mayo Ross, formally created the city in 1887.

Julian, California

Two former Confederates, cousins Drury Bailey of the 3rd Georgia Cavalry and Michael Julian of the 21st Georgia Infantry, founded the city of Julian, California, located fifty miles northeast of San Diego.

The town was named Julian in honor of Michael Julian, who later was elected San Diego County assessor. Gold was discovered in the area in 1870, triggering San

Diego's first and only gold rush, which lasted until around 1900. Although some mining continued, pioneers began farming the rich land. The area remains a famous agricultural and recreational center.

Kalispell, Montana

Charles Edward Conrad, who rode with Colonel John Singleton Mosby's Rangers, was heavily involved in the development of the state of Montana and co-founded the city of Kalispell in 1892.

Conrad built a major trading company that helped support north central and northwestern Montana. He lived in Fort Benton, Montana, and President Theodore Roosevelt was once a guest in his home. Conrad helped the endangered buffalo by starting his own herd, which eventually provided the nucleus of the National Bison Range herd.

$Part\ 6$

Officers of Professional Societies

After the Civil War, many men who had fought for the former Confederacy ascended to the highest levels of national and state professional societies, and not all of them were located in the eleven seceded states.

Before the war, many future Confederates had received training—especially in the law, the medical field, and engineering—in established and very prestigious northern universities like Harvard and Yale, as well as the University of Virginia, which at that time was the largest and most elite of all Southern colleges.

Many Confederate army surgeons returned to the private practice of medicine after the conclusion of the Civil War, while others used their training as medical educators. Likewise, former Confederate officers who were prewar attorneys returned to the practice of law and many entered politics. Several wartime engineers became prominent architects and engineers after the war and, like former Confederate physicians and attorneys, eventually held high offices in professional societies.

The national professional societies led by former Confederates in the field of medicine include the American Medical Association, the American Gynecological and Obstetrical Society, the American Neurological Association, and the American Surgical Association. In public health policy, ex-Confederates were presidents of the American Public Health Association and the Havana Yellow Fever

Convention. In science and engineering, they led the American Society of Civil Engineers, the American Association for the Advancement of Science, and the Geological Society of America. One man who had fought for the South was also a cofounder of the environmental and preservation advocacy group Sierra Club—which still exists—and another Southern intellectual and scholar was president of the Society for Classical Studies (at the time named the American Philological Association). Others were presidents of the Southern Baptist Convention and the American Saddlebred Horse Association.

American Medical Association

Several former Southern officers became presidents of the American Medical Association (AMA): Hunter Holmes McGuire, Henry Fraser Campbell, John Allan Wyeth, and Tobias Gibson Richardson. Four others served as vice presidents of the organization: John R. Deering, Robert A. Kinloch, Richard F. Michel, and Francis P. Porcher. Another, Alexander N. Talley, became chairman of the AMA's section on medical jurisprudence, chemistry, and psychology.

After an original convention of physicians was organized in 1845, the AMA was officially founded in 1847 in Philadelphia, Pennsylvania, at a meeting attended by approximately 250 delegates representing twenty-eight colleges and universities and forty-two individual medical societies across the country. By the early twenty-first century the AMA's membership stood at nearly a quarter of a million physicians and associates.

After the Civil War numerous former Confederate surgeons and physicians served as presidents and officers of the AMA and other national medical societies, as well as their state and regional-level counterparts. The first among them to serve as president of the AMA was Tobias Gibson Richardson, M.D., who during the war was medical inspector of the Army of

Tobias Gibson Richardson, M.D.

Tulane University

Tennessee, and who famously performed the amputation of Confederate General John Bell Hood's leg after the Battle of Chickamauga. Richardson was a native of Louisville, Kentucky, where in 1848 he received his medical degree from the University of Louisville. He taught and practiced medicine in Louisville until 1858, when he joined the faculty of the Medical Department of the University of Louisiana (later the Tulane University School of Medicine.) While teaching at the university he was chairman of the Department of Surgery and also was attending surgeon at Charity Hospital in New Orleans.

In December 1861 Richardson enlisted in the Confederate Army and was assigned to General Braxton Bragg's staff. In April 1863 he was assigned to the Army of Tennessee and served with that command for the balance of the war. Richardson was part of President Jefferson Davis's fleeing entourage when the Confederate chief executive was captured near Irwinville, Georgia, on May 10, 1865.

After the war Richardson returned to New Orleans and resumed his duties as attending surgeon at Charity Hospital and instructor at the University of Louisiana. He was also dean of the University of Louisiana's medical school from 1865 to 1885, chairman of its Department of Anatomy from 1865 to 1871, and chairman of its Department of Surgery from 1871 to 1888. According to Tulane University's website:

> Dr. Richardson led the medical school during the difficult post-Civil War years and brought it to national recognition. He supervised the transition of the medical department from the University of Louisiana to Tulane University of Louisiana. During this time, he served as the only physician on the Board of Administrators of the Tulane Education Fund, which oversaw Paul Tulane's Act of Donation creating Tulane University.

Dr. Richardson was also the first doctor in history known to have performed an amputation of both legs at the hip in which the patient made a complete recovery.

In 1877 Richardson was elected president of the American Medical Association and served two years in that post. He was also vice president of the American Surgical Association in 1888 and 1889. In addition to serving in national medical societies, Richardson continued to teach and practice medicine in New Orleans until his death on May 26, 1892.

The next former Confederate to lead the AMA was Henry Fraser Campbell, M.D., who had served as a surgeon in the Provisional Army of the Confederate States. Born in 1824 in Savannah, Georgia, Campbell graduated from the Medical College of Georgia and practiced medicine in Augusta. In 1852 he and his brother,

Henry Fraser Campbell, M.D.

Medical College of Georgia

Dr. Robert Campbell, established the Jackson State Hospital in Augusta specifically for the treatment of African-Americans.

From 1857 to 1861 Campbell was a professor of anatomy at the Medical College of Georgia and in 1858 was elected vice president of the AMA. Two years later he was elected to the Imperial Academy of Medicine in St. Petersburg, Russia.

In September 1861 Campbell enlisted in the Confederate Army and was appointed surgeon in the Provisional Army of the Confederate States, as well as to the organizing board for the establishment of a hospital in Richmond to treat wounded and sick Georgia soldiers. He served as director of that hospital, and throughout the war carried out his duties as a surgeon and director of various hospitals in Richmond.

After the war Campbell was professor of anatomy and surgery at the New Orleans School of Medicine, and later was professor of operative surgery and gynecology at the Medical College of Georgia. He served as president of the Medical Association of Georgia, and in 1876 founded the American Gynecological Society. In 1878 he was elected as a member of the Medical Society of Sweden, and he was elected to a two-year term as president of the American Medical Association in 1885.

Hunter Holmes McGuire was the next former Confederate to be elected president of the American Medical Association. McGuire, who is best known for being Thomas "Stonewall" Jackson's doctor, was born in 1835 and was a practicing physician by the age of twenty-two. He enlisted early in the war as a private in the 2nd Virginia Infantry. Soon thereafter he was appointed surgeon, and soon after that became chief surgeon and medical director of Major General Thomas J. "Stonewall" Jackson's Corps. After the war McGuire established several schools and hospitals that later became part of the Medical College of Virginia in Richmond (now the Virginia Commonwealth University School of Medicine). His statue sits prominently on the grounds of the Virginia state capitol in Richmond, and the

Hunter Holmes McGuire, M.D.

Wikipedia

nearby U. S. Veterans Administration McGuire Medical Center is named in his honor. In addition to serving as president of the AMA in 1893 and 1894, McGuire was also president of the American Surgical Association in 1886 and 1887.

The fourth and final former Confederate to preside over the AMA was former cavalryman John Allan Wyeth, M.D. A native of Guntersville, Alabama, Wyeth was a direct descendant of George Wyeth, a signer of the Declaration of Independence. Wyeth enlisted in the 4th Alabama Cavalry on December 16, 1862—his seventeenth birthday—and served under generals John Hunt Morgan and Joseph Wheeler before being captured in October 1863. He survived a lengthy imprisonment from October 1863 until his release in February 1865, shortly before the end of the war.

Thereafter, Wyeth enrolled at the University of Louisville's School of Medicine and graduated in 1869. After two years of additional study at Bellevue Hospital Medical College in New York, Wyeth traveled to Europe and received training in Paris, London, Berlin, and Vienna. He returned to New York in 1880 and practiced at St. Elizabeth's Hospital and Mt. Sinai Hospital. In 1881 Wyeth founded the New York Polyclinic Graduate School, which would merge with the Columbia University College of Physicians and

John Allan Wyeth, M.D.

Wikipedia

Surgeons in 1918. Wyeth's former students included Mayo Clinic founders William James Mayo and Charles Horace Mayo.

Wyeth served as president of the American Medical Association in 1901, and was also president of the New York Academy of Medicine from 1906 to 1908. He authored the important and widely read memoir *With Sabre and Scalpel: The Autobiography of a Soldier and Surgeon*, which was first published in 1914.

American Surgical Association

Two former Rebels served as president of the American Surgical Association (ASA). In addition to the aforementioned Hunter Holmes McGuire, M.D., who was president of the ASA in 1886 and 1887, Claudius Henry Mastin, M.D., was a founder of the ASA in 1880 and served as its president in 1890 and 1891.

A native of Huntsville, Alabama, Mastin attended the University of Virginia and received his medical degree from the University of Pennsylvania in 1849. He received further training in France , at the Royal College of Surgeons in England, and the University of Edinburgh, Scotland. He began the practice of medicine in Mobile, Alabama, and volunteered in April 1861 as a surgeon in the Provisional Army of the Confederate States.

Additionally, Mastin was a trustee of the Pan-American Medical Congress, a co-founder of the Congress of American Physicians and Surgeons, and a member of the Boston Gynecological Society, the American Association of Andrology, and of the Southern Surgical and Gynecological Association. Mastin was awarded an honorary doctorate degree from the University of Pennsylvania in 1875. He died in 1898 at the age of seventy-two.

Claudius Henry Mastin, M.D.

Findagrave

Francis Turquand Miles, M.D.

University of Maryland

American Neurological Association

Another former Confederate soldier and surgeon, Francis Turquand Miles, served as president of the American Neurological Association in 1880 and 1881. Born in Charleston, South Carolina, in 1827, Miles earned his medical degree from the Medical College of South Carolina in 1849 and later studied in Paris, France. He taught medicine at the Medical College of South Carolina in the 1850s and in 1860 was named chairman of its Department of Physiological Anatomy.

In March 1862 Miles enlisted in the 1st South Carolina Infantry Battalion and commissioned a captain. He was severely wounded on June 6, 1862. Once he recovered, Miles transferred to the 27th South Carolina Infantry and served with it until he was assigned as surgeon of the 17th South Carolina Infantry in November 1864.

After the war Dr. Miles returned to the Medical College of South Carolina where, in 1865, he was named chairman of the Department of Physiological Anatomy. In 1867 he moved to Baltimore, opened a private medical practice, and began teaching microscopic anatomy at Baltimore's Washington University School of Medicine. At the University of Maryland in Baltimore, Miles was named chairman of the Department of Anatomy, the Department of Diseases of the Nervous System, and the Department of Physiology. In addition to his prestigious positions at those universities, in the 1870s Miles served two terms as vice president of the Medical and Chirurgical Faculty of Maryland. In 1889 he was a consulting physician to Johns Hopkins Hospital, and the following year served as a consultant at the Presbyterian Eye, Ear, and Throat Hospital in Baltimore. When he died in Baltimore in 1903, he was a professor of physiology at the University of Maryland.

William Mecklenburg Polk, M.D.

Cornell University Alumni News

American Gynecological and Obstetrical Society

The American Gynecological and Obstetrical Society (formerly the American Gynecological Society) was led in 1896-97 by former Confederate officer William Mecklenburg Polk, M.D.

Polk was born in Maury County, Tennessee, in 1844 and graduated from the Virginia Military Institute in 1861, after which he was commissioned a captain in the Confederate Army. In May 1863 he was appointed assistant chief of artillery in his father General Leonidas Polk's Corps, and later in General A. P. Stewart's Corps, and finally served on the staff of General Joseph E. Johnston until his surrender in April 1865.

After the war Polk began the study of medicine at the Medical Department of the University of Louisiana in New Orleans (the predecessor of Tulane University Medical School) and graduated from the College of Physicians and Surgeons in New York in 1869. He established a medical practice in New York and served as professor of therapeutics and clinical medicine at Bellevue Hospital Medical College in 1875. He taught obstetrics and gynecology at New York University from 1879 to 1898, and was later dean and professor of gynecology at Cornell University Medical College. Dr. Polk was affiliated with many hospitals, and in addition to serving as president of the American Gynecological Society, he was president of the New York Academy of Medicine and the New York Obstetrical Society, vice president of the Anglo-American Medical Society of Paris, and a member of the International Society of Surgery, the Royal Society of Medicine, in England, and the Societe Belge de Gynecologic et Obstetrique of Brussels.

Dr. Polk was awarded honorary doctorate degrees from Cornell University, the University of the South, and the University of Georgia. He volunteered for U.S. military service and was commissioned a first lieutenant in the Army Reserve Medical Corps during World War , serving until his death on June 23, 1918.

American Public Health Association

The American Public Health Association was led by surgeon Henry Buckingham Horlbeck, M.D., who was the organization's president in 1896 and 1897. At the beginning of the Civil War, Horlbeck volunteered as a surgeon in the 1st South Carolina Infantry and served the entire war.

Dr. Horlbeck received his primary education in Germany and later graduated from the Medical University of South Carolina in 1859, after which he returned to Europe for a year, studying medicine in London and Paris. After his Civil War service, Horlbeck worked for twenty years as the city health officer of Charleston, South Carolina, and was instrumental in the discovery that mosquitos were the carriers of the yellow fever virus. He was a cofounder of the U.S. Quarantine Service and advocated the creation of the United States Yellow Fever Commission in 1879.

*   *   *

Many men who once served the Confederacy were not later officers of national professional associations, but are nonetheless recognized as pioneers in their medical specialties.

Stanford E. Chaille, M.D., a Confederate surgeon, was appointed by President Rutherford B. Hayes to the 1879 Havana Yellow Fever Commission and was named by the U.S. National Board of Health to be president of that international body. Chaille, the wartime surgeon general of the state of Louisiana and medical director of the Army of Mississippi, was a native of Natchez. He was educated at Phillips Academy in Massachusetts and received his undergraduate degree from Harvard University in 1851. He earned his medical degree in 1853 from the Medical Department of the University of Louisiana and returned to Harvard, where he received a second degree in 1854. He continued his medical studies in Europe between 1854 and 1857. Chaille returned to New Orleans in 1857 and was a resident physician at the Circus Street Hospital and professor of anatomy in the Medical Department of the University of Louisiana. In 1861, Dr. Chaille returned to Europe and studied for nearly two years under Dr. Claude Bernard in Paris. He returned to New Orleans in 1862 and joined the Confederate Army.

After the war Chaille resumed teaching at the University of Louisiana and, between 1865 and 1885, was a professor of obstetrics, a professor of physiology and pathological anatomy, and dean of the medical faculty. Dr. Chaille attended to Jefferson Davis during the former Confederate president's final illness and death in

New Orleans on December 6, 1889. Chaille lived another twenty-one years before dying on May 27, 1911.

Peter Bryce, M.D., a native of Columbia, South Carolina, and a distinguished former Confederate surgeon, was a pioneer in the field of psychiatry. He graduated from The Citadel in 1855, then earned a medical degree from New York Medical College (now the University of New York School of Medicine) in 1859. Afterward he traveled to Europe, developed an interest in mental health, and upon his return he worked at psychiatric hospitals in New Jersey and South Carolina before being selected as the first superintendent of the Alabama Insane Hospital in 1860. Believing that mental illness was a combination of genetic, environmental, and social causes, Bryce developed and transformed the treatment of mentally ill patients from physical restraint and isolation to a philosophy of kind treatment along with regular, constructive work. Bryce not only advocated but strictly enforced compassionate treatment of patients, and forbade excessive physical restraint.

Interrupted only by his Confederate military service, Bryce served as superintendent of the Alabama Insane Hospital for his entire career, during which he was president of various national and state medical and historical organizations. Dr. Bryce was inducted into the Alabama Hall of Fame in 1965.

Simon Baruch, M.D., was a Jewish Confederate surgeon and a pioneer in his field of study. A native of Germany, Baruch immigrated America in 1855 and began studying medicine at the Medical College of South Carolina in 1859. He earned his medical degree from the Medical College of Virginia (now Virginia Commonwealth University School of Medicine) in 1862. In April of that year

Baruch volunteered for service in the 3rd South Carolina Infantry Regiment and soon was transferred to the 13th Mississippi. When Lee's Confederate army retreated from Gettysburg on July 4, 1863, Baruch stayed behind to care for wounded Confederate soldiers and was captured. He was imprisoned, exchanged, and returned to the 13th Mississippi and served with that regiment for the remainder of the war.

Simon Baruch, M.D.

Wikipedia

After the war Baruch practiced medicine and attended postgraduate medical classes in New York City for one year before moving to Charleston, South Carolina, where he practiced medicine for sixteen years. In 1881 he moved to New York City, where he became a pioneer and vigorous proponent of public health and hygiene.

Baruch recognized the relationship between hygiene and disease, especially in densely populated, low-income areas common in nineteenth century cities. He lobbied successfully for city governments to establish public bathhouses in poor neighborhoods like the appropriately named Hell's Kitchen neighborhood of New York.

Across America, numerous civic monuments, educational institutions, and other memorials, many of which were sponsored or established by his son, financier and statesman Bernard M. Baruch, are named in Simon Baruch's honor. These include academic chairs at Clemson University, Columbia University, the New York University College of Medicine, and the Virginia Commonwealth University School of Medicine; the Simon Baruch Houses, a public housing complex in New York; and Simon Baruch Middle School in New York, which has an adjacent park called the Simon Baruch Playground and Garden.

To honor his father, in 1940 the younger Baruch endowed the Simon Baruch Auditorium on the campus of the Medical University of South Carolina. The Department of Physical Medicine and Rehabilitation at Virginia Commonwealth University also was established with funds provided by Baruch.[1]

1 Bernard Baruch served as an economic adviser for Presidents Woodrow Wilson and Franklin D. Roosevelt. During World War II, as a specialist in commodities and metals, he was appointed chairman of the War Industries Board, an institution responsible for organizing the U.S. war economy. In 1946 he was appointed by Harry Truman to prepare a plan for disarmament of nuclear weapons, but the attempt failed because it was opposed by the Soviet Union. Bernard Baruch coined the term "Cold War" to define the tension between the two superpowers. Baruch is the namesake of the elite Bernard M. Baruch College, a constituent school of the City University of New York (CUNY) system. In 1925 he established the United Daughters of the Confederacy's (UDC) Mrs. Simon Baruch University Award in honor of his mother, who had been an early member and strong supporter of the UDC.

Alexander Robert Lawton

Wikicommons

American Bar Association

Three ex-Confederates served as presidents of the American Bar Association (ABA) after the Civil War.

The ABA was founded in 1878 in Saratoga Springs, New York, by approximately one hundred attorneys from twenty-one states. "The legal profession as we know it today barely existed at that time," explains the ABA's website. "Lawyers were generally sole practitioners who trained under a system of apprenticeship. There was no national code of ethics; there was no national organization to serve as a forum for discussion of the increasingly intricate issues involved in legal practice." The ABA was formed to remedy those problems, and it currently boasts a membership of nearly half a million attorneys.

Alexander Robert Lawton was elected in 1882 to a two-year term as president of the ABA. A native of Beaufort, South Carolina, Lawton graduated from the U.S. Military Academy at West Point in 1839, and after brief service in the U.S. Army attended Harvard University Law School and graduated in 1842. Lawton was practicing law in Savannah, Georgia, when the Civil War erupted. He supported Georgia's secession, volunteered his services, and was commissioned colonel of the 1st Georgia Infantry. By April 1861 he was a brigadier general and thereafter was transferred to Virginia, where he demonstrated talent as a leader of combat troops. Lawton was seriously wounded while commanding a division at the Battle of Sharpsburg (Antietam) early on the morning of September 17, 1862, and was unable to continue serving in the field thereafter. He returned to duty in August 1863 as quartermaster general of the Confederate States.

After the war Lawton returned to Savannah, resumed the practice of law, and became active in politics. He was an unsuccessful candidate for the U.S. Senate in 1880, but was appointed to the important diplomatic position of U.S. ambassador to Austria-Hungary in 1887 by President Cleveland. Lawton died in Clifton Springs, New York, in 1896 at the age of seventy-seven.

Thomas Jenkins Semmes

Louisiana Digital Library

The next former Confederate to lead the ABA was Thomas Jenkins Semmes. Born in Washington, D.C., in 1824, Semmes was educated at Georgetown and earned a law degree from Harvard in 1845. In 1850 Semmes moved to New Orleans and, when the Civil War began, was commissioned a lieutenant in Girault's Confederate Guards of the Louisiana Militia. He resigned in 1862 to accept a seat in the Confederate Senate. During the war Semmes resided near the Confederate White House in Richmond and was a close adviser and confidant of President Jefferson Davis.

After the war Semmes returned to New Orleans to practice and teach law. He accepted a position as professor of constitutional law at Tulane University (then the University of Louisiana) and served as president of the American Bar Association in 1886 and 1887.

Uriah Milton Rose of Arkansas was the third and final former Confederate to lead the ABA. He served as its president in 1901 and 1902. Rose had been one of the founding members of the association in 1878.

Because of physical limitations Rose was unable to serve in the Confederate military, so instead he volunteered as an administrator at the Confederate War Department in Richmond. He returned to

Uriah Milton Rose

Encyclopedia of Arkansas

Arkansas during the war and served as a county judge, and afterward resumed his law practice by opening an office in Little Rock that is well known today as the Rose Law Firm.

Rose was a native Kentuckian and an 1853 graduate of Transylvania University in Lexington, Kentucky. In 1878 he co-founded and was president of the Arkansas Bar Association. In 1907, he was appointed U.S. ambassador to the Second Hague Peace Conference by President Theodore Roosevelt.

American Society of Civil Engineers

Benjamin Morgan Harrod, a lieutenant and engineer on the staff of Confederate General Martin L. Smith, became a prominent postwar engineer and architect and served as president of the American Society of Civil Engineers in 1897.

Born in New Orleans in 1837, Harrod was educated by private tutors before earning degrees from Harvard in 1856 and 1859. He volunteered for the Confederate Army in 1861 and was serving as a lieutenant with the Louisiana Crescent Rifles when he was captured at Vicksburg in July 1863. After being paroled and exchanged he joined the Second Regiment of Engineers in Petersburg, Virginia. Harrod was serving as an engineer on Robert E. Lee's staff when the

Army of Northern Virginia surrendered at Appomattox on April 9, 1865.

After the war Harrod returned to New Orleans and was chief engineer for the state of Louisiana from 1877 to 1880 and city engineer of New Orleans in 1888. He served on the federal government's Mississippi River Commission from 1879 until 1904, at which time he was appointed by President Theodore Roosevelt to the Panama Canal Commission.

Benjamin Morgan Harrod

The Cultural Landscape Foundation

John William Mallet

American Chemical Society

One of the most intellectual and accomplished Confederates veterans was John William Mallet, who served as president of the American Chemical Society in 1882.

Born in 1832 near Dublin, Ireland, Mallet received private lessons in chemistry and enrolled at Trinity College in Dublin in 1849, where he earned a bachelor of arts degree four years later. While in college Mallet assisted his father—a chemical and civil engineer—in seismological studies. He received an award in physics, and published a paper entitled "Chemical Examination of Killinite." During the summers of 1851 and 1852 he attended the University of Gottingen (in what is today Germany) and earned a degree from that institution in 1852. He also presented a paper on the chemical composition of Celtic antiquities to the Royal Irish Academy in Dublin.

In the early 1850s Mallet traveled to the United States on a research trip though he retained his British citizenship, never returned to Ireland. He was teaching analytical chemistry at Amherst College in Massachusetts in 1854, and the following year moved to Alabama and taught chemistry at the University of Alabama. At the outbreak of the Civil War Mallet enlisted as a private in a Confederate cavalry regiment but soon was assigned to serve as an aide-de-camp on the staff of General Robert E. Rodes. Mallet was transferred to an artillery company in the spring of 1862 and, when his scientific acumen was recognized, went to work in the ordnance industry. At the end of the war he held the rank of lieutenant colonel was the superintendent of the Confederate States laboratories headquartered in Macon, Georgia.

After the war Mallet resided in New Orleans, where he became professor of chemistry at the University of Louisiana and earned a medical degree in 1868. The following year the well-traveled Mallet accepted a teaching position at the University of Virginia, and conducted research in industrial and agricultural chemistry. Although he maintained a permanent residence in Charlottesville, Mallet lectured at Johns Hopkins University in 1877 and 1878, and taught chemistry and physics and was faculty chairman at the University of Texas in 1884. The industrious Irishman went on to teach chemistry at the Jefferson Medical College in Philadelphia before returning to the University of Virginia, where in 1908 he was given the title of professor emeritus.

Mallet also served as a member of the U.S. Assay Commission in 1886, 1888, and 1896. He was a member of many professional and scientific societies including the Royal Society (United Kingdom), the College of Physicians of Philadelphia, the Medical Society of Virginia, the American Academy of Arts and Sciences, the American Association for the Advancement of Science, the London Society of Arts, Societe Chimique de France, the German Chemical Society, the American Philosophical Society, and the American Chemical Society, of which he was president in 1882.

Mallet received honorary degrees from the College of William and Mary, the University of Mississippi, Princeton University, Johns Hopkins University, and the University of Pennsylvania.

Mallet's scientific research included general and applied chemistry and mineralogy. He developed methods to determine the presence of organic matter in water, and identified meteorites and rare minerals by studying the occurrence of silver ash in volcanoes. Mallet determined the density of mercury, the molecular weight of hydrofluoric acid, and the atomic weights of gold and aluminum.

The Mallet Assembly academic honors program at the University of Alabama was named in his honor in 1961. The program meets in Mallet Hall.[2]

2 According to Mallet-assembly.org, the Mallet Assembly is "A diverse group of eccentric individuals forming relationships around advocacy, service, and academics. The Mallet Assembly is an independent living community designed to enable student-led social progress. This independence empowers the Assembly to strive for an inclusive environment for not only its members, but for the University of Alabama and the world. These progressive societal ideas are applied at an organizational level to maintain a wealth of events designed to be welcoming to all. The Assembly hosts frequent gatherings from open mic nights to debates for its members and like-minded students to celebrate a common goal of inclusivity."

Joseph LeConte

Wikipedia

The Sierra Club

American Association for the Advancement of Science

Geological Society of America

Joseph LeConte, a former officer in the Confederate States Bureau of Nitre and Mining, became a prominent postwar chemist, geologist, conservationist, and educator who also co-founded the Sierra Club and served as president of the American Association for the Advancement of Science.[3]

LeConte was born in Liberty County, Georgia, in 1823, graduated from the University of Georgia (then Franklin College) in 1841, and earned a medical degree from the New York College of Physicians and Surgeons in 1845. He briefly practiced medicine in Macon, Georgia, before enrolling at Harvard to study geology. During the war LeConte produced medicines and explosives for the Confederate War Department.

After the war LeConte was chairman of the Department of Chemical Pharmacology, Minerology, and Geology at the University of South Carolina until 1868, when he accepted a position as chairman of the Department of Geology at the University of California, Berkeley (Cal-Berkeley), where he also taught physiology, geology, natural history, and botany. LeConte's brother John, who also served as a Confederate Army geologist and chemist, was president of Cal-Berkeley from 1875 to 1881.

According to the *Encyclopedia Britannica,*

---

3   In his memoirs, LeConte was himself unsure of his official rank in the Confederate Army, stating that he was commissioned as a lieutenant but received the pay rate of a major.

LeConte published a series of papers on monocular and binocular vision, and also on psychology. His chief contributions, however, related to geology. . . . He described the fissure-eruptions in western America, discoursed on earth-crust movements and their causes and on the great features of the earth's surface. As separate works he published *Elements of Geology* (1889), *Religion and Science* (1874), and *Evolution: Its History, its Evidences, and its Relation to Religious Thought* (1888).

While in California LeConte became interested in the Sierra Nevada Mountains. He was concerned about the effects of natural resource exploitation on the mountain environment and along with his close friend, the iconic conservationist John Muir, co-founded the Sierra Club in 1892. LeConte served as a director of the organization from 1892 to 1898. While involved in the founding and governance of the Sierra Club, LeConte also served as president of the American Association for the Advancement of Science in 1892 and of the Geological Society of America in 1896.

Three years after his death in July 1901, the Sierra Club built the LeConte Memorial Lodge in Yosemite National Park, but in 2016 the Sierra Club requested that his name be removed from it because of his views on race and culture. It is now named the Yosemite Conservation Heritage Center. Also named in his honor within the park is the LeConte Glacier, LeConte Canyon, LeConte Falls, and Mt. LeConte, as well as another Mt. LeConte and LeConte Lodge in the Great Smoky Mountains National Park in Sevier County, Tennessee. LeConte Hall at the University of Georgia, the LeConte College of Mathematics and Statistics at the University of South Carolina, LeConte Middle School in Hollywood, California, LeConte Avenue in Berkeley, California, and LeConte Avenue in Los Angeles are named in honor of the LeConte brothers. An elementary school in Berkeley was named for the LeConte brothers in 1892, but the name was changed to Sylvia Mendez Elementary School in 2018 because of Leconte's opinions on late nineteenth century society and culture, including his racial views.

Society for Classical Studies

Former Confederate Basil Lanneau Gildersleeve, a volunteer member of General John B. Gordon's staff, twice served as president of the American Philological Association (now named the Society for Classical Studies), in 1877 and 1908. The Society for Classical Studies is "dedicated to the study of classical literature, linguistics, history, philosophy, and cultural studies."

Basil Lanneau Gildersleeve

Wikipedia

Gildersleeve was born in Charleston, South Carolina, in 1831 and graduated from Princeton University in 1849. He earned a Ph.D. from the University of Gottingen (Germany) in 1853.

Like many college professors during the Civil War, Gildersleeve would volunteer for summer military service at the conclusion of spring classes, then return to school in the fall. According to the Johns Hopkins University newspaper, *The Gazette*, during a skirmish in the Shenandoah Valley in September 1864, Gildersleeve was delivering orders to the front when gunfire shattered his leg. "I lost my pocket Homer, I lost my pistol, I lost one of my horses and, finally, I came very near losing my life," was how Gildersleeve summed up the situation. He walked with a limp for the remainder of his life.

Before and after the war Gildersleeve was a renowned intellectual and educator. The noted scholar of Greek and Latin would go on to serve as chairman of the Department of Latin and professor of Greek at the University of Virginia, professor of Greek at Johns Hopkins University, and, in addition to serving as the philologicale association's president, was founder and editor of the *American Journal of Philology*.

The learned Gildersleeve was a member of the American Academy of Arts and Letters, and received honorary degrees from the College of William and Mary, Harvard University, Yale University, the University of Chicago, the University of Pennsylvania, the University of the South, Princeton University, as well as Oxford University and Cambridge University in England.

The Gildersleeve House dormitory at Johns Hopkins University and the Gildersleeve Portal at the University of Virginia are named in his honor. The University of Virginia's Classics program also offers a distinguished professorship in Gildersleeve's honor.

American Saddlebred Association

John B. Castleman, a major in the 2nd Kentucky Cavalry during the Civil War, served as president of the American Saddlebred Association in 1892. A postwar Kentucky lawyer and politician, Castleman became known as the "Father of the Louisville Park System." He was commissioner of the Louisville Board of Parks and established Shawnee Park, Cherokee Park, Iroquois Park, and Central Park in that city.

Castleman also was a colonel of the 1st Kentucky Volunteer Infantry during the 1898 Spanish-American War, and commanded the regiment during the invasion of Puerto Rico. After Spain's surrender, Castleman was commissioned a brigadier general and served as military governor of Puerto Rico during the Spanish evacuation.

Part 7

Higher Education

After the Civil War, many former Confederates became professional educators and administrators. Several founded colleges and universities, either as politicians who championed their establishment by signing a bill into law to create the school, or as direct benefactors.

Some of the high-profile universities founded by former Rebels include Clemson University, the Georgia Institute of Technology (Georgia Tech), the University of Florida, North Carolina State University, and the historically African-American colleges of Alcorn State University, Prairie View A&M University, the University of Arkansas at Pine Bluff, and Alabama State University. Some who wore the gray during the war founded universities exclusively for women, who in the nineteenth century were often denied a college education.

Many other Southern veterans served as presidents and chancellors of universities, some in regions not normally associated with the former Confederacy, like the University of California, Berkeley (Cal-Berkeley), while others served as members of the governing boards of such unlikely institutions as the U.S. Military Academy at West Point and the U.S. Naval Academy in Annapolis, Maryland. Former Confederates also taught at institutions of higher learning outside of the Old South, including Cal-Berkeley, Johns Hopkins University, Harvard University, Amherst College, the University of Vermont, the University of Wisconsin, the

University of Colorado, the University of San Francisco, and the University of the Pacific (San Francisco).[1]

Many nineteenth century colleges and universities have long since closed, and others merged all or part of their various departments and schools into the institutions that survive today. This complex evolution was particularly common with medical schools, many of which were initially independent but were later absorbed or merged into a university. In the latter part of the twentieth century, it became common for state medical schools to be combined into central publicly owned and regulated systems of medical education.

In addition to various organizational incarnations, college names often were changed. The current names of many public colleges and universities that existed during the antebellum period are not the same as when the institutions were founded.

Agnes Scott College (Georgia)

George Washington Scott, a former colonel in the 5th Florida Cavalry Battalion, was a postwar industrialist and a founder of Agnes Scott College, a women's liberal arts institution in Decatur, Georgia. Born in Pennsylvania in 1829, Scott moved to Leon County, Florida, in 1851 and established a mercantile exchange and a plantation. He joined the Confederate Army in 1861, and two years later took command of the battalion that would soon be called Scott's Cavalry. He served the entire war and fought in several actions in Florida, including the February 1864 Battle of Olustee, before surrendering in May 1865.

Scott was elected governor of Florida in 1868, but federal authorities refused to allow him to take his office. He turned his attention to business and industry and flourished over the next 30 years. Scott developed a revolutionary new fertilizer and the machinery to manufacture it. He sold his highly successful plantation in 1870 and moved to Atlanta, Georgia, where he built a large fertilizer manufacturing and distribution business.

Scott was the first person to recognize the commercial potential of northern Florida's vast phosphate deposits, and by the late 1880s his Atlanta-based G. W.

---

1 For clarity and simplicity, university and college teachers will most often be referred to as "professors" to differentiate them from primary and secondary school teachers.

Scott Manufacturing Company enabled him to accumulate a substantial fortune from phosphate mining and processing.

In 1889, Scott and Frank H. Gaines established the Decatur Female Seminary in Decatur, Georgia. The following year, Scott Gaines donated $100,000 to the institution, which took the name Agnes Scott College in honor of his mother. The college remains an all-female institution today.

Alabama State University and the Alabama Institute for the Deaf and Blind

Alabama State University and the Alabama Institute for the Deaf and Blind owe their existence in large part to Thomas Seay, who as governor of Alabama from 1886 to 1890 championed their creation and signed legislation chartering and funding both institutions.

Seay was born in Erie, Alabama, in 1846, and in 1858 his family moved to Greensboro, Alabama, where he attended Southern College. In 1863, he withdrew from the college and enlisted in the 1st Regiment, Alabama Reserves while still a teenager. Seay saw action at Spanish Fort and Fort Blakely, Alabama, and was captured when those forts fell to Union forces in the spring of 1865.

After the war Seay returned to Greensboro and completed his studies at Southern College. After graduation in 1867 he studied law, practicing from 1869 to 1885. He was elected to the Alabama state senate in 1876 and served for a decade, including a tenure as Senate president from 1884 to 1886. Seay then was elected to the first of two terms as governor of the state.

During his governorship Seay signed into legislation the establishment and funding for the State Normal School for Colored Students, today called Alabama State University, as well as the Alabama Academy, which is now known as the Alabama Institute for the Deaf and Blind in Talladega. Seay also advocated and approved state funding for what would become Troy University in the southern Alabama city of Troy.[2]

---

2 Thomas Seay (1886-90) (n.d.). Retrieved from www.encyclopediaofalabama.org/article/h-1533.

Alcorn State University (Mississippi)

A historically African-American institution, Alcorn State University was established in 1871 during the governorship of one of its founders, former Confederate Brigadier General James Lusk Alcorn.[3]

Alcorn was born in 1816 in Golconda along the Ohio River (in what two years became the state of Illinois) and was educated at Cumberland College in Kentucky. He served as sheriff of Livingston County, Kentucky, and was a state legislator before moving to Panola, Mississippi, in 1843. He prospered as an attorney and plantation owner there in the 1840s and 1850s, and as a member of the state legislature established and served as the first president of the state's levee board.

Alcorn strongly opposed Mississippi's secession, but like most leading citizens of the state, he supported the Confederacy once the war began. The Illinois native raised, funded, and commanded three early state militia regiments and was commissioned a brigadier general in the Confederate Army, but further promotion was blocked by a political rival. Alcorn's brigade was sent to Kentucky, but was disbanded in early 1862 and he was captured in Arkansas. He was paroled but did not return to active service. Alcorn, who had foreseen the destruction that civil war would bring upon the South, had his plantation raided during the Vicksburg Campaign. He managed to preserve his wealth by hiding his cotton and selling it to Northern speculators. Some historians estimate he was one of the fifty wealthiest Southerners after the war.

During Reconstruction, Alcorn joined the newly organized Mississippi Republican Party and became a strong advocate of full civil rights for former slaves, and he supported the passage of the Fourteenth Amendment. He was elected governor in 1869, and during his administration the Mississippi state government established a public education system and created Alcorn University (later named Alcorn State University), the nation's first land grant college for newly freed blacks. Alcorn resigned as governor in 1871 when he was elected to the U.S. Senate. He served until 1877, when he retired and returned home to practice law and manage his land holdings. He died in 1894.

---

3   G. Sansing, D. (April 13, 2018). James Lusk Alcorn. Retrieved from https://Mississippi encyclopedia.org/entries/james-lusk-alcorn/.

Auburn University

William Leroy Broun was the president of the Agricultural and Mechanical College of Alabama (then known as the Alabama Polytechnic Institute, and today as Auburn University) from 1882 to 1902, as well as a professor at Vanderbilt University and the University of Georgia. In his former life, he was a colonel and commandant of the Confederate Army's Richmond Arsenal.[4]

Averett College (Virginia)

John Tyler Averett, the namesake of Averett College, a private Baptist college in Danville, Virginia, served as the school's president from 1887 to 1892. He was a former sergeant in the 38th Virginia Infantry.

Bethel University (Tennessee)

Leslie Waggener, a former lieutenant with the 9th Kentucky Mounted Infantry, was the president of Bethel College in Kansas from 1875 to 1883, where he also served as faculty chairman and professor of English, history, and philosophy. He later was faculty chairman and professor of English and history and president at, and eventually the president of, the University of Texas. He also was the president of the Texas State Teachers Association.[5]

Blue Mountain College (Mississippi)

Blue Mountain College, which was known as Blue Mountain Female Institute until 1920, was founded in 1873 by former Confederate Brigadier General Mark Perrin Lowrey.[6]

---

4 (n.d.). Retrieved from www.lib.auburn.edu/archive/find-aid/533/wlb-bio.htm.

5 James, W. (June 15, 2010). Waggener, Leslie. Retrieved from https://tshaonline.org /handbook/online/articles/fwa06.

6 D. Cockrell, T. (September 24, 2019). Mark Perrin Lowrey. Retrieved from https:// mississippiencyclopedia.org/entries/mark-perrin-lowry/.

Lowrey was born in 1828 in McNair County, Tennessee. His family moved to Mississippi in 1843, where he became a bricklayer. He enlisted in the 2nd Mississippi Volunteer Infantry during the Mexican War, but the regiment did not see action. After the war ended Lowrey became a Southern Baptist minister in Kossuth, Mississippi, and served as a captain in the Mississippi State Militia. When the Civil War broke out, Lowrey was appointed colonel of the 4th Mississippi Infantry and later commanded the 32nd Mississippi Infantry. He fought in many major battles in the Western Theater including Shiloh, Perryville, Murfreesboro, and Chickamauga. On October 4, 1863, Lowrey was promoted to brigadier general, and acquired the nickname "Preacher General" because of his evangelical nature. His division commander, Major General Patrick Cleburne, described Lowrey as "the bravest man in the Confederate Army." Lowrey fought in the Atlanta and Nashville campaigns of 1864 but was often plagued by poor health. He resigned in April 1865 shortly before the end of the war.

Lowrey lived in Mississippi after the war and focused on his religious studies and education. In 1873 he founded the Blue Mountain Female Institute, where he taught and served as president, and from 1868 to 1877 was president of the Mississippi Baptist Convention. Lowrey's life of service included sitting on the boards of trustees of the University of Mississippi and Mississippi College.

Lowrey had a weak heart during his later years and died while buying a train ticket in Middleton, Tennessee, in 1885. He was inducted into the Mississippi Hall of Fame in 1908.

Birmingham-Southern College (Alabama)

Birmingham-Southern College was created in 1918 when Southern University in Greensboro, Alabama, merged with Birmingham College. Southern University was founded in 1855 by the Alabama Methodist Conference, of which future Confederate soldier Augustus Aurelius Coleman was a member.[7]

Coleman was born in 1826 in Camden, South Carolina, and graduated from Yale in 1844, after which he moved to Livingston, Alabama, studied law, and entered private practice. In 1855 he moved to Greensboro, was elected to a district judgeship, and became active in the founding of Southern University.

---

7 Donna R Causey Donna R. Causey. (2019, May 29). Donna R Causey. Retrieved from www.alabamapioneers.com/old-southern-university-greensboro/.

Coleman resigned from the bench in 1862 to organize what would become the 40th Alabama Infantry and was elected its colonel. Under Coleman's command the regiment served in the Mobile area in 1862 and was transferred to Mississippi in 1863. He and his 40th Alabama were captured when Vicksburg surrendered on July 4, 1863. Coleman was released by his Union captors because he was ill, and resigned from the Confederate Army to return to Greensboro.

Coleman regained his health and resumed his duties as a district judge, but Union authorities forced him from the bench at the end of the war. He resumed his law practice and during the next several years became involved in state politics. In 1888 Coleman moved to Birmingham and was elected a district judge, serving until his death in 1910.

Chowan University (North Carolina)

John C. Scarborough, a former private in the 4th North Carolina Infantry, was president of Chowan Female Institute (later Chowan University) from 1897 to 1909.[8] He also was a member of the board of trustees of Wake Forest University.

The Citadel

Former Confederate Brigadier General George D. Johnston was superintendent of The Citadel from 1885 to 1890. Johnston fought as a lieutenant at First Manassas in Virginia in July 1861 and transferred to the Western Theater, where he took part in every major battle from Shiloh to Bentonville. Just days after being promoted to brigadier general he was badly wounded in the leg at Ezra Church and was forced to use crutches during Hood's Tennessee Campaign in late 1864.[9] Johnston was succeeded at The Citadel by Asbury Coward, the former colonel of the 5th South Carolina Infantry, who served as superintendent from 1890 to 1908.

8 Taylor, R. H. (n.d.). Scarborough, John Catre. Retrieved from www.ncpedia.org/ biography /scarborough-john-catre.

9 Klein and Kara. (n.d.). Colonel Asbury Coward, CSA (1890-1908) - The Citadel - Charleston, SC. Retrieved from www.citadel.edu/root/president-past-presidents/107-info/ administration/office-of-the-president/20867-colonel-asbury-coward,-csa-1890-1908.

Clemson University

Thomas Green Clemson served as a lieutenant in the Confederate States Department of Nitre and Mining, and his wife, Anna Maria Calhoun, was the daughter of South Carolina senator and U.S. vice president John C. Calhoun. Clemson also founded the institution that bears his name today: Clemson University.[10]

Clemson was born in Philadelphia in 1807 and attended Norwich University in Vermont. After returning to Philadelphia in 1825 he studyied mineralogy, and the next year attended the Sorbonne in Paris and the Royal School of Mines in London.

He received a diploma as an assayer from London's Royal Mint. Clemson returned to America and advocated agricultural education. Being fluent in German and French, he was appointed by President John Tyler in 1844 as the country's charge'

Thomas Green Clemson

Clemson University

d'affaires to Belgium, a post he held through the James Polk, Zachary Taylor, and Millard Fillmore administrations. Before his return to America in 1853, Clemson was awarded the Order of Leopold by the king of Belgium.

Clemson purchased land in Maryland near Washington, D.C., where he could have ready access to state and national agricultural data and research. He became a nationally renowned expert on agricultural chemistry and delivered an address on the subject at the Smithsonian Institution in 1858. Two years later Clemson was appointed by President James Buchanan as the U.S. superintendent of agriculture, a position equivalent to the modern secretary of the U.S. Department of Agriculture.

10 Thomas Green Clemson. (n.d.). Retrieved from www.clemson.edu/about/history/bios/ thomas-g-clemson.html.

Anticipating Southern secession, Clemson resigned his position on March 4, 1861, and after the bombardment of Fort Sumter on April 12, 1861, moved to South Carolina. He enlisted in the Confederate Army even though he was fifty-four years old and commissioned a lieutenant. Clemson was assigned to the Army of the Trans-Mississippi and spent the entire war in Arkansas and Texas developing nitrate mines for the manufacturing of explosives. He was in Shreveport, Louisiana, when the war ended and surrendered there in June 1865.

Clemson outlived his wife and all of his children. He bequeathed a substantial portion of his estate for the creation of an institution to be named Clemson Agricultural College of the South. He also left his Fort Hill Estate property in the town of Calhoun, South Carolina, to serve as the site of the school, which opened in 1889 as a military college. The name of the town of Calhoun was changed to Clemson in 1943, and the school was renamed Clemson University in 1964.

Coker College (South Carolina)

Coker College in Hartsville, South Carolina, was founded by James Lide Coker, who was born in Society Hill, South Carolina, in 1837. He was the great grandson of two Revolutionary War officers who served in General Francis Marion's 2nd South Carolina Regiment of the Continental Army.

Coker was educated at The Citadel prior to enrolling at Harvard University, where he studied genetics and the scientific principles of farming and agriculture. At the outbreak of the Civil War, Coker enlisted in the 6th South Carolina Infantry and was later transferred to the 9th South Carolina. He fought at Malvern Hill during the Seven Days' Battles, and then at Second Manassas, Harpers Ferry, and Sharpsburg (Antietam). He was seriously wounded in the hip at Missionary Ridge in Tennessee in September 1863 and captured, imprisoned, and paroled. He

James Lide Coker

Coker College

returned home to recuperate, and although he was forced to use crutches for the rest of his life, he returned to duty late in the war delivering supplies to Confederate forces in Virginia and North Carolina.[11]

After the war Coker returned to his South Carolina plantation, which had been completely destroyed and ransacked by Major General William T. Sherman's men. He rebuilt the plantation and implemented the scientific farming principles he had learned at Harvard. His successful agricultural efforts allowed him to explore other business interests, including maritime shipping in Charleston, South Carolina, the Darlington Cotton Manufacturing Company, the Hartsville Cotton Mill, the Hartsville Oil Mill, and the Pedigreed Seed Company. Coker built a railroad line to Hartsville with his own funds, and in 1881 established the Darlington National Bank, which at that time was the only such institution in the county.

In 1893 Coker and his son successfully developed a process for refining southern pine tree pulp for the manufacture of paper. Because of the unavailability of papermaking equipment, Coker solved the problem himself by purchasing the necessary machinery to form the Carolina Fiber Company.

In 1894 Coker founded Welsh Neck High School, which in 1908 became Coker College for Women. In 1969 the school became co-educational, and the following year changed its name to Coker College. During his lifetime Coker donated more than $650,000 to the school and, while serving as its president, personally funded the construction of Davidson Hall and Memorial Hall, both of which were placed on the National Register of Historic Places in the 1980s. Coker was inducted into the South Carolina Business Hall of Fame in 1986.

The enterprising Coker also founded the Southern Novelty Company to manufacture paper and cardboard products in 1899, and the company's name was changed to Sonoco in 1923. Today, the international provider of consumer packaging is a multi-billion-dollar corporation based in Hartsville, South Carolina. Sonoco, which boasts 22,000 employees, is a component of the Standard & Poor's 400 index of the New York Stock Exchange and is the largest corporation in the state. With its 335 facilities in 34 countries, *Fortune* magazine named Sonoco to its prestigious list of the "World's Most Admired Companies" in 2013.

11 Maj James Lide Coker (1837-1918) - Find A Grave, (n.d.). Retrieved from www.finda grave.com/memorial/12291661/james-lide-coker.

College of William and Mary

The College of William and Mary, the second oldest college in the United States, was founded in 1693 but owes its presence today largely to former Confederate colonel Benjamin Stoddert Ewell, who in 1869 reopened the iconic school with his own funds.[12] The war had left the college and its buildings in ruins, and with Virginia ravaged and destitute after four years of warfare, only private funds could restore the facilities and resume operations.

Benjamin Ewell was born in Washington, D.C., in 1810, the grandson of Benjamin Stoddard, the first U.S. secretary of the navy. Ewell graduated from the U.S. Military Academy at West Point in 1832 and remained at the academy as a professor of mathematics and a professor of natural and experimental philosophy. In 1836 he accepted a position as an engineer for a railroad company before returning to academia three years later as a professor at Hampden-Sydney College. In 1846 he moved to Lexington, Virginia, to teach mathematics and military science at Washington College (later Washington and Lee University), and in 1848 accepted a teaching position at the College of William and Mary, where he was named president in 1854. Ewell remained in that prestigious position until 1888, although the school was closed during the war years.

Ewell opposed Virginia's secession, but at the onset of the war he closed the college and organized a local militia unit. In July 1861, as colonel of the 32nd Virginia Infantry, he was tasked with constructing defensive fortifications on the Peninsula near Williamsburg. Benjamin was the older brother of Confederate Brigadier General Richard Ewell, who would rise to corp command and serve much of the war as a senior commander in Lee's Army of Northern Virginia. In the summer of 1862 Benjamin was transferred to the staff of General Joseph E. Johnston, and later became adjutant on his brother's staff.

After the Battle of Williamsburg on May 5, 1862, during General George McClellan's Peninsula Campaign, the Union army converted the College of William and Mary into a hospital to deal with the 3,800 Union and Confederate casualties. Campus buildings were occupied by a Union garrison after the battle, and on September 9, 1862, the main college building was burned by Union forces.

Benjamin Ewell returned to Williamsburg once the war ended and commenced his tireless efforts to reopen the famous college. He immediately

---

12 (n.d.). Retrieved from https://web.archive.org/web/20070724173142/http://vaudc.org/ewell.html.

sought reparations from the U.S. Congress, but the school did not receive a penny until 1893. In 1869, Ewell used his own money to fund the reopening of the institution, but he had lost so much of his personal wealth in the war that he was unable to fund the school after 1881. It closed for seven years, but reopened in 1888 with support from the Commonwealth of Virginia. Confident the school would survive, Ewell retired at the age of 71. His successor, Lyon Gardiner Tyler, was the son of former U.S. President John Tyler.

Ewell remained in Williamsburg as president emeritus of the College of William and Mary until his death in 1894.

Davidson College

Former Confederate Colonel William Joseph Martin of the 11th North Carolina Infantry served as Davidson College's president in 1887 and 1888.[13] He also was chairman of the Department of Chemistry, Geology, and Natural History, as well as vice president of the college. Additionally, Martin was a professor of chemistry at the University of North Carolina at Chapel Hill.

East Carolina University

Thomas Jordan Jarvis, one of the co-founders of East Carolina University in Greenville, North Carolina, would go on enjoy a prosperous postwar career as a teacher, lawyer, governor, U.S. senator, and U.S. diplomat.[14]

Born in Currituck County, North Carolina, in 1836, Jarvis's ancestors included a colonial governor and a Revolutionary War general. He graduated from Randolph-Macon College in 1860 and earned a master of arts degree in 1861. Jarvis taught school briefly in Pasquotank County before enlisting in the 17th North Carolina Infantry. He was commissioned a lieutenant, and rose to become a captain in the 8th North Carolina Infantry. Jarvis was severely wounded in the right arm at

13 Wilson, D. B. (n.d.). Martin, William Joseph. Retrieved from www.ncpedia.org/biography/martin-william-joseph.

14 Thomas Jordan Jarvis, (n.d.). www.ncpedia.org/biography/governors/jarvis-thomas-jordan.

Thomas Jordan Jarvis

Encyclopedia of North Carolina

the Battle of Drewry's Bluff outside Richmond in May 1864, and was still recovering from his injuries when the war ended in the spring of 1865.

After the war Jarvis studied law and in 1867 opened a practice in Columbia, North Carolina. The following year he was elected to the North Carolina legislature and in 1870 was chosen as speaker of the North Carolina House of Representatives. In the early 1870s Jarvis moved to Greenville and established a law practice there while still serving in the state legislature. In 1876 he was elected lieutenant governor and ascended to the governorship two years later when Governor Zebulon Vance was elected to the U.S. Senate.

As governor, Jarvis advocated and succeeded in founding mental health facilities in Goldsboro and Morganton, as well as teachers' programs at Davidson College, Trinity College (later Duke University), and Wake Forest College. His administration also organized the State Board of Health. During his second term Jarvis championed the establishment of a new system of county superintendents, elected boards of education, and teacher certification standards.

The ex-Rebel captain was a forceful advocate of North Carolina's growing agricultural and industrial position in the postwar South, but in 1884 he resigned the governorship to accept an appointment by President Grover Cleveland as U.S. ambassador to Brazil. He served in that capacity until the end of Cleveland's first term and returned to Greenville in 1888 to resume his law practice. The following year he was offered the presidency of North Carolina State University, but declined. Five years later, in 1894, he was appointed to fill the U.S. Senate seat left vacant by the death of Senator Vance. In 1900 Jarvis again resumed his private law practice, and in 1904 was offered the deanship of the law department at Trinity College, but he declined the position because of his advanced age. Jarvis died in Greenville in 1915.

During his lifetime Jarvis was heavily involved in the Methodist Church, representing North Carolina's devotees at national Methodist conferences. While Jarvis was a member of the board of trustees of Trinity College, he and his friend William Ragsdale wrote the legislative bill that resulted in the opening of a teacher's college in Greenville in 1907 that would become East Carolina College (later East Carolina University). Jarvis Hall at the university and Jarvis Street in Greenville are named in his honor, as is Greenville's Jarvis Memorial Methodist Church.

Georgia Institute of Technology

The Georgia Institute of Technology, commonly known as Georgia Tech, owes its existence to Nathaniel Edwin Harris, a former Confederate major in the 16th Virginia Cavalry.[15]

Harris, a native of Jonesboro, Tennessee, was born in 1846. His family moved south to Georgia during the early days of the Civil War to escape the depredations of federal troops and Tennessee Unionists. After his sixteenth birthday in 1862 he

enlisted in the Confederate Army and served in the 16th Virginia, a cavalry regiment that saw service under Jeb Stuart in Lee's Virginia army.

After the war Harris enrolled in the University of Georgia and graduated in 1870. In 1873 he opened a law practice in Macon, Georgia, and was elected to the Georgia state legislature in 1882. He firmly believed Georgia was in need of a technological and scientific school to face the challenges of rebuilding the state after the devastation brought by the Civil War.

Nathaniel Edwin Harris

Georgia Institute of Technology

15 Nathaniel Edwin Harris. (n.d.). Retrieved from www.nga.org/governor/nathaniel-edwin-harris/.

After several failed attempts, the persistent Harris finally succeeded in passing legislation to fund the new school, and the bill was signed on October 12, 1885, by Governor Henry D. McDaniel, who was himself a former Confederate officer in the 11th Georgia Infantry. Atlanta was chosen as the site for the Georgia School of Technology. Its initial board of trustees included Harris, who served in that position until his death in 1929. The school's name was changed to Georgia Institute of Technology (Georgia Tech) in 1948.

Harris was elected to the Georgia state senate in 1894, served as a superior court judge from 1896 to 1912, and in 1914 he was elected the sixty-first governor of Georgia.

Georgia Military College

Former Confederate Major General Daniel Harvey Hill, a native of South Carolina, served as one of the first presidents of the University of Arkansas from 1877 to 1884, and then as president of the Georgia Military College in Milledgeville from 1885 to 1889 (which today is a junior college, high school, and middle school). Hill resigned because of his declining health, died a month later, and was buried in Charlotte, North Carolina.[16]

Hardin-Simmons University (Texas)

Hardin-Simmons University in Abilene, Texas, was established as Abilene Baptist College in 1891 by a group of local ranchers and businessmen. One of its original founders was Claiborne Walker Merchant, a former captain in the 14th Texas Cavalry.

A native of Nacogdoches County, Texas, Merchant became a successful rancher and land speculator after the war. His role as co-founder of the city of Abilene in 1881 earned him the moniker "Father of Abilene." Merchant donated

16 Daniel Harvey Hill (1821-1889). Retrieved from https://northcarolinahistory.org/ency-clopedia/daniel-harvey-hill-1821-1889/.

the land on which Abilene Baptist College was built, and served on its board of trustees. In 1934 the school's name was changed to Hardin-Simmons University.[17]

Owen Clinton Pope, a former private in the 1st Florida Cavalry, also was a president of the university, from 1898 to 1901.

Harvard University

Although no former Confederates were president of Harvard College (as it was then known), two former Rebel soldiers taught at the school. John McCrady, chairman and professor of zoology at Harvard, had been a captain in the Engineering Corps, Provisional Army of the Confederate States. McCrady also was a professor of mathematics at the College of Charleston, and a professor of biology at the University of the South in Sewanee, Tennessee.

Crawford Howell Toy was the Hancock Professor of Arabic, Semitic languages and Muslim law, as well as the Dexter Lecturer in Biblical Literature, both at Harvard. Toy was a former corporal in the Norfolk (Virginia) Light Artillery, and later was chaplain of the 53rd Georgia Infantry. Toy also was a professor of natural philosophy and astronomy at the University of Alabama, taught Greek at Furman University, and was a professor of Old Testament interpretation at the Southern Baptist Theological Seminary in Louisville, Kentucky.

Jacksonville State University (Alabama)

Former Confederate Brigadier General William Henry Forney served as president of Jacksonville State University (formerly Calhoun College) in 1871.[18] He also was a member of the U.S. House of Representatives from Alabama, and was appointed by President Cleveland to the Gettysburg Battlefield Commission. Forney saw extensive action during the war in Lee's Army of Northern Virginia and was wounded and left on the field at Gettysburg, where he was captured and imprisoned for more than a year. Forney surrendered at Appomattox.

---

17 Daniel, J. (2010, June 15). MERCHANT, CLAIBORNE WALKER. Retrieved from https://tshaonline.org/handbook/online/articles/fme26.

18 William Forney. (n.d.). Retrieved from www.encyclopediaofalabama.org/article/h-3321.

Johns Hopkins University

No former Confederates served as president of Johns Hopkins, but two taught at the prestigious Baltimore university. Basil Lanneau Gildersleeve, a former aide-de-camp to Major General John B. Gordon, was a professor of Greek at Johns Hopkins and also taught and was chairman of the Department of Latin at the University of Virginia. Gildersleeve was president of the Society for Classical Studies, an organization founded in the nineteenth century as the American Philological Association. The highly respected scholar was awarded honorary doctorate degrees from the College of William and Mary, Harvard, Yale, the University of Chicago, the University of Pennsylvania, the University of the South, Princeton University, Oxford University, and Cambridge University.

Colonel John William Mallet (who was described more extensively earlier in this study) was a professor of chemistry and physics at Johns Hopkins. In addition to serving in various national and international scientific societies, Mallet also taught at Amherst College in Massachusetts, the University of Alabama, the University of Louisiana (Tulane), the University of Virginia, the Jefferson Medical College in Philadelphia, and was faculty chairman and professor at the University of Texas.

Judson College (Alabama)

Samuel Wooten Averett led an interesting life at sea before settling into academia. He was born in Virginia on March 1, 1838, graduated from the U. S. Naval Academy in 1859, and was posted to the screw-sloop USS *Wyoming* in the U.S. Navy's Pacific Squadron. When the *Wyoming* docked in San Francisco in May 1861, news swept through the ship that the country was embroiled in a civil war. Averett resigned, traveled to New Orleans, and enlisted as a lieutenant in the Confederate Navy.

His first command was the small tugboat *Watson*, which was used to help erect the city's defenses. Averett then was put in command of a floating battery at Island No. 10 between Tennessee and Kentucky on the Mississippi River, and was captured there when the stronghold fell in April 1862. When he was exchanged four months later he joined the CSS *Florida*, a successful Southern raider that plied the Atlantic. The ship and crew were captured in Brazilian waters in October 1864, ending Averett's military career.

After the war, Averett taught at the Culpeper Female Academy and was president of Judson College in Alabama from 1887 until his death in 1896. Prior to moving to Judson College, he taught and was co-principal at Averett College in Virginia.[19]

Lander College (South Carolina)

John Owens Willson, president of Lander College from 1904 to 1915, had served as a private in the 3rd South Carolina Cavalry during the war. In addition to Lander, Willson was a member of the board of trustees of Columbia College in South Carolina.[20]

Louisiana State University

Three former Confederate officers served as presidents of Louisiana State University (LSU).

David F. Boyd, a former major on the staff of General Harry Thompson Hays, was president of LSU from 1865 to 1880; David Boyd Hall on LSU's campus is named after him.

Boyd was succeeded by William Preston Johnston, a former colonel in the 1st Kentucky Infantry who was president of the college from 1880 to 1883. Johnston, the son of General Albert Sidney Johnston, who was killed at Shiloh, had been an aide-de-camp to President Jefferson Davis. The younger Johnston also was president of Tulane University and a professor of history, literature, and political economy at Washington and Lee University.

Johnston was succeeded by James W. Nicholson, who served as president from 1883 to 1896. He was a former sergeant in the 12th Louisiana infantry.[21] Nicholson was the first dean of the LSU's College of Arts and Sciences, professor

---

19 Judson College. (n.d.). Retrieved from www.encyclopediaofalabama.org/article/h-2492.

20 Dr John Owens Willson (1845-1923) - Find A Grave. (n.d.). Retrieved from www.findagrave.com/memorial/116770168/john-owens-willson.

21 Louisiana State University, & LSU (n.d.). Louisiana State University. Retrieved from www.lsu.edu/president/history.php.

and chairman of the Mathematics Department, and a world-renowned mathematician. According to one source,

> He was a member of the London Mathematical Society, and also of the Mathematical Society of New York. A partial list of his mathematical works, formulas, etc., includes: A series of arithmetic and an elementary algebra, adopted and in exclusive use in the public schools of Louisiana. A treatise on "Isoperimetrical Geometry" in 1869, one on the "Calculus of Finite Differences" in 1871, and one on "Directed Quantities" in 1885. In 1868 he published a pamphlet on the "Trigonometrical Circle," a formula which he devised for expressing the relation between the sides and functions of the angles of right-angled triangles, which has been incorporated into some of the standard works on trigonometry. In 1880 he published a pamphlet entitled "A New and Complete Demonstration of the Binomial Theorem." He published a pamphlet on the "Multisector," an instrument which he invented for dividing an angle into any number of equal parts, and his paper on "a simple and direct method of separating the roots of ordinary equations" was read before the Mathematical Society of New York, May 7, 1892. His last great contribution to mathematics is "A Direct and General Method of finding the Real Roots of Numerical Equations to any Degree of Accuracy.[22]

James W. Nicholson Hall on the LSU campus is named in his honor.

Millsaps College (Mississippi)

A former major in Confederate service named Reuben Webster Millsaps founded Millsaps College in Jackson, Mississippi.[23]

Millsaps, a native of Copiah County, Mississippi, was born in 1833 and attended Hanover College in Madison, Indiana, before transferring to Asbury College (later DePauw University) in Greencastle, Indiana, where he graduated in 1854. Millsaps returned home to Mississippi for two years and enrolled at Harvard, earned a law degree in 1858, and practiced in Pine Bluff, Arkansas, until the beginning of the Civil War.

---

22 Biographical and Historical Memoirs of Louisiana, Vol. II, Chicago, Goodspeed Publishing, 1892, 278-279 (Author not given.)

23 Major Reuben Webster Millsaps. (n.d.). Retrieved from www.millsaps.edu/admissions/major-reuben-webster-millsaps.php.

Millsaps was commissioned a lieutenant in the 9th Arkansas Infantry and was wounded at Shiloh in April 1862. He returned to action and fought at Champion Hill during the Vicksburg Campaign. The 9th Arkansas was part of Major General William Loring's Division, so Millsaps avoided capture when Vicksburg surrendered on July 4, 1863. He fought at the subsequent siege of Jackson and was later transferred to Georgia, where he was promoted to major and fought in the Atlanta and Tennessee campaigns of 1864. Millsaps was again wounded at the Battle of Nashville but returned to duty and served in North Carolina under General Joseph E. Johnston. He surrendered with what little was left of the Army of Tennessee on April 26, 1865.

After receiving his parole, Millsaps returned to Mississippi and embarked on a remarkable career as a churchman, businessman, and educator. He entered the cotton brokerage and shipping business in Brookhaven, Mississippi, and in 1880 sold the business and moved to St. Louis, where he opened a wholesale grocery and cotton commission business. He returned to Hazelhurst, Mississippi, in 1885, and in 1887 became president of the Capitol State Bank in Jackson.

In addition to his banking interests, Millsaps was involved in the management of the Illinois Central Railroad, the Jackson Fertilizer Company, and the Jackson Light, Heat, and Water Company, and served on the Jackson Board of Trade. He also was a large landowner in the Mississippi Delta region and donated the property on which the Mississippi Methodist Children's Home was built.

Millsaps was a lifelong active member of the Methodist Episcopal Church, of which he was a major benefactor. Because of his keen interest in education, in 1889 he pledged $50,000 for the establishment of a Methodist college in Mississippi. Three years later Millsaps College opened in Jackson, where he had once fought with his regiment twenty-six years earlier. Before his death in 1916 Millsaps supported his namesake school, and ultimately donated in excess of $500,000 toward the construction of various college facilities.

Mississippi State University

Stephen Dill Lee, widely regarded as the Founding Father of Mississippi State University, experienced one of the most remarkable and varied careers of any Confederate soldier.

Lee was born in Charleston, South Carolina, in 1833, raised in Abbeville, and graduated from West Point in 1854. He served in the U.S. Army in Florida, Kansas, and the Dakota Territory before resigning to join the Confederacy in 1861 as a

Stephen Dill Lee

Wikipedia

captain in the South Carolina Militia. Lee was involved in the command decisions that led up to the bombardment of Fort Sumter on April 12, 1861, and was soon thereafter placed in command of Confederate artillery in the Army of Northern Virginia. He fought with that army from the outskirts of Richmond in the Seven Days' Battles through the push north to Second Manassas and into Maryland at Sharpsburg, earning a promotion to colonel.

November 1862 brought with it a promotion to brigadier general and a transfer west to Mississippi, where Lee led an infantry brigade and then a division. He was captured with the rest of the Vicksburg garrison in early July 1863. After his exchange that August, Lee was promoted to major general and placed in command of a cavalry force that saw hard service in Mississippi, Alabama, and Tennessee. In June of 1864 Lee was promoted to lieutenant general—the youngest at that rank in the Confederate Army—and the following month he was assigned to command an infantry corps in General John Bell Hood's Army of Tennessee. Lee led his new command in the unsuccessful defense of Atlanta and then moved north with the rest of the army on Hood's ill-fated Tennessee Campaign that November and December. Lee was wounded by artillery fragments during the army's retreat from Nashville. When he recovered Lee joined General Joseph Johnston's army in North Carolina, but a reorganization left him without a formal command. He surrendered with the rest of Johnston's men on April 26, 1865.

After the war Lee moved to Columbus, Mississippi, where he engaged in planting and served as a Mississippi state legislator. He recognized the state's need for an agricultural and technical college and strongly advocated for its establishment and initial funding. He got his wish in 1878 when the Agricultural and Mechanical College of the State of Mississippi was chartered. Lee's passion for the new institution was so strong that he became the school's first president and he served for twenty-two years in that capacity until 1899. The school's name was changed to Mississippi State College in 1932. As it grew in size and prestige, its name was changed again in 1958, this time to Mississippi State University.[24]

Stephen Lee also was a delegate to the Mississippi constitutional convention in 1890, and in 1895 became the first chairman of the Vicksburg National Park Association. The former lieutenant general also was a driving force behind the creation of the Mississippi Historical Commission in 1900, which was the forerunner of the Mississippi Department of Archives and History. Recognized as a pioneer in industrial education in the South, Lee was inducted into the Mississippi Hall of Fame in 1903. Lee Hall at Mississippi State University is named in his honor.

The old soldier and indefatigable educator died in Vicksburg in 1908 from a cerebral hemorrhage while addressing former Union soldiers he had fought in the battles around Vicksburg in July 1863.

Missouri Military Academy

The Missouri Military Academy owes its existence to a former Confederate colonel named Alexander Frederick Fleet.[25]

Born in Virginia in 1843, Fleet volunteered to serve the Confederacy and joined the 26th Virginia Infantry as a sergeant in June 1861. He soon was commissioned a lieutenant and served on the staff of Brigadier General Henry A. Wise. Fleet rose to the rank of colonel and surrendered with Lee's army at Appomattox in April 1865.

Fleet received his education at the University of Virginia (where he was enrolled before the war and to which he returned once the war ended) and earned his degree in 1867. He briefly taught school in Fredericksburg before moving to Liberty, Missouri, where he taught Greek and was faculty chairman at William Jewell College from 1868 to 1873. Fleet served as president of Baptist Female College in Lexington, Missouri, from 1873 to 1879, and was chairman and professor of Greek at the University of Missouri from 1879 to 1890. In 1891, he founded the Missouri Military Academy in Mexico, Missouri, and served as its

24 https://mississippiencyclopedia.org/entries/stephen-d-lee/.

25 Col Alexander Frederick Fleet (1843-1911). Retrieved from www.findagrave.com/memorial/154131077/alexander-frederick-fleet#view-photo=130728628.

superintendent until 1910, at which time ill health forced him to move to Atlanta, Georgia, to be near his children. Fleet died in 1911.

North Carolina State University

Confederate veteran Sydenham Benoni Alexander, together with fellow North Carolinian Ashley Horne, is recognized as a co-founder of North Carolina State University.[26]

Alexander was a native of Mecklenburg County, North Carolina, born in 1840. He graduated from the University of North Carolina at Chapel Hill in 1860. In April of the following year he enlisted as a private in the 1st North Carolina Infantry and in June of 1862 was elected a captain in the 42nd North Carolina Infantry. In 1864, Alexander transferred to the staff of General Robert F. Hoke, but he returned to the 42nd North Carolina during the siege of Petersburg in early 1865. He surrendered with Robert E. Lee's Virginia army at Appomattox.

After the war Alexander returned to North Carolina and became a successful farmer. He was elected to the North Carolina Senate in 1879, served on several powerful committees, and was reelected several times. Alexander strongly advocated for the establishment of a technical university in the state and his efforts were realized in 1887 with the creation of the North Carolina College of Agriculture and Mechanical Arts, later renamed North Carolina State University. In addition to serving on the new college's board of trustees, Alexander also was president of the North Carolina Railroad

Sydenham Benoni Alexander

Encyclopedia of North Carolina

26 Noblin, S. (n.d.). Alexander, Sydenham Benoni. Retrieved from www.ncpedia.org/biography/alexander-sydenham-benoni.

Ashley Horne

Yale University Alumni Magazine

and the North Carolina Farmers Alliance. He was an unsuccessful candidate for governor in 1888, but was elected to the U.S. House of Representatives in 1890 and served two terms until his retirement in 1894.

Ashley Horne, Alexander's fellow Southern veteran, is considered a founder of North Carolina State University. Horne was born near Clayton, North Carolina, in 1841, and was one of six brothers to serve in the Confederate Army. Only three survived. Horne received little formal education but was one of North Carolina's wealthiest citizens by the turn of the century.

In 1861 Horne enlisted as a private in the 50th North Carolina Infantry, but was soon transferred to the 53rd North Carolina where his older brother Sam was a lieutenant. The younger Horne served the entire war and was a sergeant when Lee's army surrendered at Appomattox. Horne led a detachment of ten paroled soldiers to North Carolina to ensure that General Joseph Johnston was informed of Lee's capitulation.

Horne returned to his family's North Carolina home after the war and became a successful farmer and politician. His business prowess was renowned, and during his career he was involved in farming, banking and finance, cotton milling, phosphate processing, and fertilizer manufacturing. Horne also was involved in the formation of the insurance industry in North Carolina and was a director of an insurance company. His involvement in politics and his position as an influential member of the North Carolina Senate Finance Committee in 1884-85 allowed him to shepherd the creation and funding of the college that would become North Carolina State University.

Horne personally funded a monument honoring the North Carolina women of the Confederacy in Raleigh. The monument was vandalized and spray-painted with graffiti in 2015, and was the subject of hearings in 2018 as to whether it was so offensive that it should be taken down. After public hearings, during which a majority of attendees demanded the statue remain, the monument (and two others) were left in place. Horne also helped established and fund the Horne Memorial United Methodist Church in Clayton, North Carolina, which is named in his honor.

Another Confederate veteran, Alexander Quarles Holladay, served as president of North Carolina State University from 1889 to 1899. Holladay, a former lieutenant in the 19th Virginia Infantry, also was a postwar president of the University of Florida.

Prairie View A&M University (Texas)

Ashbel Smith, a strong advocate for the education of women and African-Americans, is credited as one of founders of Prairie View A&M University. His successful career left an indelible mark on the development of Texas.

Smith was born in Hartford, Connecticut, in 1805 and graduated from Yale University in 1824. He taught school briefly in North Carolina before returning to Yale to earn a medical degree in 1828. He traveled overseas to France for further studies and while there treated victims of the Paris cholera epidemic of 1832. He returned to North Carolina later that year and established a medical practice in Salisbury before moving to Texas in 1836.

Once in Texas Smith became one of President Sam Houston's close friends and was appointed surgeon general of the Republic of Texas. During his service Smith established the first hospital in the settlement that would later become the city of Houston. His advocacy of medical science and public education led to him being a charter member and first vice president of the Texas Philosophical Society. The organization immediately began lobbying the Texas state government to establish a system of public education. Smith treated victims of a yellow fever

Ashbel Smith

Texas Literary Institute

epidemic in Galveston in 1839, a harrowing experience that would later inspire him to fight for the retention of a hospital in the city, whose subtropical climate was conducive to fevers and disease.

In 1841 President Houston appointed Smith as the republic's ambassador to the United Kingdom and France, and as emissary to the Vatican. After his return from Europe in 1845 Smith was appointed secretary of state of the Republic of Texas, but served only briefly before Texas joined the United States in December 1845.

When war was declared on Mexico in April 1846, Smith volunteered and served as a U.S. Army surgeon. After the war he was appointed a member of the board of visitors of the U.S. Military Academy at West Point, and in 1853 he co-founded the Texas Medical Association. Two years later he was elected to the U.S. House of Representatives.

Smith supported the secession of Texas. When war erupted in 1861, he organized a company in the 2nd Texas Infantry and was elected its captain. He was severely wounded at the Battle of Shiloh in early April 1862 and after his recovery was promoted to colonel and given command of the regiment. Smith and the 2nd Texas fought at Vicksburg and were captured when the city fell on July 4, 1863. He was later exchanged, returned to duty, and served the rest of the war in the defense of Galveston. During the waning days of the war his name was submitted for promotion to brigadier general, but the rank was never confirmed. At the war's end Smith and fellow Confederate William P. Ballinger were dispatched by the Texas governor to New Orleans to negotiate peace with the federal government.

In 1866 Smith and his cousin Henry Gillette founded the Bayland Orphans Home for children of deceased Confederate soldiers. Four years later in 1870 he co-founded the Texas Historical Society and served as its first president. In 1876, while serving as a member of the Texas state legislature, Smith championed the establishment of the Stuart Female Seminary and the Alta Vista Agricultural and Mechanical College for the Benefit of Colored Youths—the school now named Prairie View A&M University.[27]

Smith's commitment to higher education earned him the moniker "Father of the University of Texas." He served as president of the University of Texas Board of Regents and was president of the Texas Medical Association, and along with Greensville Dowell, he succeeded in saving the financially imperiled Galveston

---

27 Silverthorne, E. (2010, June 15). SMITH, ASHBEL. Retrieved from https://tshaonline.org/handbook/online/articles/fsm04.

Medical College by merging it with the Texas Medical College, a part of the University of Texas.

Richmond Academy of Medicine

Founded in 1820 as a medical school, the Richmond Academy of Medicine is now exclusively a professional association. Edwin S. Gaillard, a surgeon in the 1st Maryland Infantry of the Confederate Army, was appointed the first professor of pathology at the Richmond Academy of Medicine in 1867—the same year he became the institution's president. The following year he moved to Kentucky and served as dean of the Louisville Medical College. Gaillard founded the *Richmond and Louisville Medical Journal* that same year and the *American Medical Weekly* in 1874. He was declared legally insane in 1885, and died that same year.[28]

Samford University (Alabama)

Jabez L. M. Curry, the aforementioned Confederate colonel and United States diplomat, served as president of Samford University from 1865 to 1868. Curry served on the staffs of Generals Joseph E. Johnston and Joe Wheeler. He was a prolific postwar teacher and education advocate.[29]

Shepherd University (West Virginia)

One of the founders of Shepherd University in Shepherdstown, West Virginia, was Alexander Robinson Boteler, a former Confederate colonel who served on the staffs of Generals Robert E. Lee, Thomas J. "Stonewall" Jackson, and J.E.B. Stuart. Boteler, a Shepherdstown native and Princeton University graduate, returned home after the war and helped found Shepherd College in 1871. In addition to his law practice and philanthropic activities, Boteler served on the U.S. Tariff Commission in the Chester Arthur administration, and on the staff of U.S.

28 Dr Edwin Samuel Gaillard (1827-1885), retrieved from www.findagrave. Com/memorial/ 135610201/edwin-samuel-gaillard.

29 Jabez Lamar Monroe Curry, (n.d.), Retrieved from www.encyclopediaofalabama.org/ article/h-1154.

Attorney General Benjamin H. Brewster. Former Private Dudley D. Pendleton of the 1st Virginia Cavalry served as president of Shepherd University from 1882 to 1885.[30]

Southwestern University (Texas)

Southwestern University in Georgetown, Texas, was co-founded by former Confederate captain Emzy Taylor. According to the Texas State Historical Association, "No matter what was going on in Georgetown in the 1870s and 1880s, Emzy Taylor was probably involved with it. The former Confederate officer helped start Georgetown's First National Bank, its water works, its college, its first rail line, and served as the town's first fire chief."

Born in Little Rock, Arkansas, in 1841, Taylor's family moved to rural Williamson County, Texas, in the late 1840s, and by 1849 resided in Georgetown. Taylor worked in the family store until 1861, when he volunteered for the Confederate Army as a member of the 4th Texas Infantry, part of Hood's Texas Brigade. Taylor was discharged because of illness in late 1862 or early 1863 and returned home. Once he recovered, he formed a company of infantry that would become part of the 16th Texas Infantry in the Army of the Trans-Mississippi. Taylor fought in the Red River Campaign in Louisiana at the battles of Mansfield and Pleasant Hill.

After the war Taylor returned to Georgetown and took over the family's mercantile business when his father died in 1868. In the 1870s he established a waterworks business as well as a nursery and produce company, and helped found the Georgetown Railroad Company, which brought the first rail service to the city in 1878. Taylor went on to start the First National Bank of Georgetown in the following decade.

Taylor was instrumental in the creation of Southwestern University in 1873, which was created by consolidating four Texas educational institutions: Wesleyan College in San Augustine, Soule University in Chappell Hill, Rutersville College in Rutersville, and McKenzie College in Clarksville. The new institution, built in Georgetown, was named Texas University. The state legislature was planning a

---

30 Shepherd Chronological Highlights. (n.d.). Retrieved from www.shepherd.edu/about-shepherd/chronology.

new university in Austin to be named the University of Texas, so in 1875 Texas University's name was changed to Southwestern University.[31]

Texas A&M University

John Garland James, a former corporal in the VMI Corps of Cadets at the Battle of New Market, was president of Texas A&M University from 1879 to 1883. He also taught at the Kentucky Military Institute, co-founded the Texas Military Institute, and served on the board of visitors of the U.S. Naval Academy.[32]

Another VMI cadet and New Market veteran, Hardaway Hunt Dinwiddie, was president of Texas A&M from 1883 to 1887, as well as faculty chairman and professor of chemistry and physics. He and his brother John Garland James were also co-founders of the Texas Military Institute.

Lawrence Sullivan "Sul" Ross was president of Texas A&M from 1891 to 1899.[33] Ross, a member of the Texas Rangers before the war, was an infantry and cavalry officer, and eventually attained the rank of brigadier general by the end of 1863. He also served as governor of Texas, was a state senator, and was a sheriff of McLennan County.

Texas Christian University

Confederate veteran Addison Clark, along with his brother Randolph, are recognized as co-founders of Texas Christian University.[34]

Both brothers were members of the 16th Texas ("Fitzhugh's") Cavalry Regiment. Addison was born in Morris County, Texas, in 1842, and received most of his education from his mother. He volunteered for Confederate military service in 1862 and served until the end of the war.

---

31 Retrieved from https://williamson-county-texas-history.org/Georgetown_Texas /Emzy_Taylor_Historical_Marker_Georgetown_Texas_in_Williamson_County.html.

32 Morley, D. (2010, June 15). James, John Garland. Retrieved from https:// tshaonline.org/handbook/online/articles/fja18.

33 Benner, & Ann, J. (2010, June 15). Ross, Lawrence Sullivan [Sul]. Retrieved from https:// tshaonline.org/handbook/online/articles/fro81.

34 Carey. (2010, June 12). Clark, Randolph. Retrieved from https://tshaonline.org/handbook/online/articles/fcl12; M. J. (2010, June 12). Clark, Addison. Retrieved from https://tshaonline.org/handbook/online/articles/fcl02.

Once the fighting ended he enrolled at Carlton College in Bonham, Texas, graduating in 1869. Addison moved to Fort Worth, Texas, and founded a school under the auspices of his religious denomination, the Disciples of Christ. In 1874 Addison, his brother Randolph, and their father moved to Thorp Spring, Texas, and opened the AddRan Male and Female College, with Addison acting as its first president. The school grew quickly and the Clark brothers gave the institution to the Disciples of Christ of Texas in 1889. Addison remained president. Over his objections the name was changed to AddRan University. In 1895 the university was moved to Waco, which Addison also opposed. He remained its president until 1899. Three years later the school's name was officially changed to Texas Christian University.

Addison taught ancient languages at the university until 1904, when he resigned and opened AddRan Jarvis College at the old Thorp Spring campus. The new college closed just five years later, after which Addison served as a pastor of a Disciples of

Addison Clark

Texas Christian University

Christ church in Mineral Wells, Texas, until his death in 1911.

Addison's younger brother Randolph was born in Waskom, Texas, in 1844, and like his older brother was a member of the 16th Texas Cavalry. After the war Randolph attended school in Kentucky Town, Texas, and joined Addison at Carlton College in Bonham. As noted above, the brothers established the college that would eventually bear the name Texas Christian University.

Randolph became a prolific founder of educational institutions during his career as an educator and administrator. In 1876 he enrolled at Bethany College in West Virginia and completed studies in physical science. He returned to AddRan University, which was then at the Thorp Spring campus, and served as its vice president and as a teacher for 20 years.

In 1873 Randolph, like his older brother, was an ordained minister in the Disciples of Christ church and as a pastor oversaw numerous churches in central and north Texas. At the request of the citizens of Lancaster, Texas, he opened Randolph College in 1898 and in 1902 founded Hereford College in Hereford, Texas. In 1923 Randolph served as chaplain of the Texas Senate. He died in 1935.

Troy University (Alabama)

The establishment of Troy University is credited in large part to Thomas Seay, who as governor of Alabama from 1886 to 1890 championed its creation and signed legislation chartering and funding the institution.[35] Seay, whose career was discussed earlier in this study, is also considered a founder of Alabama State University and the Alabama Institute for the Deaf and Blind. He was elected to the Alabama State Senate in 1876. His ten years of service with that body included a stint as senate president from 1884 to 1886. Seay was elected governor of Alabama twice, in 1886 and 1888.

Tulane University

As noted earlier, William Preston Johnston (former colonel in the 1st Kentucky Infantry, son of General Albert S. Johnston) was the president of Tulane University from 1884 to 1899. He also served as president of Louisiana State University and was a professor of history, literature, and political economy at Washington and Lee University.[36]

Tulane University School of Medicine

The Tulane University School of Medicine was established by one of the most famous American physicians of the nineteenth century, the previously mentioned Tobias Gibson Richardson, M.D., of New Orleans. During the Civil War, Dr.

35 Thomas Seay (1886-90). (n.d.). Retrieved from www.encyclopediaofalabama.org/article/h-1533.

36 Past Presidents. (n.d.). Retrieved from https://tulane.edu/past-presidents.

Richardson was the medical inspector of the Army of Tennessee and performed the difficult and successful amputation of General John Bell Hood's right leg after the Battle of Chickamauga.

"Dr. Richardson led the medical school during the difficult post-Civil War years and brought it to national recognition," explains Tulane University's website. "He supervised the transition of the medical department from the University of Louisiana to Tulane University of Louisiana. During this time, he served as the only physician on the Board of Administrators of the Tulane Education Fund, which oversaw Paul Tulane's Act of Donation creating Tulane University."[37]

In addition to his teaching duties, Richardson practiced medicine in New Orleans from 1866 until his death in 1892.

United States Military Academy (West Point, NY)

Three former Confederates (all mentioned earlier) served on the board of visitors of West Point. Fitzhugh Lee, a former cavalry major general in the Army of Northern Virginia, also was governor of Virginia, the U.S. consul general to Havana, a U.S. Army major general of volunteers during the Spanish- American

War, and the military governor of Havana and Pinar del Rio, Cuba. Lee also was a post-Civil War U.S. Army brigadier general and commander of the Division of Missouri, and the keynote speaker at the Battle of Bunker Hill centennial celebration in 1875 in Boston, Massachusetts.

Also serving as West Point board of visitors members were Daniel Ruggles, a former brigadier general in the Army of Tennessee, and Scott Shipp, a former major in the 21st Virginia Infantry who commanded the VMI cadet corps at the

Scott Shipp

Library of Congress

37 (n.d.). www.tulane.edu/~matas/historical/medschool/doctors/ richardson.htm.

Battle of New Market. Shipp also was the president of Virginia Tech, and a member of the board of visitors of the U.S. Naval Academy.

United States Naval Academy (Annapolis)

The U.S. Naval Academy at Annapolis, Maryland, was founded in 1845 by Captain Franklin Buchanan, who would resign from the U.S. Navy to serve the Confederacy during the Civil War as an admiral and the commander of two of its more famous ironclads: the CSS *Virginia* and the CSS *Tennessee*.

Ex-Confederate John Garland James was a member of the board of visitors of the Naval Academy. He was a corporal in the VMI corps of cadets at New Market, and after the war served as president of Texas A&M University, co-founded the Texas Military Institute, and taught at the Kentucky Military Institute.

Another VMI cadet, Thomas Staples Martin, served on the Naval Academy's board of visitors. Martin was majority leader and chairman of the Appropriations Committee in the U.S. Senate. He co-authored the United States Declaration of War against Germany in 1917, and later served as a member of the board of visitors of the University of Virginia.

The aforementioned Scott Shipp was yet another former Confederate who served on the academy's board of visitors.

University of Alabama

A series of Southern veterans served as postwar presidents of the University of Alabama. William Russell Smith, president from 1869 to 1871, was a former colonel in the 26th Alabama Infantry and a member of the Confederate House of Representatives from Alabama.

Smith was succeeded by the famous American mariner and oceanographer Matthew Fontaine Maury, who was interim president of the university in 1871. Before the war Maury was called the "Father of Modern Oceanography and Naval Meteorology," and "Scientist of the Seas" in recognition of his extensive work, especially his groundbreaking 1855 book *The Physical Geography of the Sea*. At the outbreak of the Civil War, Maury resigned from the U.S. Navy to join the Southern cause and was appointed Confederate Chief of Sea Coast, River and Harbor Defenses.

Nathaniel Thomas Lupton, the former superintendent of the Confederate Nitre and Mining Bureau in Selma, Alabama, was named president of the university in 1871. Before leading the University of Alabama Lupton had been a professor of chemistry and pharmacy at Vanderbilt University and a professor of chemistry at Auburn University. He served as state chemist of Alabama.

The next former Confederate to preside over the University of Alabama was Josiah Gorgas, who began his two-year tenure in 1878. Gorgas was one of the most important officers in the Southern Army, yet one of the least known. He rose to become a brigadier general and served throughout the war as chief of the Ordnance Department. Succeeding Gorgas as president of the university was Burwell Boykin Lewis, a former captain in the 2nd Alabama Cavalry whose tense lasted from 1880 to 1885.

The Confederate lineage of University of Alabama presidents continued when Henry DeLamar Clayton was named to the position in 1886. The former major general in the Army of Tennessee led the university until 1889. Clayton was succeeded by the last Confederate to serve as president, Richard Channing Jones, formerly a lieutenant in the 44th Alabama Infantry. Jones served in his position from 1890 until 1897.[38]

One of the most famous chemists of the nineteenth century, the aforementioned former Confederate Colonel John William Mallet, was a professor of chemistry at the University of Alabama in addition to all of the other schools at which he taught. (For more on Mallet, see page. 117.)

Another ex-Confederate and renowned scholar, Crawford Howell Toy, was professor of Hebrew at the university. (For more on Toy, see page. 136.)

University of Alabama School of Medicine

The University of Alabama School of Medicine, located in Birmingham, traces its origins to the founding of the Medical College of Alabama in 1859 by Josiah Clark Nott, M.D., a Confederate Army surgeon and medical director on the staffs of Generals Daniel Ruggles and Braxton Bragg.[39]

38 The University of Alabama. (n.d.). Retrieved from www.ua.edu/legends/list_ presidents. php.

39 Josiah C. Nott. (n.d.). Retrieved from www.encyclopediaofalabama.org/article/h-1484.

Born in Columbia, South Carolina, Nott's life was filled with familial tragedy. He received his medical degree from the University of Pennsylvania and later studied in France. He returned to America and lived in Mobile, Alabama, where he established a practice. Nott was among the early pioneers who theorized that yellow fever was a mosquito-borne disease. Tragically, he and his wife lost four of their seven children to the disease in a one-week period in 1853. Two of his three remaining sons died during the Civil War: Henry "of exposure and fatigue on the battlefield at Shiloh," in 1862, and James, "while leading a charge" at the Battle of Chickamauga in 1863. Just prior to the war, Nott had successfully lobbied the state legislature to charter and provide funding for the medical school. After the war Nott returned to Mobile, practiced medicine, and was a professor at the Medical College of Alabama until his death in 1873.

Assisting Nott with establishment of the Medical College of Alabama was fellow former Confederate George A. Ketchum. A surgeon in the 5th Alabama Infantry, Ketchum was later faculty dean and professor of the theory and practice of medicine at the school. Ketchum co-founded the Alabama Medical Association, served as president of the Mobile Board of Health, and was a member of the Alabama State Board of Health. He also was president of the Mobile County Medical Society and the Medical Association of the State of Alabama, as well as a member of the International Medical Congress.

In the early 1900s the Medical College of Alabama, then located in Mobile, became affiliated with the University of Alabama, and the school was moved to the university's main campus in Tuscaloosa in the 1920s. The medical college remained there until 1945, when it was moved to Birmingham and became a component of the University of Alabama at Birmingham, itself a part of the University of Alabama System.

University of Arkansas

Daniel Harvey Hill, president of the University of Arkansas from 1887 to 1884, was a former major general in the Army of Northern Virginia. Hill also was president of Georgia Military College.[40]

---

40 Daniel Harvey Hill (1821-1889). Retrieved from https://northcarolinahistory.org/encyclopedia/daniel-harvey-hill-1821-1889/.

University of Arkansas at Pine Bluff

Another Arkansas college established by an ex-Confederate was the University of Arkansas at Pine Bluff, an historically African-American institution founded in 1873 at the insistence of Arkansas governor Augustus Hill Garland.[41] A native of Covington, Tennessee, and a practicing attorney in Little Rock at the outbreak of the Civil War, Garland opposed Arkansas' secession but remained loyal to his state. Although he did not serve in the Confederate military, he was elected to the Confederate Congress and Senate.

As stated previously, after the war Garland served in the U.S. Senate, and was U.S. attorney general in the Grover Cleveland administration. As governor of Arkansas he urged the legislature to support education for the blind and deaf, and was instrumental in the establishment and initial funding of the Branch Normal College, now named the University of Arkansas at Pine Bluff.

University of Arkansas College of Medicine

Six of the eight founders of the University of Arkansas College of Medicine, which initially was named the Medical Department of the Arkansas Industrial University, were Confederate veterans.[42] According to the university, the medical school was founded by former Confederates Augustus Louis Breysacher, Philo Oliver Hooper, Claiborne Watkins, Roscoe Green Jennings, John Josephus McAlmont, and James Henry Southall. The two other co-founders were Arkansan James Anthony Dibrell Jr., who was too young to serve in the war, and Connecticut native Edwin Bentley, who served as a Union army surgeon.

Dr. Augustus Louis Breysacher, the son of German immigrants, was born in Canton, Ohio, in 1831 and raised in St. Louis. He graduated from Xavier University in Cincinnati, Ohio (then St. Xavier College) and the Missouri Medical College in St. Louis (later Washington University School of Medicine). After one year of service with the U.S. Army Breysacher returned to St. Louis and practiced

41 Garland, Augustus Hill. (n.d.). Retrieved from https://encyclopediaofarkansas.net/entries/augustus-hill-garland-106/.

42 University of Arkansas for Medical Sciences (UAMS). (n.d.). Retrieved from https://encyclopediaofarkansas.net/entries/university-of-arkansas-for-medical-sciences-uams-2395/.

Dr. Augustus Louis Breysacher

University of Arkansas for Medical Sciences

medicine. In addition to being a medical doctor, he also was a chemist and pharmacist.

At the outbreak of the Civil War Breysacher declined a commission in the U.S. Army and enlisted in the Confederate Army, where he served for the entire war as a surgeon and medical director. After the war Breysacher moved to Pine Bluff, Arkansas, and then to Little Rock, where he became a highly respected obstetrician, gynecologist, and educator. One notable event in his career occurred on January 26, 1880, when he delivered baby Douglas MacArthur, the future legendary U.S. Army general. Douglas's father, Arthur MacArthur, had been a Union officer in the Civil War, and at the time of Douglas's birth was a U.S. Army officer stationed at the Little Rock Barracks.

In addition to co-founding the Medical Department of the University of

Arkansas, Breysacher was a professor of obstetrics and diseases of women and children at the university. For several years he was treasurer of the Arkansas Medical Association and a member of the American Medical Association. He served as a delegate from the latter organization to the International Medical Congress in Philadelphia in 1876.

According to the University of Arkansas for Medical Sciences, College of Medicine, "Though some may not

Douglas MacArthur

Library of Congress

remember Dr. Breysacher by name, thousands of physicians and suffering patients will reap the benefits of his intelligence, foresight, judgment, and determination as manifested in medical education and medical regulation organizations for ages to come."[43]

Another co-founder, Philo Oliver Hooper, was born in Little Rock in 1833, studied at the University of Nashville (now Vanderbilt University), and graduated from the Jefferson Medical College in Philadelphia in 1856. Later that year he began the practice of medicine in Little Rock.

Hooper entered Confederate service at the outbreak of the Civil War. He was commissioned a major and appointed as medical director of Confederate forces in the Indian Territory on the staff of General Albert Pike. He was later assigned to hospital duty in Memphis and Little Rock, and was head of the Confederate medical examination boards in Arkansas, Louisiana, Texas, and the Indian Territory. He served until the end of the war.

Hooper resumed his medical practice in Little Rock in 1865 and, along with a dozen other physicians, organized the Little Rock and Pulaski County Medical Society in 1866. Four years later the Arkansas State Medical Association was formed and Hooper served as its first president.

In 1879 Hooper approached Arkansas Industrial University's president, former Confederate General Daniel Harvey Hill, and proposed the establishment of a medical school. On June 17, 1879, Hill recommended to the university's trustees that the proposed medical training school be organized; the trustees approved and the new school welcomed its first medical students in October of that year. Hooper served as dean of the medical school until 1885 when he resigned to become superintendent of the state lunatic asylum.

Hooper held a deep concern for the mentally ill and was a respected and influential member of the American Medico-Psychological Association. He was sympathetic to the plight of mentally impaired Arkansans, and Arkansas was one of only three states that had no institutions for their housing and treatment. At Hooper's urging, in 1873 and 1876 the state legislature appropriated funds for the construction of the Arkansas Lunatic Asylum. Hooper became superintendent of the facility in 1886 and served until 1893. He resumed the position of superintendent in 1897 and held it until shortly before his death in 1902.

43 Augustus L. Breysacher, M.D. (n.d.). Retrieved from https://medicine. Uams.edu/about-the-college/college-of-medicine-history/founders/augustus-l-breysacher-m-d/.

The main thoroughfare through the campus of the University of Arkansas medical schools and the University of Arkansas Medical Psychiatric Research Institute is named Hooper Drive in honor of Dr. Philo O. Hooper.

Another founder of the medical school at the University of Arkansas was former Confederate surgeon Roscoe Green Jennings, M.D., a native of Leeds, Maine. Jennings attended Dartmouth Medical College in New Hampshire and graduated from the Medical School of Maine in 1856. With his formal education complete he moved to Camden, Arkansas (where his brother was an attorney), opened a medical practice, and purchased and operated a drugstore.

When the Civil War began in 1861 Jennings enlisted in the Confederate Army and was appointed surgeon of the 12th Arkansas Infantry. He was ordered to Vicksburg, Mississippi, to organize Confederate hospitals there and was captured when the Vicksburg bastion fell in July 1863. Jennings was imprisoned but escaped in 1864. His health had deteriorated during his time as a prisoner and he was discharged from the Confederate Army.

Jennings was a physician in Fort Steele, Arkansas, after the war, and became an expert on smallpox. He was appointed surgeon general of Arkansas State Militia troops during civil unrest in 1874. In 1879, he joined with seven other physicians to found the School of Medicine of Arkansas Industrial University where he was secretary and professor of clinical surgery and venereal diseases until his death in 1899.

John Josephus McAlmont was another of the eight founders of the School of Medicine of Arkansas Industrial University. McAlmont, a native of Hornellsville, New York, was born in 1821 and graduated from Geneva Medical College in New York in 1843. He earned a second medical degree from Case Western Reserve School of Medicine (then named the Medical Department of Western Reserve College) in 1849. The following year he moved to Little Rock and opened a medical practice.

When the Civil War began, Dr. McAlmont volunteered for Confederate service and joined the Arkansas Militia with the rank of major. He participated in the surrender of federal facilities at Fort Smith and Little Rock and served as the Confederate Army's enrolling officer at the latter location. McAlmont and his wife Martha allowed their home to be used as a hospital for sick and wounded Confederate soldiers until Little Rock fell to Union forces in 1863.

Before the war Dr. McAlmont had owned and operated a drug store, and after the war he resumed his medical practice and retail drug operations. In 1879 he and seven other physicians established a new medical school at Arkansas Industrial University. Because of his knowledge and expertise in pharmacology, McAlmont was named professor of pharmacology and therapeutics, as well as treasurer of the school, holding both positions until his death in 1896.

During his eventful life the doctor also was mayor of Little Rock in 1866 and 1867, a trustee at St. John's College in Little Rock, a member of the board of directors of the Arkansas Female Academy, and attending physician and member of the board of directors of the Arkansas School for the Blind. McAlmont, who was active in pharmaceutical politics, co-founded the Arkansas Association of Pharmacists in 1883, and served as its first president.

Yet another former Rebel also participated in the founding of the medical school at the Arkansas Industrial University. James Henry Southall, M.D., was born in Smithfield, Virginia, in 1841. His grandfather was a Revolutionary War veteran and his father fought in the War of 1812. Southall spent much of his early years in Virginia and North Carolina and got his early education there as well. He earned his medical degree from the University of Louisiana (later Tulane University) in March 1861 at the young age of nineteen.

Soon after graduating, Southall enlisted in the 55th Virginia Infantry and was wounded and taken prisoner at Gettysburg. He was exchanged in December 1863, rejoined his unit, and was with the army until Lee's surrender at Appomattox on April 9, 1865.

After the war Southall opened a medical practice in Norfolk, Virginia, but soon moved to Memphis, Tennessee. In 1872, he relocated to Little Rock, where he became active in city and state medical affairs and served as president of the Arkansas Medical Society in 1882. In 1879 Dr. Southall and seven other Little Rock physicians formed the new medical school at the Arkansas Industrial University. Southall was a professor of physiology until 1886, when he became professor of the theory and practice of medicine. He retired in 1900 and died the following year.

The sixth former Confederate to co-found the Arkansas Industrial University medical school was Claiborne Watkins, M.D., a native Arkansan from a prominent family. His father was a veteran of the War of 1812, and his uncle was Robert Anderson Watkins, a former Arkansas commissioner of education and secretary of state. Another of Claiborne's uncles, George Claiborne, was chief justice of the Arkansas Supreme Court and the state's attorney general.

Claiborne Watkins attended school at the prestigious St. Timothy's Hall in Catonsville, Maryland, and was only two weeks away from graduating in 1861 when he left to return to Little Rock to volunteer for the Confederate Army. He enlisted as a private in the 11th Arkansas Infantry and was soon promoted to captain and placed in command of a company. Watkins and his unit were captured in April 1862, imprisoned, and exchanged in October of that year. After returning to duty he was captured again at Port Hudson, Louisiana, in July 1863 but escaped a month later. He returned to duty once again and served for the rest of the war in Mobile, Alabama, surrendering with General Richard Taylor's army on May 8, 1865.

After the war Watkins enrolled at Jefferson Medical College in Philadelphia, graduated in 1867, and opened a medical practice and infirmary in Little Rock. After several years, he became disenchanted with state medical certification and licensing politics and established a pharmacy. In 1879, he joined the organizers of the new medical school at Arkansas Industrial University, and because of his knowledge and experience in pharmacology was appointed professor of chemistry and toxicology. Watkins died in 1908.

University of California, Berkeley

The LeConte brothers contributed substantially to the field of higher education. John LeConte was president of the University of California, Berkeley

twice (1869 to 1870, and 1875 to 1881).[44] The former major in the Bureau of Nitre and Mining also served as a chemistry professor at the Columbia University College of Physicians and Surgeons and at the University of Georgia, and as professor of physics at the University of South Carolina, and professor of physics and the first faculty member at Cal-Berkeley.[45]

John's brother Joseph was chairman of the Department of Geology at Cal- Berkeley, and like his brother had been a major in the

John LeConte

Wikipedia

44 Douglass, J., & Thomas, S. (n.d.). U.C. Presidents Overview. Retrieved from www.lib. berkeley.edu/uchistory/general_history/overview/presidents/index.html#leconte.

45 Neither John LeConte nor his brother Joseph were sure of their official ranks in the Confederate Army. Both believed they were lieutenants, but both received a major's pay.

Confederate Bureau of Nitre and Mining. He also was chairman of the Department of Chemical Pharmacology, Minerology, and Geology at the University of South Carolina. (For more detail on Joseph LeConte, see pages 117-118.)

University of California Hastings College of the Law

Among those heavily involved in the establishment of the University of California Hastings College of the Law in San Francisco was Oliver Perry Evans, a former Virginia Military Institute cadet and veteran of the Battle of New Market.[46]

Evans was born in Jackson County, Virginia (later West Virginia) in 1842 and graduated from VMI in 1865. After the war he studied law at Washington College (later Washington and Lee University) and in 1868 moved to San Francisco, California, where he opened a law practice to immediate success. One of his prestigious clients was Judge Serranus Clinton Hastings, who employed Evans to shepherd the organization of a new law school through the California legislature. Judge Hastings provided the original funding for the new school, which was established on March 28, 1878 and named in his honor. Evans was appointed one of the first directors of Hastings College of the Law, and also served as a professor at the school.

Evans was appointed by the governor of California to the judgeship of the Fourth District Court for San Francisco and was elected Superior Court judge for San Francisco in 1880. He served three years before resigning to return to his private law practice. Judge Evans died on May 15, 1911—the forty-seventh anniversary of the Battle of New Market.

University of Colorado School of Medicine

The state of Colorado was the postwar home of William Riddick Whitehead, M.D., a former Confederate surgeon and administrator and co-founder of the Denver College of Medicine (which later became the University of Colorado School of Medicine).[47]

---

46 W. Couper, *The Corps Forward: The Biographical Sketches of the VMI Cadets Who Fought in the Battle of New Market* (Buena Vista, VA: Mariner Pub. 2005).

47 Dr William Riddick Whitehead (1831-1902) (n.d.). Retrieved from www.findagrave.com/ memorial/120221997/william-riddick-whitehead.

Whitehead was born in Suffolk, Virginia, in 1831, graduated from VMI in 1851, and received a medical degree from the University of Pennsylvania in Philadelphia in 1853 (his thesis was entitled "Digestion"). He traveled overseas to serve as a surgeon in the Russian army during the Crimean War from 1853-1854 and was knighted into the Imperial Order of St. Stanislaus by the Russian tsar Nicholas I in recognition of his service.

Once the Crimean War ended Whitehead traveled to France to continue his medical studies in Paris, where he earned a second medical degree in 1860. He returned to America and was appointed professor of clinical medicine at New York Medical College. The outbreak of civil war convinced him to leave New York for his native state, where he enlisted in the 44th Virginia Infantry in July 1861 and was appointed regimental surgeon. Dr. Whitehead served the entire war in various medical capacities and was president of the Confederate Army Board of Medical Examiners when it ended.

After the Civil War Whitehead returned to the practice of medicine in New York City and in 1872 moved to Denver, where five years later he was elected president of the Denver Medical Association. In 1881 he co-founded the Denver College of Medicine, which merged with the University of Colorado Medical School in 1883. He was chairman of the medical school's Department of Medicine and Surgery, and from 1887 to 1893 worked as a professor of medicine at the University of Denver. From 1883 to 1884 Dr. Whitehead served as president of the Colorado State Medical Society. During this time he also managed to maintain a private medical practice. He died on October 12, 1902.

University of Florida

Brigadier General Evander McIver Law was a brigade and division commander in the Army of Northern Virginia and a postwar railroad executive who founded the South Florida Military College, which is considered a predecessor of the University of Florida.[48]

---

48 South Florida Military College. (n.d.). Retrieved from www.schoolandcollegelistings. com/US/Bartow/103785712993560/South-Florida-Military-College.

Law was born in Darlington, South Carolina, the grandson and great grandson of three Revolutionary War soldiers who served under the legendary Continental Army guerrilla commander Francis Marion. He graduated from the Citadel in 1856, taught school for four years, and in 1860 moved to Tuskegee, Alabama, to found his own military school.

At the outbreak of the war Law enlisted in the Alabama militia and was soon promoted to colonel and commander of the 4th Alabama Infantry. He was wounded at First Manassas (First Bull Run), recovered, and was promoted to brigadier general in command of an infantry brigade. Law fought in most of the Army of Northern Virginia's major battles including the Seven Days' Battles, Second Manassas (Second Bull Run), Sharpsburg (Antietam), Fredericksburg, and Gettysburg, where his brigade attacked Little Round Top. Law's command, which was part of Lieutenant General James Longstreet's First Corps, was later sent with the bulk of the corps to Georgia. There, Law played a prominent role at Chickamauga and took part in operations around Chattanooga. He had a falling out with General Longstreet and nearly resigned. Law returned to Virginia with Longstreet's detached command in early 1864 and participated in the Overland Campaign. Law was wounded in the head at Cold Harbor. He recovered and fought during the Petersburg siege and ended the war leading cavalry in South Carolina. He was promoted to major general in the final weeks, but the promotion was not confirmed by the Confederate senate.

Immediately after the war Law administered his father-in-law's estate, which

EVANDER McIVER LAW

included large agricultural holdings and railroad interests in South Carolina. In the late 1860s he returned to Alabama and in 1881 moved to Bartow, Florida, where he established and administered the South Florida Military College, which he modeled after the Citadel. The school closed in 1905 when the Florida legislature consolidated the state's six independent colleges and universities into the newly created State University System of Florida.

Evander McIver Law

State Library and Archives of Florida

Evander Law also was heavily involved in Bartow and Polk county public and private education, and worked as the editor of the *Courier Informant* newspaper until his death in 1920.

Ex-Rebel officer Alexander Quarles Holladay of the 19th Virginia Infantry was, from 1885 to 1888, president of another predecessor institution of the University of Florida: Florida State Agricultural College in Lake City. Holladay, who ended the war as a lieutenant, also served as president of North Carolina State University.

University of Georgia

William Ellison Boggs, a former chaplain of the 6th South Carolina Infantry who was born in India in 1838, served as chancellor of the University of Georgia from 1889 to 1898. He also was a professor at Columbia Theological Seminary in South Carolina, and secretary of schools and colleges in Savannah, Georgia. His son Gilbert would go on to play a vital role in Georgia Tech's chemistry department.[49]

University of Maryland

Four former Confederates served as presidents of the University of Maryland.[50] Franklin Buchanan, president in 1868 and 1869, was a former Confederate admiral. Before the Civil War, Buchanan had founded the U.S. Naval Academy and was its first superintendent. (For more details on Buchanan's life and contributions, see page 153.)

Franklin had succeeded Charles Landon Carter Minor, who was president of the university in 1867 and 1868. Minor, who had been a captain on the staff of Brigadier General Albert G. Jenkins, also served as president of Virginia Tech and was a professor at the University of the South in Sewanee, Tennessee.

49 William Ellison Boggs (1838-1920) (n.d.). Retrieved from www.findagrave.com/memorial /3358282/william-ellison-boggs.

50 University Presidents. (2018, January 18). Retrieved from www.umd.edu/history-and-mission/university-presidents.

Samuel Jones served as president of the University of Maryland from 1873 to 1875. The former major general is best known for commanding the Department of Western Virginia and defending the Virginia and Tennessee Railroad and nearby salt mines, which were vital to the Confederacy. Jones later commanded the the District of South Carolina and during the war's final months was in command of the Department of Florida and South Georgia.

Jones was succeeded as president of the university by yet another former Confederate named William Harwar Parker, who served in that capacity from 1875 to 1882. Parker was a prominent captain in the Confederate States Navy and was superintendent of the Confederate States Naval Academy. After the Civil War, Parker served as U.S. ambassador to Korea.

Thomas Marshall Jones, a former colonel of the 27th Mississippi Infantry, was among several professors at the University of Maryland who had served the Confederacy. Jones also was superintendent of a school for Native Americans in Santa Fe, New Mexico, and taught various Native American tribes in New Mexico, Wyoming, Arizona, and Oklahoma.

University of Maryland School of Medicine

Harvey Leonidas Byrd, a prominent nineteenth century Maryland physician and educator, was a co-founder of the Baltimore Medical College and the College of Physicians and Surgeons, both of which merged with the University of Maryland School of Medicine in 1913 and 1915, respectively.[51] Byrd had founded Oglethorpe Medical College in Savannah, Georgia in 1856.

Born in Salem, South Carolina, in 1820, Byrd was awarded a medical degree in 1840 from the Pennsylvania Medical College and moved to Georgetown, South Carolina. He moved again in the mid-1850s to Savannah, Georgia, where he practiced medicine and taught *materia medica* (pharmacology) at Savannah Medical College.

In September 1861 Dr. Byrd enlisted in the 23rd Georgia Infantry and in May 1862 was appointed surgeon of the 4th Georgia Cavalry. That same year he also worked as a surgeon in the hospital in Waynesville, Georgia. In April of 1863 he was transferred to Mobile, Alabama, where he worked as surgeon in charge of

---

51 Dr Harvey Leonidas Byrd (1820-1884) (n.d.). Retrieved from www.findagrave.com /memorial/91909456/harvey-leonidas-byrd.

Moore Hospital. In March of 1864 Dr. Byrd was ordered back to Georgia, where he served in hospitals in both Macon and Augusta. He was inspecting hospitals in the Georgia towns of Athens, Jefferson, Danielsville, Carnesville, Greensboro, Elberton, Lexington, Crawfordsville, and Madison when the war ended.

In 1867, Dr. Byrd earned a second medical degree from the University of Pennsylvania in Philadelphia. Later that year he moved to Baltimore, Maryland, where he opened a private medical practice. He also co-founded the Washington University Medical School, where he was dean and professor of obstetrics from 1867 to 1872. He was one of the founders of the College of Physicians and Surgeons in 1872, and worked there as a professor of medical practice and of diseases of women and children. In 1881, he founded Baltimore Medical College. Both institutions would merge with the University of Maryland School of Medicine.

University of Mississippi

Former Confederate Lieutenant General Alexander Peter "A. P." Stewart was chancellor of the University of Mississippi from 1874 to 1887.[52] He would also serve as a commissioner of the Chickamauga and Chattanooga National Military Park.

Stewart graduated from West Point in the outstanding Class of 1842 (12th out of 56) but resigned from the service three years later to become a professor of mathematics and experimental philosophy at Cumberland University in Lebanon, Tennessee. He saw extensive action during the Civil War as a general in the Western Theater. Stewart ended the war in North Carolina with the Army of Tennessee.

After the war Stewart moved to Missouri and worked as an insurance executive, which he found unrewarding. The restless academic moved again in 1874, this time to Mississippi, where he served as the chancellor of the University of Mississippi. From 1890 to 1908 he served as the commissioner of the Chickamauga and Chattanooga National Military Park. He returned to Missouri in 1906, and died two years later in Biloxi, Mississippi.

---

52 Maness, L. E. (2018, March 1). Alexander P. Stewart. Retrieved from https://tennesseeen cyclopedia.net/entries/alexander-p-stewart/.

Stewart was succeeded as chancellor by Edward Mayes, a former private in the 4th Mississippi Cavalry. Mayes led the university from 1887 until 1891.[53] He also taught law at Millsaps College in Jackson.

University of North Carolina at Greensboro

Jabez Lamar Monroe Curry was one of the founders of the University of North Carolina at Greensboro. The ex-Rebel colonel and native of Georgia served as a staff officer to two Southern generals during the Civil War. He was born in 1825 to a prominent Southern family that included Mirabeau Bounaparte Lamar, the second president of the Republic of Texas, and Lucius Q. C. Lamar, a postwar U.S. secretary of the interior and associate justice of the U.S. Supreme Court.[54]

After the war Curry became an ordained minister but focused his time and energy on public education throughout the South. He lobbied state legislatures for the establishment of colleges, rural schools, and a system of graded public schools. In 1881 he became an agent for the Peabody Education Fund and the John F. Slater Fund, which aided schools in the South after the Civil War. Curry was instrumental in the creation of the Southern Education Board and the first normal school in North Carolina, now known as the University of North Carolina at Greensboro.

"Education is the fundamental basis of general and permanent prosperity," argued Curry in a speech before the Alabama state legislature in 1889. "Poverty is the inevitable result of ignorance. Capital follows the schoolhouse."[55] From 1885 to 1888 Curry served as U.S. ambassador to Spain. He received the Royal Order of Charles III from the king of Spain, and during his lifetime he was awarded several honorary doctorate degrees from universities.

Two years after Curry's death in 1905 the iconic industrialist and financier John D. Rockefeller, Sr. funded a college of education at the University of Virginia, stipulating that its name be the Curry School of Education. The Longwood

53 Chancellors of UM. (n.d.). Retrieved from https://inauguration.olemiss.edu/ about-um/ chancellors/.

54 Cox, R., and University Libraries. (n.d.). Retrieved from http://library.uncg.edu/map/ details/Curry_Building.aspx.

55 Sutori. (n.d.). Retrieved from www.sutori.com/story/southern-education-foundation-150-years—tesc3sqyoeeo8dd863cfujte.

University Alumni Association bestows the Jabez Lamar Monroe Curry Humanitarian Award annually. (For additional details on Curry, see pages 40-41.)

University of San Francisco

Alfred W. Perry was born in Massachusetts and earned his medical degree from the New Orleans School of Medicine in 1862. He served the Confederacy during the war as the assistant surgeon in the 7th Mississippi Infantry. After the war he lectured and taught chemistry at the New Orleans Dental College before moving west to become a professor of chemistry at the University of San Francisco. He died in 1929.

University of South Carolina

Four Confederate veterans served as presidents of the University of South Carolina.[56] The first, William Porcher Miles, led the university from 1880 to 1882. Miles was a colonel on the staff of General P. G. T. Beauregard. John McLaren McBryde succeeded Miles as president, serving from 1883 to 1891. During the war McBryde was a private in the 1st South Carolina Infantry and later was a supervisor at the Confederate Tax Department in Richmond. McBryde also was president and president emeritus of Virginia Tech and a professor of botany and agriculture at the University of Tennessee. He received honorary doctorate degrees from both institutions.

James Woodrow served as president from 1891 to 1897. He also was dean of the School of Liberal Arts and taught chemistry, geology, pharmacy, mineralogy, botany, and zoology there. Woodrow, the uncle of future president Woodrow Wilson, had been a pharmacologist with the Confederate Medical Department in Columbia, South Carolina. The last ex-Confederate to serve as president of the University of South Carolina was Benjamin F. Sloan Jr., a former major and chief of artillery in General W. H. C. Whiting's Division. Sloan led the university from 1902 to 1908.

56 List of Presidents of the University of South Carolina. (2019, August 6). Retrieved from https://en.wikipedia.org/wiki/List_of_Presidents_of_the_University_of_South_Carolina.

University of Texas

Confederate veteran Ashbel Smith is often called The Father of the University of Texas.[57] His remarkable postwar life was one of advocacy of public education, notably for women and African-Americans. According to the Texas State Historical Association, in the 1870s Smith, a member of the Texas legislature, "championed public education for blacks and women," and was instrumental in the founding of both the Stuart Female Seminary and Prairie View A&M University, a historically African-American institution.[58] Smith also was instrumental in saving the financially distressed Galveston Medical College from closure. In 1881 Smith was elected president of the newly created University of Texas Board of Regents and immediately set out to establish curriculum and recruit highly qualified professors. He hoped to make the university, which at that time was on the remote western frontier of the United States, an institution of national prominence. (For more details on Smith, see pages 144-145.)

After Smith's death on January 21, 1886, a special meeting of the Board of Regents passed a resolution declaring the university "a living monument" to Ashbel Smith. "It may be said of him," concluded the regents, "that he was insofar as the practical inauguration of the University is concerned, the 'Father of the University of Texas.'"[59]

The Ashbel Smith Building ("Old Red") on the campus of the University of Texas at Austin is named in his honor, and the University of Texas Medical Branch at Galveston annually bestows the Ashbel Smith Distinguished Alumnus Award. There are multiple Ashbel Smith professorships throughout the University of Texas System, and in Baytown, Texas, Ashbel Smith Elementary School and Ashbel Street are named in his honor.

Another ex-Confederate, Leslie Waggener, who had served as a lieutenant in the 9th Kentucky Mounted Infantry, was the president of the University of Texas in 1895 and 1896. Waggener also was faculty chairman and professor of English and history. He served as faculty chairman and professor of English, history, and

57 Ashbel Smith, M.D. (n.d.). Retrieved from www.utsystem.edu/board-of-regents/former-regents/ashbel-smith-md.

58 Silverthorne, E. (2010, June 15). SMITH, ASHBEL. Retrieved from https:// tshaonline.org/handbook/online/articles/fsm04.

59 Ibid.

philosophy at Bethel College in Kentucky, and as president of the Texas State Teachers Association.[60]

University of the Pacific (San Francisco)

John T. Douglass, professor of English at the University of the Pacific, was a former sergeant in the Virginia Military Institute (VMI) cadet corps and a veteran of the Battle of New Market. Douglass also served as a professor at, and commandant of, the Maryland Military Institute.

The University of the South

Located in Sewanee, Tennessee, the University of the South is often referred to as Sewanee University or Sewanee: The University of the South—even by the university itself. Thomas Underwood Dudley was chancellor of the university from 1893 to 1904. He had been a Confederate commissary officer during the war. After the fighting ended Dudley served as the Episcopal bishop of Kentucky.[61]

Ellison Capers, born in Charleston, South Carolina, graduated from the South Carolina Military Academy (now The Citadel) in 1857 and taught mathematics at his alma mater. He enlisted in the Confederate Army and served along the Atlantic coast, in the Vicksburg Campaign, and with the Army of the Tennessee. He was promoted to brigadier general during the closing weeks of the war and was captured at the Battle of Bentonville in North Carolina in March of 1865.

After the war Capers served as chancellor of the University of the South from 1904 to 1908. He also was secretary of state of South Carolina, a professor at Furman University, and a rector in the Episcopal Church. Capers Hall at The Citadel is named in his honor.[62]

60 Leslie Waggener. (2019, December 3). Retrieved from https://president.utexas.edu/past-presidents/leslie-waggener.

61 Thomas Underwood Dudley. (2019, September 30). Retrieved from https://en.wikipedia.org/wiki/Thomas_Underwood_Dudley.

62 Anderson, P. C. (n.d.). Capers, Ellison. Retrieved from www.scencyclopedia.org/sce/entries/capers-ellison/.

University of Virginia

The University of Virginia (UVA), founded in 1819, was governed by its faculty in consultation with the board of visitors until 1905, at which time it adopted the position of president to serve as the chief executive of the institution.

Among those who were members of the university's Board of Visitors was Thomas Staples Martin, a former private in the VMI corps of cadets, U.S. Senate majority leader, chairman of the Senate Appropriations Committee, and co-author of the United States Declaration of War against Germany in 1917. Martin also served on the Board of Visitors of the U.S. Naval Academy. (For more information on Martin, see pages 65-66.)

Another member of the UVA Board of Visitors was William Henry White, a former private in the VMI cadet corps who had fought at New Market. White also was the U.S. district attorney for the Eastern District of Virginia. William Elisha Peters, a former colonel in the 21st Virginia Cavalry, also served on the UVA Board of Visitors.

Still another former VMI cadet and New Market veteran was Charles J. Faulkner, a member of the Board of Trustees of the University of Virginia Alumni Endowment Fund. Faulkner had served on the staff of Brigadier General Henry A. Wise. After the war Faulkner was elected U.S. senator from the new state of West Virginia. He was chairman of the Democratic Congressional Campaign Committee as well as a member of the International Joint High Commission of the United States and Great Britain in 1898.

University of Vermont, Larnar College of Medicine

Albert Freeman Africanus King, a former surgeon in the 15th Alabama Infantry, was a professor of surgery at the University of Vermont medical school.[63] King also served in many other educational capacities, including: professor at Georgetown University; dean and professor at the George Washington University School of Medicine and Health Sciences (at the time the National Medical College

---

63 King did not enlist in the Confederate Army, rather, he entered into a contract with the Confederate government to serve as a surgeon and was assigned to the 15th Alabama Infantry. When his contract expired in late 1864 King moved north to Washington, D.C., where he accepted a position as a physician in a public hospital.

Albert Freeman Africanus King

Virginia Polytechnic Institute and State University

of Columbian University); president of the Medical Association of Washington D.C.; president of the Washington Obstetrical and Gynecological Society; as a fellow in the British Gynecological Society, and the American Gynecological Society, and the American Society for the Advancement of Science.

In a remarkable coincidence, Dr. King was in attendance at Ford's Theater on April 14, 1865, when President Abraham Lincoln was shot by John Wilkes Booth, and he was among the group of physicians who immediately attended to the mortally wounded president.

University of Wisconsin-Madison

James Reeve Stuart, a former private in the 9th South Carolina Infantry, was a professor of art at the University of Wisconsin-Madison.

Vanderbilt University (University of Nashville)

Edmund Kirby Smith had a significant influence on the course of the Civil War because of his long tenure as commander of the Trans-Mississippi Department, a region so distant from Richmond that it was called "Kirby Smithdom." Before assuming command there, he took part in the fighting in Kentucky during Braxton Bragg's failed autumn of 1862 invasion. Smith was the last full general to surrender his command in May 1865. After fleeing to Mexico and eventually to Cuba, he returned and swore an oath of amnesty in November 1865. Smith served as chancellor of the University of Nashville (later Vanderbilt University) from 1870 to

1875, and also was a professor of mathematics at the University of the South.[64] A dormitory on the Louisiana State University campus in Baton Rouge is named Edmund Kirby Smith Hall, and a portrait of the former general hangs in the Wyatt Center at Vanderbilt University.

Bushrod Rust Johnson also had ties to Vanderbilt. Johnson was born in Ohio to abolitionist Quakers but sided with the South. He served in the Western Theater from Fort Donelson and Shiloh through Chickamauga and Longstreet's East Tennessee Campaign. In the spring of 1864 he was sent east, where he fought around Petersburg with Lee's Army of Northern Virginia and surrendered at Appomattox as a major general. Johnson was chancellor of the University of Nashville in 1866, and later worked as a professor there.[65]

Virginia Tech

Four former Confederates served as presidents of Virginia Tech.[66] Charles Landon Carter Minor, a captain of the staff of Brigadier General Albert G. Jenkins, was Virginia Tech's president from 1872 to 1879. Minor also was president of the University of Maryland and taught at the University of the South.

Scott Shipp, who served briefly as president in 1880, was a major in the 21st Virginia Infantry and commanded the VMI cadets at the Battle of New Market. Shipp was a member of the Board of Visitors of both the U.S. Naval Academy and the U.S. Military Academy.

Confederate veteran John McLaren McBryde was a longtime president of Virginia Tech (1891 to 1907). He is known as "The Father of the Modern Virginia Tech," and oversaw the major growth of the institution, including the construction of the campus's signature structure, "The Grove," which is the home of the university's president. When he retired in 1907, McBryde was named the school's first President Emeritus, and received Virginia Tech's first honorary doctorate degree. McBryde Hall on the Virginia Tech campus is named in his honor. Prior to his tenure at Virginia Tech, McBryde was president of the University of South

---

64 Edmund Kirby Smith. (n.d.). Retrieved from www.aoc.gov/art/national- statuary-hall-collection/edmund-kirby-smith.

65 (n.d.). Retrieved from www.thelatinlibrary.com/chron/civilwarnotes/johnson1.html.

66 Past Presidents. (n.d.). Retrieved from https://www.president.vt.edu/presidents.html.

John McLaren McBryde

Virginia Polytechnic Institute and State University

Carolina and a professor at the University of Tennessee, from which he received an honorary doctorate degree.

Lunsford Lindsay Lomax, an ex-Confederate brigadier general of cavalry in Robert E. Lee's Army of Northern Virginia, served as president of Virginia Tech from 1886 to 1891. Lomax also was a commissioner of the Gettysburg National Military Park.

Washington College (later Washington and Lee University)

Robert E. Lee, the iconic former commander of the Army of Northern Virginia and general in chief of the Confederate States Army, was asked to serve as

president of impoverished Washington College in Lexington, Virginia, in 1865. He was hesitant to accept because the war had only recently ended, and his presence "might draw upon the College a feeling of hostility," though he also added, "I think it the duty of every citizen in the present condition of the Country, to do all in his power to aid in the restoration of peace and harmony." According to the university's website, Lee provided "innovative educational leadership during his

Robert E. Lee

LOC

transformational tenure as president of Washington College from 1865 to 1870." After he died in 1870, the college's trustees voted to change the school's name from Washington College to Washington and Lee University.

George Washington Custis Lee succeeded his father as president of the university and served in that capacity from 1871 to 1897. The younger Lee was a major general and aide to Jefferson Davis, the Confederate president. Lee was teaching at VMI at the time of his father's death and left that school to assume the presidency of Washington and Lee University.

Another former Confederate, Private William Lyne Wilson of the 12th Virginia Cavalry, succeeded the younger Lee as president in 1897 and served until shortly before his own death in 1900.[67] Wilson had already carved out an admirable postwar career as president of West Virginia University, a member of the House of Representatives from West Virginia, postmaster general of the United States in the Grover Cleveland administration, and a member of the Board of Regents of the Smithsonian Institution.

Western Kentucky University

William A. Obenchain, a former captain in the Provisional Army of the Confederate States, was president of Ogden College in Bowling Green, Kentucky, from 1883 to 1906.[68] Ogden merged with Western Kentucky State Normal School and Teachers College in 1927 to form what would ultimately be named Western Kentucky University.

West Virginia University

William Lyne Wilson (mentioned on page 176) was president of West Virginia University from September 1882 until March 1883.

---

67 (n.d.). Retrieved from www.wvculture.org/hiStory/government/wilsonwilliam04.html.

68 Maj William Alexander Obenchain (1841-1916) - Find... (n.d.). Retrieved from www.findagrave.com/memorial/88919198/william-alexander-obenchain.

William Peace University (North Carolina)

James Dinwiddie, an officer in Brigadier General Henry Wise's Legion and the Charlottesville Light Artillery, was a postwar educator and president of Peace College (later William Peace University) in Raleigh, North Carolina, from 1890 until his death in 1907.[69] Dinwiddie had previously served as a professor of mathematics at the University of Tennessee and as principal of the Sayre School in Lexington, Kentucky. The James Dinwiddie Chapel on the campus of William Peace University is named in his honor.

*   *   *

See the Appendix for a complete list of college and university professors.

69 Carroll, G. L. E. (n.d.). Dinwiddie, James. Retrieved from www.ncpedia.org/biography/dinwiddie-james.

Part 8

Native Americans, Philanthropists, Industrialists, and Others

*M*any Native Americans from the Cherokee, Choctaw, Seminole, Chickasaw, and Creek nations fought for the Confederate Army and several veterans became high-ranking postwar tribal officials. Among them was Allen Wright, a former member of the Confederate Choctaw and Chickasaw Mounted Rifles who was chief of the Choctaw Nation from 1866 until 1870.

Wright was born in Mississippi in 1826, orphaned at age thirteen, and adopted by a Presbyterian minister in the town of Doaksville in Indian Territory (present-day Oklahoma.) He attended Delaware College and Union Theological Seminary in New York City and became an ordained Presbyterian minister. Wright returned to Indian Territory and was a member of the Choctaw Council from 1856 to 1862, and was elected treasurer of the Choctaw Nation in 1859. In 1861 Wright signed the treaty allying the Choctaw tribe with the Confederate States of America.

At the end of the war Chief Peter Pitchlynn appointed Wright as the Choctaw Nation's representative to sign an armistice with federal authorities in Fort Smith, Arkansas. Wright served in several elected positions within the tribal government including chief and delegate to the Choctaw House of Representatives. He was superintendent of schools for the Choctaw Nation from 1880 to 1884, and is

Jackson Frazier McCurtain

Choctawnation.com

credited with naming the state of Oklahoma, which is taken from the Native American term meaning "Land of the Red Man."[1]

Colonel Jackson Frazier McCurtain of the 3rd Choctaw Cavalry, Army of the Trans-Mississippi, was the chief of the Choctaw Nation as well as president of the Choctaw Senate.

McCurtain was born in Mississippi in 1830 and moved with his family to Indian Territory in 1833. In 1859 he was elected as a representative to the Choctaw National Council, and in June 1861 he volunteered for the 1st Regiment of Choctaw and Chickasaw Mounted Rifles. McCurtain was commissioned as a captain and in 1862 promoted to colonel in command of the First Choctaw Battalion.

After the war McCurtain was elected Choctaw senator from Sugar Loaf County, Indian Territory. In 1878, upon the death of Chief Garvin, McCurtain, as Senate president pro tem, ascended to the position of tribal chief. McCurtain remained in office at the close of Garvin's unexpired term in 1882 and was elected chief of the Choctaw Nation, a position he held until his death on November 14, 1885.

William Penn Adair, a colonel in the 2nd Cherokee Mounted Rifles in the Trans-Mississippi Department, was a postwar lawyer and assistant chief of the Cherokee Nation. Adair was born on the Cherokee Nation lands in New Echota, Georgia, and his family was moved to the Indian Territory in 1838 during the infamous forced march known to history as the "Trail of Tears." After studying law in Cherokee schools, he enlisted in the Confederate Army in 1861 and was assigned to the 1st Regiment of Cherokee Mounted Volunteers under Cherokee Brigadier

---

1 1866: Allen Wright: Choctaw Nation. (n.d.). Retrieved from www.choctawnation.com/chief/1866-allen-wright.

William Penn Adair

LOC

General Stand Waite. Adair attained the rank of colonel. He organized and led the 2nd Regiment of Cherokee Mounted Volunteers, and saw considerable action.

After the war Adair became a strong advocate of Cherokee interests. He was assistant chief, tribal senator, a justice on the tribal supreme court, and the Cherokee Nation's delegate to Washington, D.C. Adair co-founded the Texas Cherokees and Associated Bands in the 1850s, and served as president of the Texas Cherokee tribe from 1871 until his death in 1880. Legendary American humorist William Penn Adair Rogers, better known as Will Rogers, was named after William Penn Adair.

William Adair's brother Walter Thompson Adair, M.D., was a surgeon in the 2nd Cherokee Mounted Volunteers. As a postwar physician he served as medical superintendent of the Cherokee Male and Female Seminaries in Tahlequah, Cherokee Nation West, Oklahoma Territory. The town of Adair, Oklahoma, is named in honor of William Penn Adair and Walter Thompson Adair, and Adair County, Oklahoma, is named for the Adair family.

Another Confederate veteran, James Madison Bell, was a colonel in the 1st Cherokee Mounted Volunteers and a postwar member of the Cherokee Nation Senate.

Two members of the Creek Indian Nation who served in the Confederate military were also active in postwar tribal governance. Daniel Newman McIntosh, a colonel in the 1st Creek Mounted Volunteers, was a member of the Creek Nation House of Representatives, and Timothy Barnett, a colonel in the 2nd Creek Mounted Volunteers, was a postwar treasurer of the Creek Nation.

* * *

Samuel D. Shannon

LOC

After the war Confederate veterans, like many other Americans, spread across the United States and assimilated into their various communities. Many prospered, and some attained positions of high public trust.

In addition to the previously identified prominent ex-Rebels who emigrated to the non-Confederate states and territories of Alaska, Colorado, Oklahoma, California, Montana, Wyoming, New Mexico, Minnesota, Utah, and Kansas, many others helped build their newly adopted local communities.

Samuel D. Shannon, a native of South Carolina and a captain on the staff of Brigadier General Robert H. Anderson, was appointed by President Cleveland as secretary of state of the Wyoming Territory, and held that post from 1887 to 1889.

Several former Confederates are known to have emigrated to the Union state of California after the war, where they attained positions of prominence. One of them was George W. Gretter, a lieutenant in the VMI cadet corps and a Battle of New Market veteran. Gretter was a postwar educator in Pacific Grove, California and served for a dozen years as a member of the Monterey County Board of Education, including a term as its president. Gretter later moved to Watsonville, California, and was president of the Pajaro Valley Chamber of Commerce.

Native Virginian George Fletcher Maynard moved to San Francisco in the 1850s. He returned to Virginia at the outbreak of the war and served as a major and quartermaster in Richmond. At the end of hostilities he returned to California, and in the 1870s held the position of City Services Auditor of San Francisco. Maynard's fellow Virginian, George Hugh Smith served as a colonel in the 62nd Virginia Infantry and was a postwar judge in San Francisco and Los Angeles, as well as a California state senator.

A former captain in the 12th Mississippi Infantry, Rufus Shoemaker, was a postwar newspaperman who co-founded the *Evening Telegraph* in Grass County,

California. In 1889 Shoemaker was appointed captain of the Nevada Rifles in the California State Militia.

Isaac Williams Smith, who served as a captain in the Confederate Engineering Office in Richmond, was an engineer and surveyor after the war. He became chief engineer of the California Board of State Harbor Commissioners, a member of the California Board of Railroad Commissioners, and chief engineer of the Sacramento River Drainage Commission. Smith, who also worked as chief engineer for the City of Portland (Oregon) Water Works, is known as the "Father of the Portland Water System."

A surgeon in the 8th Tennessee Cavalry, Travis Witt Pendergrass, M.D., moved to California after the war and served as coroner of Tulare County from 1884 to 1891. He was also a member of the Board of Public Instruction of Visalia, California.

In Montana, in addition to the aforementioned co-founder of the city of Kalispell, Charles Conrad, a former member of Lieutenant General Richard Ewell's staff named Benjamin H. Greene served as a surveyor general of Montana after the war. Charles William Turner, a VMI cadet and New Market veteran, became adjutant general of Montana and organized and commanded the state's militia.

In Arizona, Joel Brown Watkins, a former volunteer aide on the staff of Major General George W. C. "Custis" Lee (Robert E. Lee's son), was a postwar merchant and educator who also served as superintendent of Arizona schools.

New York City became the postwar home of several former Confederates of note. In addition to the previously mentioned Isidor Straus, Henry K. Douglas, William Polk, John Wyeth, and Simon Baruch, former Confederate major John Denis Kelley Jr. served as City Treasurer of Brooklyn. Kelley had been quartermaster of Lieutenant General James Longstreet's Corps in Lee's Army of Northern Virginia.

New York also was the postwar destination of Mayer Lehman, a Jewish-Confederate state commissioner from Alabama who had been appointed by Alabama Governor Thomas H. Watts to inspect Northern prisoner of war camps holding Alabama soldiers. After the war Mayer, along with his brother Emanuel, co-founded the Lehman Brothers investment firm in New York City. Mayer Lehman's son, Henry Lehman, became governor of New York and was elected to the Senate.

James Jasper Phillips, who had served the Confederacy as a colonel in the 9th Virginia Infantry, as another postwar New York businessman and financier. Phillips became president of the New York City Board of Trade.

Joseph Bardwell Lyman, a botanist and publisher who had served as a private in Scott's 1st Louisiana Cavalry, also settled in New York. Lyman later became the agricultural editor of the *New York Weekly Tribune*, agricultural editor of the *New York World* newspaper, managing editor of *Hearth and Home* magazine, and author of the book *Resources of the Pacific States*.

Another ex-Rebel who went on to postwar fame in New York was publisher Virginius Dabney, Sr., who had served as a captain on the staff of General John B. Gordon. After the war Dabney was president of the American Newspaper Publishers Association, the predecessor of the present-day News Media Alliance. At the time of his death in 1894, Dabney held the position of Collector of the Port of New York.

Roger Atkinson Pryor, a brigadier general in the Army of Northern Virginia early in the war, was a postwar lawyer and judge who served as a justice on the Supreme Court of the State of New York.

Baltimore, Maryland, was home to former Confederates involved in public education administration as well as engineering. Henry A. Wise, a major and adjutant of the 46th Virginia Infantry, was Baltimore's superintendent of schools after the war, and Joseph Packard, Jr., a corporal in the 1st Rockbridge (Virginia) Artillery, worked as an attorney after the war and served as president of the Baltimore School Board.

A lieutenant in Page's Virginia Artillery, John Donnell Smith, gained fame as an internationally renowned botanist. He held the position of Honorary Associate in Botany at the Smithsonian Institution and also served as a trustee of the Peabody Institute of Baltimore.

John Ellicott, a former captain in the Confederate Nitre and Mining Bureau, worked as an architect and engineer in Baltimore. He designed and built the clubhouse and grounds at the Pimlico Race Course.

The former Confederate state of Florida was the postwar home to ex-Rebels who had a significant impact upon the Sunshine State's economic development and culture. In addition to City of Naples co-founder John S. Williams and University of Florida co-founder Evander Law, Jewish-Confederate David Levy Yulee made marked contributions to the state's progress. The prewar U.S. Senator did not hold an official position in the Confederate military or government, but Yulee did work as a close advisor to Confederate President Jefferson Davis and was imprisoned for nine months after the war. He was eventually pardoned by President Andrew Johnson. In Florida, Yulee worked as a pioneer in the development of the early railroads in the state and as such is considered the "Father of Florida Railroads." The city of Yulee is named in his honor, as is Levy County. In

David Levy Yulee

Wikipedia

the year 2000—114 years after his death—Yulee was inducted into the Florida Department of State's Great Floridians honorary program.

William Wing Loring joined Yulee in the Great Floridians honorary program in 2000. The former Confederate major general served in three armies: the U.S. Army before the Civil War, the Confederate Army, and, after the Civil War, in the Egyptian army for nine years. He eventually attained the equivalent rank of major general while serving in Egypt. The World War II Liberty Ship SS *William W. Loring* was named in his honor.

Francis Littlebury Dancy, a colonel and Confederate quartermaster general of Florida, was a postwar engineer, geologist, agronomist, and farmer who is recognized as one of the most significant figures in the establishment of Florida's citrus industry. In addition to being a successful citrus grower and prewar mayor of St. Augustine, he was also the Florida state engineer and geologist. According to the Florida Citrus Hall of Fame, into which Dancy was inducted in 2013, "In 1872 Dancy educated fellow growers on more effective growing methods and contributed to the industry with the 'Dancy Tangerine,' developed in Dancy's grove in Orange Mills, Florida, between 1867 and 1871."[2]

Abraham Charles Myers, a Jewish-Confederate colonel and quartermaster general of the Confederate Army, is the namesake of the city of Fort Myers. The city was named after the former colonel by its founder, Manuel A. Gonzales, a merchant marine captain who delivered supplies to Union military forces in Florida during the Civil War. Myers was a graduate of the U.S. Military Academy at West Point, and his son, John Twiggs Myers, would go on to become a lieutenant general in the U.S. Marine Corps. The younger Myers was commander of the Department

2   Col. Francis L. Dancy. (n.d.). Retrieved from https://floridacitrushalloffame.com/inductees/col-francis-l-dancy/.

Samuel Henry Lockett

Battleofchampionhill.org

of the Pacific and served in several conflicts, including the Spanish-American War, the Philippine Insurrection, the Boxer Rebellion (China), and World War I.

*　*　*

Former Confederates Amory Coffin, Jr. and Samuel Lockett were also prominent architects and engineers in the postwar era.

Coffin, a sergeant major in Parker's South Carolina Light Artillery, was a postwar chief engineer of the Phoenix Iron Company of Phoenixville, Pennsylvania. He supervised the structural design of many famous buildings including the Crocker Building in San Francisco, Madison Square Garden and the New York Stock Exchange building in New York City, the Wisconsin state capitol, and the Provident Life and Trust Company building in Philadelphia.

Samuel Henry Lockett, a colonel and chief engineer of the Confederate Army's Department of Alabama, Mississippi, and East Louisiana, was a postwar educator and engineer who designed the structural features of the base of the Statue of Liberty in New York Harbor. Lockett also taught at East Tennessee State University and Louisiana State University, and worked as an engineer for the U.S. Army in Egypt and South America.

*　*　*

Several former Confederates attained postwar prominence in business, commerce, and philanthropy like industry magnates John Lide Coker, Thomas Green Clemson. Washington Duke was another who deserves to be remembered.

An officer in the Confederate Navy and a postwar industrialist, Duke founded the American Tobacco Company, and in 1892 persuaded Trinity College to move to Durham, North Carolina, where it was renamed Duke University in his honor. As a vigorous proponent of women's rights he was way ahead of his time, and he

Washington Duke

North Carolina Museum of History

insisted that the university admit females. Because of his efforts he was offered the vice presidency of the National Suffrage Association, but declined.

James Edward Hanger, a private during the war's early weeks in the Churchville (Virginia) Cavalry Regiment, was the conflict's first amputee when he lost his left leg at the Battle of Philippi, Virginia (now West Virginia), on June 2, 1861. After his discharge he returned home to Churchville and invented and patented the "Hanger Limb" prosthesis. In 1863 he founded the J. E. Hanger Company and during the war opened facilities in Richmond and Staunton, Virginia.

After the war Hanger's prosthetics operations in Virginia grew rapidly and in 1915 the company was moved to Washington, D.C. It moved once more some years later to Austin, Texas. By 2018 Hanger Incorporated had 677 locations in the United States with more than 4,600 employees.

Ambrosio Jose Gonzales was a native of Cuba and later a resident of South Carolina. He began the war as a volunteer staff officer for General P. G. T. Beauregard, who attended the same small school with Gonzales in New York City when they were young boys. He was active during the Fort Sumter bombardment and was later assigned as an inspector of Confederate coastal defenses in Georgia, South Carolina, and North Carolina. President Davis declined Gonzales' promotion to brigadier general six times because the colonel of artillery was one of Beauregard's favorites, and the general and the president were bitter enemies.

After the war Gonzales worked as a journalist and a scholar of the African-American dialect of the Gullah people of the South Carolina and Georgia Low Country.[3] Two of his sons, Ambrose and Narciso, founded *The State* newspaper in

---

3 Rob. (2018, February 16). Gullah History: Beaufort Historic Culture: Gullah Culture. Retrieved from www.beaufortsc.org/guides/gullah-history/. "The Gullah are African

GENERAL AMBROSIO JOSE GONZALEZ.

Ambrosio Jose Gonzales

LOC

Columbia. In 1986 Ambrosio Gonzales was inducted into the South Carolina Business Hall of Fame.

William Payne Thompson, a colonel in the 19th Virginia Cavalry, was a postwar lawyer and businessman who became vice president of Standard Oil Company.

Native New Yorker Lewis Ginter, a former major and commissary officer on the staff of generals Joseph R. Anderson, Cadmus Wilcox, and A. P. Hill, was a prominent postwar philanthropist. Because of his gallantry in battle and tactical advice to commanders, Ginter earned the nickname "The Fighting Commissary." Ginter served the entire war and surrendered with Lee's army at Appomattox.

After the war Ginter became a prominent citizen of Richmond and accumulated a considerable fortune there in business enterprises and real estate development. Ginter built Richmond's Jefferson Hotel, which is listed on the National Register of Historic Places, as well as Ginter Park, a residential subdivision in Richmond.

Ginter established the Lakeside Wheel Club in Richmond, which later became the Lewis Ginter Botanical Garden. When he died in 1897, he left much of his fortune to his niece Grace Arents, who continued his philanthropic efforts by funding the development of the Lakeside Wheel Club into the Lewis Ginter Botanical Garden. Today, the complex contains a visitor center, library and education center, classical glass-domed conservatory, rose garden, children's

---

Americans who live in the Low Country region of South Carolina and Georgia, which includes both the coastal plain and the Sea Islands. The Gullah are known for preserving more of their African linguistic and cultural heritage than any other black community in the United States. They speak an English-based creole language with many African loanwords and significant influences from African languages in grammar and sentence structure. Gullah storytelling, cuisine, music, beliefs, crafts, farming and fishing traditions all show strong influences from western and central African cultures."

garden, sunken garden, Asian garden, Victorian garden, and healing garden. Ginter also donated land for the campus of the Union Theological Seminary in Richmond.

Louisville, Kentucky, was the postwar home of philanthropist Bennett Henderson Young, a lieutenant in the cavalry of Brigadier General John Hunt Morgan, led the St. Albans (Vermont) Raid, staged from Canada by Confederate agents on October 19, 1864. After the war Young lived in Louisville, where he became a successful lawyer, businessman, and renowned philanthropist. Young was a leader in the establishment of the Home for Colored Orphans in Louisville in 1879, and served as the orphanage's president for twenty-four years. He established Louisville's Booker T. Washington Community Center for African-American children and co-founded a Presbyterian school for orphan girls in Anchorage, Kentucky, while also serving as president of the Kentucky School for the Blind. In the 1870s Young's financial support helped save the Louisville Free Public Library from closure.

John Peter Smith, a colonel in the 7th Texas Cavalry, was a lawyer, real estate investor, and philanthropist called the "Father of Fort Worth." He served as mayor of the city for six terms and donated land for Fort Worth area cemeteries, schools, and parks. The John Peter Smith Hospital in Fort Worth is named in his honor.

Another former Confederate much renowned for humanitarian deeds was Reverend Hampden Coit DuBose. A former Citadel cadet and member of the South Carolina Battalion of State Cadets, DuBose fought in several battles during Sherman's March to the Sea. After the war he became a Presbyterian missionary, and in that capacity performed pioneering work against the opium trade.

DuBose was born in South Carolina and attended The Citadel and the Columbia Theological Seminary, and after the war he and his wife went to Suzhou, China, as missionaries with the Southern Presbyterian Church. Witnessing firsthand the destructive consequences of opium addiction, he joined with other missionaries and founded the Anti-Opium League

Reverend Hampden Coit DuBose

Wikipedia

in China and became its first president. By the end of the nineteenth century his work turned public opinion against opium use and trade. DuBose's advocacy attracted the attention and support of President Theodore Roosevelt, the U.S. Congress, the British Parliament, the International Opium Commission, and eventually the Chinese emperor himself, who in 1906 signed an imperial edict banning the opium trade—an edict written by DuBose.

This proclamation led to the first international drug control convention in 1909 and, in 1912, the first treaty prohibiting the opium trade was signed at the International Opium Commission in The Hague, Netherlands.

*   *   *

A proud former Confederate became one of the world's most famous and celebrated sculptors.

Moses Jacob Ezekiel was a Richmond native and the first Jewish cadet at the Virginia Military Institute. Ezekiel fought in the Battle of New Market and served in the defenses of Richmond in 1865. After the war Ezekiel returned to VMI and graduated in 1866. After spending a year at the Medical College of Virginia, he moved to Cincinnati, Ohio, to study sculpting. He followed the advice of Cincinnati artists and later went to Berlin for further training at the Royal Art Academy.

At the age of 29 Ezekiel became the first non-German to win the Michel Beer Prix de Rome award for a bas relief entitled "Israel." He moved to Rome, where he maintained a home for the rest of his life. Ezekiel was knighted by King Victor Emmanuel of Italy and received awards from Italian King Umberto. Ezekiel's other awards included the Crosses for Merit and Art from the emperor of Germany and another from the Grand Duke of Saxe-Meiningen. In 1910, the Italian king bestowed upon him the titles of Chevalier

Moses Jacob Ezekiel

Wikipedia

and Officer of the Crown of Italy. Ezekiel also received the Gold Medal of the Royal Society of Palermo and the Raphael Medal from the Art Society of Urbino.

Ezekiel created some 200 works of art during his career. Among his most admired were "Religious Liberty" (also known as "Religious Freedom"), a marble work sculpted for the 1876 Centennial Exposition in Philadelphia that is now displayed at the National Museum of American Jewish History in Philadelphia.

Some of the most acclaimed artworks by Ezekiel were "Christ Bound for the Cross," "Christ in the Tomb," "Homer Reciting the Iliad," and "Eve Hearing the Voice," now at the University of Virginia. His sculptures are also displayed at the Corcoran Gallery of Art in Washington, D.C.

Several of Ezekiel's works were related to his ties to Virginia, VMI, and the American South, including a statue of Thomas Jefferson in Louisville, Kentucky, a replica of which can be found at the University of Virginia. His bronze of General Thomas J. "Stonewall" Jackson stands on the West Virginia State Capitol grounds, and a tribute to the fallen cadets of the Battle of New Market, "Virginia Mourning Her Dead," resides on the VMI campus.

Another bronze work entitled The Outlook depicts a Confederate soldier looking out upon Lake Erie from the Confederate cemetery at the site of the former prisoner of war camp at Johnson's Island, Ohio—resting place of some of Ezekiel's fellow VMI cadets.

Ezekiel's last visit to the United States was in 1910 when he attended the commencement ceremonies at VMI. His final work was a bronze of Edgar Allan Poe, created in 1917 and now residing in Wyman Park in Baltimore.

During his career Ezekiel was honored not only by European monarchs but by Presidents Grant, Roosevelt, Taft, and Wilson. Late in his life, Ezekiel's sentiments returned to Virginia in general, and—according to him—one place in particular: "VMI, where every stone and blade of grass is dear to me, and the name of the cadet of VMI is the proudest and most honored title I can ever possess."[4]

Ezekiel suspended his artwork during World War I and from his home in Rome helped organize the American-Italian Red Cross. He died shortly afterward on March 27, 1917. He was temporarily buried in Rome and later, per his wishes, was re-interred in the Confederate section of Arlington National Cemetery on March 31, 1921. The ceremony was presided over by U.S. Secretary of War John W. Weeks, who read a message from President Warren G. Harding praising Ezekiel as "a great Virginian, a great artist, a great American, and a great citizen of world

4 (n.d.). Retrieved from http://jewish-history.com/civilwar/moses_ezekiel.html.

fame."[5] An honor guard comprised of eight VMI cadets was present, one of whom was future U.S. Marine Corps commandant Randolph M. Pate.

Ezekiel's small headstone reads simply,

> Moses J. Ezekiel
> Sergeant of Company C
> Battalion of Cadets of the
> Virginia Military Institute

5 Ibid.

Appendix

Public Officials and Educators

Governors
(by state, chronologically)

Alabama

Rufus W. Cobb, captain, 10th Alabama Infantry Regiment. Governor, 1878-1882.

Edward A. O'Neal, colonel, 26th Alabama Infantry Regiment. Governor, 1882-1886.

Thomas J. Seay, sergeant, 62nd Alabama Infantry Regiment (1st Alabama Reserves.) Governor, 1886-1890.

Thomas Goode Jones, lieutenant, staff of General John B. Gordon, Governor, 1890-1894. Also U.S. district judge for the Northern District of Alabama.

William Calvin Oates, colonel, 15th Alabama Infantry Regiment. Governor, 1894-1896. Also U.S. House of Representatives from Alabama and brigadier general of volunteers, U.S. Army, Spanish-American War.

Joseph F. Johnston, lieutenant, 18th Alabama Infantry Regiment. Governor, 1896-1900. Also U.S. senator from Alabama.

William J. Samford, lieutenant, 46th Alabama Infantry Regiment. Governor, 1900-1901. Also U.S. House of Representatives from Alabama.

Alaska Territorial Region

Mottrom Dulany Ball, colonel, 11th Virginia Cavalry Regiment. U.S. Department of the Treasury senior administrator and de facto governor, 1878-1879.

Arkansas

Thomas J. Churchill, major general. Governor, 1881-1883. Also state treasurer of Arkansas.

James Henderson Berry, lieutenant, 16th Arkansas Infantry Regiment. Governor, 1883-1885. Also U.S. senator from Arkansas.

Simon Pollard Hughes, colonel, 23rd Arkansas Infantry Regiment. Governor, 1885-1889.

James P. Eagle, colonel, 1st Consolidated Arkansas Mounted Rifles. Governor, 1889-1893. Also president, Southern Baptist Convention.

Daniel Webster Jones, colonel, 20th Arkansas Infantry Regiment. Governor, 1897-1901. Also attorney general of Arkansas.

Colorado

Charles Spalding Thomas, private, Georgia State Militia. Governor, 1899-1901. Also U.S. senator from Colorado and chairman, Senate Committee on Women's Suffrage.

Florida

William Dunnington Bloxham, captain, Leon County Militia. Governor, 1881-1885, 1897-1901. Also U.S. consul to Bolivia and U.S. surveyor general for the state of Florida.

Edward A. Perry, brigadier general. Governor, 1885-1889.

Henry Laurens Mitchell, captain, 4th Florida Infantry Regiment. Governor, 1893-1897.

Georgia

James Milton Smith, colonel, 13th Georgia Infantry Regiment. Governor, 1872-1877.

Alfred Holt Colquitt, brigadier general. Governor, 1877-1882. Also U.S. senator from Georgia.

Alexander H. Stephens, vice president, Confederate States of America. Governor, 1882-1883. Also U.S. House of Representatives from Georgia.

James Stoddard Boynton, colonel, 30th Georgia Infantry Regiment. Governor 1883.

Henry Dickerson McDaniel, major, 11th Georgia Infantry Regiment. Governor 1883-1886.

John Brown Gordon, major general. Governor 1886-1890. Also U.S. senator from Georgia.

Nathaniel Harris, major, 16th Virginia Cavalry Regiment. Governor 1915-1917.

Kentucky

Simon Bolivar Buckner, lieutenant general. Governor, 1887-1891.

James Bennett McCreary, major, 11th Kentucky Cavalry Regiment. Governor, 1911-1915. Also U.S. House of Representatives and U.S. Senator from Kentucky.

Louisiana

Samuel Douglas McEnery, lieutenant, 2nd Louisiana Infantry Regiment. Governor, 1881-1888. Also U.S. senator from Louisiana.

Mississippi

James Lusk Alcorn, brigadier general, Mississippi Militia. Governor, 1870-1871. Also U.S. senator from Mississippi.

Robert Lowry, brigadier general. Governor, 1882-1890.

Anselm Joseph McLaurin, private, 3rd Regiment Mississippi Cavalry Regiment (Militia.) Governor 1896-1900. Also U.S. senator from Mississippi. (Great-great grandfather of the late comedian/actor Robin McLaurin Williams.)

John Marshall Stone, colonel, 2nd Mississippi Infantry Regiment. Governor, 1876-1882.

Missouri

John S. Marmaduke, major general. Governor, 1885-1887.

New Mexico Territory

William Taylor Thornton, sergeant, Wood's Battalion Missouri Cavalry. Governor, 1893-1897. Also first mayor of Santa Fe in 1891.

North Carolina

Curtis Hooks Brogden, brigadier general, North Carolina Militia. Governor, 1874-1877. Also U.S. House of Representatives from North Carolina.

Zebulon Baird Vance, colonel, 26th North Carolina State Troops. Governor, 1877-1879. Also U.S. senator from North Carolina.

Thomas Jordan Jarvis, captain, 8th North Carolina State Troops. Governor, 1879-1885. Also U.S. senator from North Carolina.

Alfred Moore Scales, brigadier general. Governor, 1885-1889. Also U.S. House of Representatives from North Carolina.

Daniel G. Fowle, colonel, 31st North Carolina State Troops. Governor, 1889-1891.

Daniel Lindsay Russell, captain, 2nd North Carolina Artillery. Governor, 1897-1901. Also U.S. House of Representatives from North Carolina.

Oklahoma Territory

William Cary Renfrow, sergeant, 50th North Carolina Infantry Regiment. Governor, 1893-1897.

Panama Canal Zone

Joseph Clay Stiles Blackburn, colonel, Blackburn's Cavalry Regiment. Governor, 1907-1909. Also U.S. senator and House of Representatives from Kentucky, chairman, Senate Rules Committee, chairman, House Committee on War Department Expenditures.

South Carolina

Franklin J. Moses Jr., colonel, conscription officer, South Carolina. Governor, 1872-1874. Also speaker, South Carolina House of Representatives.

Wade Hampton III, lieutenant general. Governor, 1876-1879. Also U.S. senator from South Carolina.

William Dunlap Simpson, major, 14th South Carolina Infantry Regiment. Governor, 1879-1880. Also chief justice, South Carolina Supreme Court.

Thomas Bothwell Jeter, captain, 5th South Carolina Infantry. Governor, 1880. Also chief justice, South Carolina Supreme Court.

Johnson Hagood, brigadier general. Governor, 1880-1882. Also comptroller general of South Carolina.

Hugh Smith Thompson, captain, commander of The Citadel cadet battalion. Governor, 1882-1886. Also assistant secretary of the U.S. Department of the Treasury, U.S. Civil Service Commission, comptroller of the New York Life Insurance Company.

John Peter Richardson III, captain, staff of General James Cantey. Governor, 1886-1890. Also treasurer of the State of South Carolina.

Tennessee

John C. Brown, major general. Governor, 1871-1875.

William B. Bate, major general. Governor, 1883-1887. Also U.S. senator from Tennessee.

John P. Buchanan, private, 4th Alabama Cavalry Regiment. Governor, 1891-1893.

Peter Turney, colonel, 1st Tennessee Infantry Regiment. Governor, 1893-1897. Also chief justice, Tennessee Supreme Court.

Texas

James W. Throckmorton, captain, 6th Texas Cavalry Regiment. Governor, 1866-1867. Also U.S. House of Representatives from Texas.

Richard Coke, captain, 15th Texas Infantry Regiment. Governor, 1874-1876. Also U.S. senator from Texas.

Oran Milo Roberts, colonel, 11th Texas Infantry Regiment. Governor, 1879-1883. Also chief justice, Texas Supreme Court.

John Ireland, colonel, Texas State Troops. Governor, 1883-1887.

Lawrence Sullivan Ross, brigadier general. Governor, 1887-1891. Also sheriff of McLennan County.

Samuel Willis Tucker Lanham, sergeant, 3rd South Carolina Infantry. Governor, 1903-1907. Also U.S. House of Representatives from Texas.

Utah Territory

Caleb Walton West, sergeant, 1st Kentucky Infantry Regiment. Governor 1886-1889, 1893-1896.

Virginia

James Lawson Kemper, major general. Governor, 1874-1878.

Frederick William Mackey Holliday, colonel, 33rd Virginia Infantry Regiment. Governor, 1878-1882.

William E. Cameron, captain, staff of General William Mahone. Governor, 1882-1886.

Fitzhugh Lee, major general. Governor, 1886-1890. Also major general of volunteers, U.S. Army, Spanish-American War and U.S. consul-general, Havana, Cuba.

Philip Watkins McKinney, captain, 4th Virginia Cavalry Regiment. Governor, 1890-1894.

Charles Triplett O'Ferrall, major, 23rd Virginia Cavalry Regiment. Governor, 1894-1898. Also U.S. House of Representatives from Virginia.

West Virginia

Henry Mason Mathews, lieutenant, staff of General William W. Loring. Governor, 1877-1881. Also attorney general of West Virginia.

United States Senators

(by state, alphabetically)

Alabama

Joseph Forney Johnston, lieutenant, 18th Alabama Infantry Regiment. Senator, 1907-1913. Also, governor of Alabama.

James Lawrence Pugh, private, 1st Alabama Infantry Regiment. Senator, 1880-1897. Chairman, Judiciary Committee.

Arkansas

James Henderson Berry, lieutenant, 16th Arkansas Infantry Regiment. Senator, 1885-1907. Chairman, Committee on Public Lands. Also governor of Arkansas.

James Kimbrough Jones, private, 3rd Arkansas Cavalry Regiment. Senator, 1885-1903. Chairman, Committee on Indian Affairs. Also member, U.S. House of Representatives from Arkansas and chairman, Democratic National Committee, 1896-1904.

James David Walker, colonel, 4th Arkansas Infantry Regiment. Senator, 1879-1885.

Colorado

Charles Spalding Thomas, private, Georgia State Militia. Senator, 1913-1921. Chairman, Committee on Women's Suffrage and Committee on Coastal Defenses. Also governor of Colorado. According to the *Biographical Directory of the United States Congress*, Thomas was the "Last Confederate veteran to serve in the United States Senate." His Confederate service details unknown.

Florida

Wilkinson Call, captain, staff of General Patton Anderson. Senator, 1879-1897. Chairman, Committee on Civil Service and Retrenchment, Committee on Patents.

Samuel Pasco, sergeant, 3rd Florida Infantry Regiment. Senator, 1887-1899. Chairman, Committee on Claims. Also member of Isthmian Canal Commission (later named the Panama Canal Commission.)

James Piper Taliaferro, private, 5th Virginia Cavalry Regiment. Senator, 1899-1911. Chairman, Committee on Claims.

Georgia

Middleton Pope Barrow, lieutenant, Carlton's Georgia Artillery. Senator, 1882-1883.

Alfred Holt Colquitt, brigadier general. Senator, 1883-1894. Also governor of Georgia.

John Brown Gordon, major general. Senator, 1873-1880, 1891-1897. Chairman, Committee on Commerce, Committee on Coastal Defense. Also governor of Georgia.

Benjamin Harvey Hill, former member of the Confederate States Senate. U.S. senator, 1877-1882. Also member, U.S. House of Representatives from Georgia.

Homer V. M. Miller, surgeon and medical instructor, Provisional Army of the Confederate States. Senator in 1871.[1]

Patrick Walsh, lieutenant, Meagher Guards, South Carolina Militia. Senator, 1894-1895.

Kansas

William Alexander Harris, VMI cadet and ordnance officer on the staff of General Robert E. Rodes. Senator, 1897-1903. Also member, U.S. House of Representatives from Kansas.

Kentucky

Joseph Clay Stiles Blackburn, judge advocate and colonel, Blackburn's Cavalry Regiment. Senator 1885-1897, 1901-1907. Chairman, Senate Rules Committee. Also member, U.S. House of Representatives from Kentucky, chairman, House Committee on Rules. Also governor, Panama Canal Zone.

William Lindsay. quartermaster, 7th Kentucky Mounted Infantry Regiment. Senator, 1893-1901. Chairman, Committee on Claims.

Willis Benson Machen, member, Confederate States House of Representatives. U.S. senator, 1872-1873.

James Bennett McCreary, colonel, 11th Kentucky Cavalry Regiment. Senator, 1903-1909. Also, member, U.S. House of Representatives, governor of Kentucky. Appointed by President Benjamin Harrison as U.S. delegate to the International Monetary Conference in Brussels, Belgium, 1892.

John Stuart Williams, brigadier general. Senator, 1879-1885.

Louisiana

Donelson Caffery, lieutenant, 13th Louisiana Infantry Regiment. Senator, 1892-1901.

James Biddle Eustis, lieutenant, staff of generals Joseph E. Johnston and John Bell Hood. Senator, 1876-1879, 1885-1891. Also U.S. ambassador to France.

Randall Lee Gibson, brigadier general. Senator 1883-1892. Also member, U.S. House of Representatives, member, board of regents, Smithsonian Institution.

Benjamin Franklin Jonas, captain, Fenner's Louisiana Artillery. Senator, 1879-1885. Chairman, Committee on Interior and Insular Affairs. First practicing Jew to serve in United States Senate. Also city attorney of New Orleans.

Samuel Douglas McEnery, lieutenant, 2nd Louisiana Infantry Regiment. Senator, 1897-1910. Also governor of Louisiana.

Mississippi

James Lusk Alcorn, brigadier general, Mississippi Militia. Senator, 1871-1877. Also governor of Mississippi.

---

1 Miller's term was a mere seven days, the second shortest tenure in U.S. Senate history.

James Zachariah George, colonel, 5th Mississippi Cavalry Regiment. Senator, 1881-1897. Chairman, Committee on Agriculture and Forestry. Also chief justice, Mississippi Supreme Court.

James Gordon, colonel, 2nd Mississippi Cavalry Regiment. Senator, 1909-1910.

Lucius Q. C. Lamar II, former colonel, 19th Mississippi Infantry Regiment. Senator, 1877-1885. Also associate justice, U.S. Supreme Court, U.S. secretary of the interior, member, U.S. House of Representatives.

Anselm Joseph McLaurin, private, 3rd Regiment, Mississippi Cavalry (Militia). Senator, 1894-1895, 1901-1909. Also governor of Mississippi, member, U.S. Immigration Commission. (The great-great grandfather of the late comedian/actor Robin Williams.)

Hernando De Soto Money, private, 11th Mississippi Infantry Regiment. Senator, 1897-1911. Also member, U.S. House of Representatives.

Missouri

Francis Marion Cockrell, brigadier general. Senator, 1875-1905. Chairman, Committee on Claims, Committee on Appropriations. Also member, Interstate Commerce Commission. Appointed by President Theodore Roosevelt to negotiate the border between Texas and the New Mexico Territory.

George Graham Vest, judge advocate and member, Confederate House of Representatives. Senator, 1879-1903.

New Mexico

Thomas Benton Catron, lieutenant, 3rd Missouri Artillery Battalion. Senator, 1912-1917. Also member, U.S. House of Representatives, mayor of Santa Fe, U.S. district attorney, New Mexico Territory, attorney general, New Mexico Territory.

North Carolina

Thomas Jordan Jarvis, captain, 8th North Carolina State Troops. Senator, 1894-1895. Also governor of North Carolina and speaker, North Carolina House of Representatives.

Augustus Summerfield Merrimon, private, 14th North Carolina Infantry Regiment. Senator, 1873-1879. Also chief justice, North Carolina Supreme Court.

Matt Whitaker Ransom, brigadier general. Senator, 1872-1895. Senate president pro tempore, chairman, Committee on Commerce. Also United States ambassador to Mexico.

Zebulon Baird Vance, colonel, 26th North Carolina State Troops. Senator, 1879-1894. Also governor of North Carolina. Namesake, World War II liberty ship USS Zebulon B. Vance.

South Carolina

Matthew Calbraith Butler, major general. Senator, 1877-1895. Also major general of volunteers, U.S. Army, Spanish-American War.

Joseph Haynsworth Earle, sergeant, Kemper's South Carolina Artillery. Senator in 1897. Also attorney general of South Carolina.

Wade Hampton III, lieutenant general. Senator, 1879-1891. Also governor of South Carolina.

Tennessee

James Edmund Bailey, colonel, 49th Tennessee Infantry Regiment. Senator, 1877-1881. Chairman, Committee on Education and Labor.

William Brimage Bate, major general. Senator, 1887-1905. Chairman, Committee on Military Affairs. Also governor of Tennessee.

David McKendree Key, colonel, 43rd Tennessee Infantry Regiment. Senator, 1875-1877. Also member, U.S. House of Representatives, U.S. district judge, U.S. postmaster general.

Thomas Battle Turley, private, 154th Tennessee Infantry Regiment. Senator, 1897-1901.

Washington Curran Whitthorne, captain, staff of General Robert H. Anderson. Senator, 1886-1887. Chairman, Committee on Naval Affairs. Also member, U.S. House of Representatives.

Texas

Samuel Bell Maxey, brigadier general. Senator, 1875-1887.

Roger Quarles Mills, colonel, 10th Texas Infantry Regiment. Senator, 1892-1899. Chairman, Committee on Ways and Means, Committee on Interstate and Foreign Commerce.

John Henninger Reagan, Confederate postmaster general and secretary of the treasury. U.S. Senator, 1887-1891. Chairman, Committee on Commerce.

Virginia

John Strode Barbour Jr., volunteer on the staff of General Philip S. Cocke. Senator, 1889-1892.

John Warwick Daniel, major, staff of General Jubal Early. Senator, 1887-1910. Also member, U.S. House of Representatives.

John Warfield Johnston, Confederate States Receiver in Abingdon, Virginia. Senator, 1870-1883. Chairman, Committee on Agriculture.

Thomas Staples Martin, VMI cadet. Senator, 1895-1919. Senate Majority Leader, coauthor of the United States Declaration of War against Germany in 1917, chairman, Appropriations Committee.

Harrison Holt Riddleberger, captain, 23rd Virginia Cavalry Regiment. Senator, 1883-1889. Chairman, Commerce Committee.

Robert Enoch Withers, private, 18th Virginia Infantry Regiment. Senator, 1875-1881. Also U.S. consul to Hong Kong, lieutenant governor of Virginia.

West Virginia

Allen Taylor Caperton, Confederate States senator from Virginia. Senator, 1875-1876.

Charles James Faulkner, VMI cadet and Battle of New Market veteran, later staff of General Thomas J. "Stonewall" Jackson. Senator, 1887-1899. Also member, International Joint High Commission of the United States and Great Britain, 1898.

John Edward Kenna, private, 23rd Battalion Virginia Infantry. Senator, 1883-1893.

Secretary of the United States Senate

The Secretary of the Senate is an elected officer of the U.S. Senate who supervises administrative offices and services related to the day-to-day operations of the Senate. Similar to the clerk of the United States House of Representatives, duties of the Senate secretary include keeping the minutes and records of Senate proceedings, receiving and transmitting correspondence to and from the executive branch and the House of Representatives, as well as purchasing equipment, supplies, consumables, and support services and hiring, training, and supervising pages, clerks and curators.

John Christopher Burch, colonel, staff of General Nathan Bedford Forrest. Secretary of the U.S. Senate, 1879-1881. Also comptroller, state of Tennessee.

William Ruffin Cox, brigadier general. Secretary of the U.S. Senate, 1893-1900. Also member, U.S. House of Representatives from North Carolina.

United State House of Representatives
(by state, alphabetically)

Alabama

Newton Nash Clements, colonel, 50th Alabama Infantry Regiment.

George Paul Harrison Jr., colonel, 32nd Georgia Infantry Regiment.

Thomas Hord Herndon, major, 36th Alabama Infantry Regiment.

William Calvin Oates, colonel, 15th Alabama Infantry Regiment. Also governor of Alabama and brigadier general of volunteers, U.S. Army during the Spanish-American War.

William J. Samford, lieutenant, 46th Alabama Infantry Regiment. Also governor of Alabama.

Charles M. Shelley, brigadier general. Also sheriff of Dallas County, Alabama.

Joseph Wheeler, major general; major general of vols., U.S. Army, Spanish- American War.

Arkansas

Jordan Edgar Cravens, colonel, 1st Arkansas Consolidated Infantry Regiment.

Lucien C. Gause, colonel, 32nd Arkansas Infantry Regiment.

James Kimbrough Jones, private, 3rd Arkansas Cavalry Regiment. Also U.S. senator, chairman, Committee on Indian Affairs and chairman, Democratic National Committee.

Albert Rust, brigadier general.

William Ferguson Slemons, colonel, 2nd Arkansas Cavalry Regiment.

Florida

Robert Bullock, brigadier general.

Jesse Johnson Finley, brigadier general.

Georgia

Hiram Parks Bell, colonel, 43rd Georgia Infantry Regiment.

Philip Cook, brigadier general.

Dudley McIver DuBose, brigadier general.

Thomas Hardeman Jr., colonel, 45th Georgia Infantry Regiment. Also speaker, Georgia House of Representatives.

Benjamin Harvey Hill, Confederate senator from Georgia.

Julian Hartridge, lieutenant, Chatham's Alabama Light Artillery.

Alexander H. Stevens, vice president, Confederate States of America. Also governor of Georgia.

Kansas

William A. Harris, VMI cadet and ordnance officer on the staff of General Robert E. Rodes. Also U.S. senator.

Kentucky

Joseph Clay Stiles Blackburn, judge advocate and colonel, Blackburn's Cavalry Regiment. Also U.S. senator and governor, Panama Canal Zone.

William Campbell Preston Breckinridge, colonel, 9th Kentucky Cavalry Regiment.

John William Caldwell, colonel, 9th Kentucky Infantry Regiment.

Edward Crossland, captain, 1st Kentucky Infantry Regiment and colonel, 7th Kentucky Mounted Infantry Regiment.

Joseph Horace Lewis, brigadier general. Also chief justice, Kentucky Supreme Court.[2]

James Bennett McCreary, major, 11th Kentucky Cavalry Regiment. Also U.S. senator and governor of Kentucky.

Louisiana

Randall Lee Gibson, brigadier general. Also U.S. senator and member, board of regents, Smithsonian Institution.

Carleton Hunt, lieutenant, Louisiana Heavy Artillery.

William Mallory Levy, colonel, staff of General Richard Taylor. Also associate justice, Louisiana Supreme Court.

Mississippi

James Ronald Chalmers, brigadier general.

Charles Edward Hooker, colonel, staff of General A. P. Stewart.

Lucius Q. C. Lamar II, colonel, 19th Mississippi Infantry Regiment. Also U.S. senator, U.S. secretary of the interior, associate justice, U.S. Supreme Court.

Hernando Desoto Money, private, 11th Mississippi Infantry Regiment. Also U.S. senator.

Henry Lowndes Muldrow, colonel, 11th Mississippi Cavalry Regiment. Also assistant U.S. secretary of the interior.

---

2 Lewis served on the Kentucky Court of Appeals which was, until 1975, the equivalent of the Kentucky Supreme Court.

Missouri

John Bullock Clark, colonel, Provisional Army of the Confederate States.
Jeremiah V. Cockrell, colonel, 7th Missouri Infantry Regiment.

New Mexico

Thomas B. Catron, lieutenant, 3rd Missouri Artillery Battalion. Also U.S. senator, mayor of Santa Fe, and U.S. district attorney for New Mexico.

New York

Isidor Straus, Confederate commissioner to Europe. Also vice president, New York City Chamber of Commerce and member, New York Board of Trade.

North Carolina

Sydenham B. Alexander, captain, 1st Brigade, North Carolina Reserves.
Risdon Tyler Bennett, colonel, 14th North Carolina Infantry Regiment.
Curtis Hooks Brogden, brigadier general, North Carolina Militia. Also governor of North Carolina.
William Ruffin Cox, brigadier general.
William Henry Forney, brigadier general. Also member, Gettysburg Battlefield Commission.
Louis Charles Latham, captain, 1st North Carolina Infantry Regiment.
Sion Hart Rogers, colonel, 47th North Carolina Infantry Regiment. Also attorney general of North Carolina.
Daniel Lindsay Russell, captain, 2nd North Carolina Artillery. Also governor of North Carolina.
Alfred Moore Scales, brigadier general. Also governor of North Carolina.

South Carolina

David Wyatt Aiken, colonel, 7th South Carolina Infantry Regiment.
William B. Butler, colonel, 3rd South Carolina Artillery. Also librarian, U.S. House of Representatives.
Edward Croft, colonel, 14th South Carolina Infantry Regiment.
George William Croft, colonel, Citadel Battalion of Cadets.
George W. Dargan, private, Citadel Battalion of Cadets.
William Elliott, captain, staff of General Stephen D. Lee.
George Johnstone, private, Citadel Battalion of Cadets.
William Hayne Perry, private, 2nd South Carolina Cavalry Regiment.
Eli Thomas Stackhouse, colonel, 3rd South Carolina Consolidated Infantry Regiment.
George D. Tillman, private, 2nd South Carolina Heavy Artillery.

Tennessee

John Goff Ballentine, colonel, Ballentine's Mississippi Cavalry Regiment.

Nicholas N. Cox, colonel, 10th Tennessee Cavalry Regiment.

George Gibbs Dibrell, brigadier general.

George Washington Gordon, brigadier general.

David McKendree Key, colonel, 43rd Tennessee Infantry Regiment. Also U.S. postmaster general, U.S. district judge and U.S. senator.

Josiah Patterson, colonel, 5th Alabama Cavalry Regiment.

Washington Curran Whitthorne, captain, staff of General Robert H. Anderson. Also U.S. senator.

Texas

Nathaniel Macon Burford, colonel, 19th Texas Cavalry Regiment. Also speaker, Texas House of Representatives.

Richard Coke, captain, 15th Texas Infantry Regiment. Also governor of Texas, U.S. senator.

David Browning Culberson, colonel, 18th Texas Cavalry Regiment.

George Washington Jones, colonel, 17th Texas Infantry Regiment.

James Henry Jones, colonel, 11th Texas Infantry Regiment.

Samuel Willis Tucker Lanham, sergeant, 3rd South Carolina Infantry Regiment. Also governor of Texas.

William H. "Howdy" Martin, major, 4th Texas Infantry Regiment.

Roger Quarles Mills, colonel, 10th Texas Infantry Regiment. Chairman, Ways and Means Committee, U.S. senator from Texas. Namesake of Roger Mills County, Oklahoma.

John Henninger Reagan, postmaster general and secretary of the treasury, Confederate States of America. Also U.S. senator.

James W. Throckmorton, captain, 6th Texas Cavalry Regiment. Also governor of Texas.

Virginia

Richard L. Beale, brigadier general.

John Warwick Daniel, major, staff of General Jubal Early. Also U.S. senator.

Richard Thomas Walker Duke, colonel, 46th Virginia Infantry Regiment.

Abram Fulkerson, colonel, 63rd Tennessee Infantry Regiment.

John Goode, private, 2nd Virginia Cavalry Regiment, later on the staff of General Jubal Early. Also U.S. solicitor general.

Joseph Eggleston Johnston, general.

Robert Murphy Mayo, colonel, 47th Virginia Infantry Regiment.

Charles Triplett O'Ferrall, major, 23rd Virginia Cavalry Regiment. Also governor of Virginia.

Auburn Lorenzo Pridemore, colonel, 64th Virginia Cavalry Regiment.

Campbell Slemp, colonel, 64th Virginia Infantry Regiment.

West Virginia

Eustace Gibson, captain, 49th Virginia Infantry Regiment. Also speaker, West Virginia House of Delegates.

Alpheus Haymond, major, commissary officer for General John Pegram. Also associate justice, West Virginia Supreme Court.

John Edward Kenna, private, 23rd Battalion Virginia Infantry. Also U.S. senator.

College and University Professors
(by school, alphabetically)

Auburn University

William H. Chambers, captain, Alabama "Pioneer Guard". Professor of literature.

Robert Hardaway, major, chief of artillery for General Robert H. Anderson. Professor of agriculture.

James H. Lane, brigadier general. Professor and professor emeritus of engineering. Lane also taught at Virginia Tech and the University of Missouri, and received honorary doctorate degrees from Duke University and West Virginia University.

Nathaniel Thomas Lupton, superintendent, Confederate Nitre and Mining Bureau, Selma, Alabama. Professor of chemistry. Lupton also was president of the University of Alabama, professor of chemistry at Vanderbilt University, and the state chemist of Alabama.

College of William and Mary

Van Franklin Garrett, VMI cadet and Battle of New Market veteran. Professor of chemistry.

Frank Preston, VMI cadet and Battle of New Market veteran. Chairman, Department of Modern Languages.

Thomas L. Snead, lieutenant, staff of General Robert H. Anderson. Professor of mathematics.

Davidson College

William W. Carson, sergeant major, 4th Louisiana Cavalry Regiment. Professor of mathematics. Carson also was professor of civil engineering and professor emeritus of mathematics at the University of Tennessee.

Louisiana State University

Samuel H. Lockett, colonel and chief engineer, Department of Alabama, Mississippi, and East Louisiana. Professor of engineering. Lockett also taught at East Tennessee State University and was a postwar engineer for the United States Army in Egypt, Chile, and Bolivia.

Millsaps College (Mississippi)

Edward Mayes, private, 4th Mississippi Cavalry Regiment. Professor of law. Mayes also was chancellor of the University of Mississippi.

Richmond Academy of Medicine

John Nottingham Upshur, VMI cadet and New Market veteran. Professor of medicine. Upshur was a charter member and president of the Virginia State Medical Society, a professor at the Medical College of Virginia, and attending physician at the Female Humane Association of Virginia.

Tulane University

James L. Cross, major, staff of General Robert Hoke.

Edward Cunningham Jr., colonel, chief of artillery for General E. Kirby Smith.

John Williams Walker Fearn, colonel, staff of General E. Kirby Smith. Professor and chairman, Department of Spanish and Italian. Fearn also was U.S. ambassador to Greece, Romania, and Serbia.

Tulane University School of Medicine

Stanford E. Chaille, surgeon, Ocmulgee Confederate Hospital, Macon, Georgia. Dean of faculty, professor of physiology and pathological anatomy, and professor of obstetrics. Chaille served as president of the Havana Yellow Fever Commission and was a member of the National Board of Health.

John William Mallet, colonel, superintendent of ordnance laboratories for the Confederate War Department. Professor of chemistry. Mallet also taught at Amherst College, the University of Alabama, Johns Hopkins University, the University of Virginia, the Jefferson Medical College in Philadelphia, and was faculty chairman and a professor at the University of Texas.

University of Maryland School of Medicine

John Julian Chisolm, surgeon, Manchester (Virginia) Hospital. Faculty dean, professor of materia medica and professor of eye and ear surgery. Chisolm cofounded the Baltimore Eye and Ear Hospital and founded the Presbyterian Charity Eye, Ear and Throat Hospital in Baltimore. He is considered one of the fathers of American ophthalmology.

Francis Turquand Miles, surgeon, 17th South Carolina Infantry. Chairman, Department of Anatomy, chairman, Department of Diseases of the Nervous System, and chairman, Department of Physiology. Miles also was president of the American Neurological Association and chairman of the Department of Physiological Anatomy at the Medical University of South Carolina.

Russell Murdoch, surgeon, 1st Confederate Engineers, Petersburg. Professor of diseases of the eye and ear. He also cofounded the Presbyterian Eye, Ear, and Throat Charity Hospital in Baltimore and was chairman of the Department of Ophthalmology and Otology at the Woman's Medical College in Baltimore.

Henry R. Noel, surgeon of the 60th Virginia Infantry. Professor of physiology and hygiene.

Isham R. Page, surgeon, 18th Virginia Infantry Regiment. Professor of principles and practice of surgery.

John Randolph Page, surgeon, Provisional Army of the Confederate States. Professor of the practice of medicine. Page also was treasurer of the Richmond Academy of Medicine, and professor of natural history and agriculture, professor of zoology and agriculture, and professor of pharmacy at the University of Virginia.

J. William Walls, surgeon, 5th Virginia Infantry Regiment. Professor of anatomy and physiology.

University of Mississippi

Lucius Q. C. Lamar II, colonel, 19th Mississippi Infantry Regiment. Professor of metaphysics and professor of social science. Lamar also taught law at the University of Mississippi School of Law and was an associate justice on the U.S. Supreme Court, U.S. secretary of the interior, and a U.S. senator and member of the U.S. House of Representatives.

Wistar Claudius Sears, brigadier general. Professor of mathematics.

Francis Asbury Shoup, brigadier general. Professor of mathematics and physics. Shoup also taught at the University of the South and was a rector in the Episcopal Church.

University of South Carolina

Edward Porter Alexander, brigadier general. Professor of civil and military engineering and professor of mathematics. Alexander also was a U.S. special envoy to Nicaragua and Costa Rica during the Grover Cleveland administration.

John G. Barnwell, major, staff of General John C. Pemberton. Librarian, University of South Carolina.

John LeConte, major, Confederate Bureau of Nitre and Mining. Professor of physics. LeConte also was professor of chemistry and president of the University of California, Berkeley, professor of chemistry at the Columbia University College of Physicians and Surgeons and professor of chemistry at the University of Georgia.

Joseph LeConte, major, Confederate Bureau of Nitre and Mining. Chairman of the Department of Chemical Pharmacology, Minerology, and Geology. LeConte also was chairman of the Department of Geology at the University of California, Berkeley.

University of Texas

William Leroy Broun, colonel, commandant of the Richmond (Virginia) Arsenal. Professor of chemistry. Broun also was president of Auburn University and a professor at Vanderbilt University.

James Benjamin Clark, private, 18th Mississippi Infantry Regiment. University Librarian and proctor.

Robert L. Dabney, major, staff of General Thomas J. "Stonewall" Jackson. Professor of history. Dabney also taught at Union Theological Seminary.

John William Mallet, colonel, superintendent of ordnance laboratories for the Confederate War Department. Professor of chemistry and faculty chairman. Mallet also taught at Amherst College, the University of Alabama, Tulane University, the University of Virginia, the Jefferson Medical College in Philadelphia, and Johns Hopkins University.

John F. Y. Paines, surgeon, 21st Alabama Infantry Regiment. Faculty dean and professor of obstetrics and diseases of women and children and professor of obstetrics and gynecology. Paines also was president of the Texas State Medical Association, a fellow of the American Association of Obstetricians and Gynecologists, and honorary member of the Louisiana State Pharmaceutical Association, an honorary member of the Alabama State Surgical and Gynecological Association, and a fellow of the Texas Academy of Science.

The University of the South[3]

John Roberts Deering, surgeon, 20th Tennessee Infantry Regiment. Chairman, Department of Physiology and Clinical Medicine, chairman, Medical Department and chairman, Department of

---

3   Located in Sewanee, Tennessee, the University of the South is often referred to as "Sewanee" and "Sewanee: The University of the South," even by the university itself.

Theory and Practice of Medicine. Deering also was postwar physician of the Tennessee State Prison, a member of the Nashville Board of Health, professor at the Vanderbilt University School of Medicine and professor at the University of Tennessee Graduate School of Medicine. He also was vice president of the American Medical Association and treasurer of the Tennessee State Medical Society.

William Porcher DuBose, chaplain, Kershaw's (South Carolina) Brigade. Dean of the Theology Department and professor in the School of Moral Science and the Evidences of the Christian Religion. DuBose also was a professor of Greek at Mt. Zion College (South Carolina).

John McCrady, captain, Engineering Corps of the Provisional Army of the Confederate States. Professor of biology. McCrady also was chairman and professor of zoology at Harvard and professor of mathematics at the College of Charleston (South Carolina.)

Charles Landon Carter Miller, captain, staff of General Albert G. Jenkins. Professor of Latin. Miller also was president of the University of Maryland and Virginia Tech.

James B. Murfree, surgeon in charge, Emory and Henry Hospital, Emory, Virginia. Professor of principles and practices of surgery. Murfree also was president of the Tennessee State Medical Association and mayor of Murfreesboro, Tennessee.

Francis Asbury Shoup, brigadier general. Professor of mathematics and professor of physics. Shoup also taught at the University of Mississippi and was a rector in the Episcopal Church.

Edmund Kirby Smith, general and commander of the Department of the Trans-Mississippi. Professor of botany and professor of mathematics. Smith also was president of the University of Nashville (later Vanderbilt University).

University of Virginia

William M. Fontaine, captain and ordnance officer for General Patton Anderson. Chairman of the Department of Geology and Natural History. Fontaine also taught at West Virginia University.

Basil Lanneau Gildersleeve, volunteer aide-de-camp, staff of General John B. Gordon. Professor and chairman of the Department of Latin. Gildersleeve also was a professor at Johns Hopkins University and president of the Society for Classical Studies (then named the American Philological Association.) Gildersleeve was awarded honorary doctorate degrees from the College of William and Mary, Harvard University, Yale University, the University of Chicago, the University of Pennsylvania, the University of the South, Princeton University, and Oxford University and Cambridge University in England.

Otis Allan Glazebrook, corporal, VMI cadet and Battle of New Market veteran. University chaplain. Glazebrook also was chaplain of the 3rd New Jersey Regiment of Volunteers in the U.S. Army during the Spanish-American War and a U.S. diplomat.

John William Mallet, colonel, superintendent of ordnance laboratories for the Confederate War Department. Professor of analytical, industrial, and agricultural chemistry. Mallet also taught at Amherst College, the University of Alabama, Tulane University, Johns Hopkins University, the Jefferson Medical College in Philadelphia, and was faculty chairman and professor at the University of Texas.

John Randolph Page, surgeon, Provisional Army of the Confederate States. Professor of natural history, agriculture, zoology, and pharmacy. Page also was treasurer of the Richmond Academy of Medicine, professor at the Louisiana Military Academy and professor at the University of Maryland School of Medicine.

Thomas Randolph Price Jr., lieutenant, staff of General J. E. B. Stuart. Professor of engineering. Price also taught at the University of Richmond and Randolph Macon College.

Charles E. Vawter, sergeant, 27th Virginia Infantry Regiment. Professor of Hebrew and professor of mathematics. Vawter also cofounded The Miller School Orphanage in Albemarle County, Virginia, served as chairman of the board of trustees of the Normal and Industrial School for Girls in Farmville, Virginia, and was chairman of the board of trustees of the Normal and Industrial School for Negroes in Petersburg, Virginia. Vawter also was rector and trustee at Virginia Tech and a trustee at Emory and Henry College.

Charles Scott Venable, colonel, staff of General Robert E. Lee. Professor of mathematics.

Vanderbilt University (The University of Nashville)

William Leroy Broun, colonel and commandant, Richmond (Virginia) Arsenal. Professor of chemistry. Broun also was president of Auburn University and a professor at the University of Texas.

John Roberts Deering, surgeon, 20th Tennessee Infantry Regiment. Chairman of the Department of Physiology and Clinical Medicine, chairman of the Medical Department and chairman of the Department of Theory and Practice of Medicine at the Nashville Academy of Medicine (later merged with Vanderbilt University.) Deering also was a vice president of the American Medical Association, treasurer of the Tennessee State Medical Society, surgeon of the Tennessee State Prison, member of the Nashville Board of Health, and professor at the University of Tennessee Graduate School of Medicine.

Paul F. Eve, surgeon general. Professor of operative and clinical surgery. Before the war, Eve had performed the first successful hysterectomy in the United States.

Nathaniel Thomas Lupton, superintendent of the Confederate Nitre and Mining Bureau in Selma, Alabama. Professor of chemistry and chairman of the Department of Pharmacy. Lupton also was president of the University of Alabama, professor of chemistry at Auburn University and was the state chemist of Alabama.

James Merrill Safford, former officer in the Confederate States Ordnance Bureau. Chairman, Department of Chemistry. Safford also was Tennessee state geologist and a member of the Tennessee State Board of Health.

Virginia Tech

William W. Blackford, colonel, 1st Confederate Engineers. Professor of mechanics.

William R. Boggs, brigadier general. Professor of mechanics.

James H. Lane, brigadier general. Professor of mathematics. Lane also was professor and professor emeritus at Auburn University and a professor at the University of Missouri. Lane received honorary doctorate degrees from Duke University and West Virginia University.

William M. Patton, sergeant, VMI cadet and Battle of New Market veteran. Dean and professor of engineering. Patton Hall on the campus of Virginia Tech is named in his honor.

Washington and Lee University

William Allan, colonel, staff of generals Richard Ewell and Jubal Early. Professor of mathematics. Allan also was president of The McDonogh School in Owings Mills, Maryland.

Edmund Berkeley, Jr., former VMI cadet. Professor of civil engineering.

Cuthbert Grady, sergeant, 6th Virginia Cavalry Regiment. Professor of Latin.

William Preston Johnston, colonel, 1st Kentucky Infantry Regiment and aide-de-camp to President Jefferson Davis. Professor of history, literature, and political economy. Johnston also was president of Louisiana State University and trustee of Tulane University.

Nathaniel Alpheus Pratt, captain, Confederate States Bureau of Nitre and Mining. Chairman of the Department of Applied Science. Pratt also was Georgia state chemist and geologist for the Georgia Department of Agriculture.

College/University Governing Boards

College of William and Mary

David Wyatt Aiken, colonel, 7th South Carolina Infantry Regiment.
William B. Taliaferro, brigadier general, Department of Florida.

Davidson College

James Douglass Blanding, colonel, 9th South Carolina Infantry Regiment.

Judson University (Georgia)

William T. McAllister, surgeon, Buckner Hospital in Newnan, Georgia.

Georgia Tech

William E. Simmons, captain, 3rd Battalion, Georgia Sharpshooters.

University of Arkansas

Virgil Y. Cook, private, 12th Kentucky Cavalry Regiment. After the Civil War Cook was a brigadier general in the Arkansas Reserve Militia, a major general in the Arkansas State Guard, and colonel of the 2nd Regiment of Arkansas Volunteers in the U.S. Army during the Spanish-American War.

University of Georgia

Middleton Pope Barrrow, lieutenant, Carlton's Georgia Artillery. Barrow also was a U.S. senator from Georgia.
James Henry Fannin, colonel, 1st Georgia Reserves.
Abda Johnson, captain, 40th Georgia Infantry Regiment.
Homer V.M. Miller, surgeon and hospital inspector, Georgia Division. Miller also was a professor at the Emory University School of Medicine and a U.S. senator from Georgia.

University of Mississippi

William Thompson Martin, major general.

University of South Carolina

Franklin J. Moses Jr., colonel, Confederate Army Conscription Office. Moses also was governor of South Carolina and speaker of the South Carolina House of Representatives.

James Simons, brigadier general, 4th Brigade, South Carolina Militia.

Nathaniel B. Barnwell, private, 7th South Carolina Cavalry Regiment.

University of Texas

George Washington Littlefield, captain, 8th Texas Cavalry Regiment, "Terry's Texas Rangers." Littlefield was a legendary benefactor of the university, donating over three million dollars to the school in the early 1900s. The Littlefield House and the Littlefield Fountain at the University of Texas are named in his honor. Littlefield also was founder of the Littlefield Fund for Southern History. The city of Littlefield in Lamb County, Texas, is named in his honor.

Vanderbilt University (University of Nashville)

David Campbell Kelley, colonel, 26th Tennessee Cavalry Regiment.

Virginia Tech

Leonard A. Slater, surgeon, 15th Virginia Cavalry Regiment.

John Philip Smith, surgeon, 2nd Virginia Infantry Regiment.

Charles E. Vawter, sergeant, 27th Virginia Infantry Regiment. Vawter also was a professor at the University of Virginia, cofounder of The Miller School Orphanage in Albemarle County, Virginia; chairman of the board of trustees of the Normal and Industrial School for Girls in Farmville, Virginia; chairman of the board of trustees of the Normal and Industrial School for Negroes in Petersburg, Virginia; and a trustee of Emory and Henry College.

Confederate Veterans Killed while Serving as Postwar Law Enforcement Officers

The following information was provided by Mr. Jim Huffman of Picayune, Mississippi. His research is titled "The Thin Gray Line, The Thin Blue Line: Confederate Veterans Killed in the Line of Duty as Postwar Peace Officers." The list is grouped by state; the city or county shown indicates the location of the officer's death.

Alabama

Sergeant John M. Awtrey, 50th Alabama Infantry. Tuscaloosa County.

Private Hansford P. Gipson, 11th Alabama Cavalry. Tuscumbia.

Lieutenant William A. Russell, 4th Alabama Cavalry. Madison County.

Corporal William J. Street, 4th Alabama Cavalry. Huntsville.

Arkansas

Sergeant Major William F. Beattie, 1st Virginia Cavalry. Crittenden County.
Private Abraham G. Byler, Missouri State Guard. Gainesville.
Private John I. Mount, 16th Arkansas Infantry. Fayetteville.

Florida

Private David U. L. Alvarez, 2nd Florida Cavalry. Bradford County.
Private William Beasley, 1st Florida Cavalry. Orlando.
Captain Daniel J. Brownell, Holmes County Home Guard. Prosperity.
Private Jesse W. Dickson, 1st Florida Infantry. Quincy.
Private William P. Edwards, 6th Georgia Infantry. Volusia County.
Corporal David W.L. Mizell, 8th Florida Infantry. Orange County.
Private Thompson B. Simkins, 3rd Battalion Florida Cavalry. Jefferson County.
Private James W. Williams, 5th Florida Infantry. Orlando.

Georgia

Private William C. Barrow, 12th Georgia Infantry. Americus.
Corporal James A. Carter, 23rd South Carolina Infantry. Toccoa.
Private William Dooley, 1st Georgia Cavalry. Hartwell.
Private Robert H. Goodson, Stephens' Cavalry, Georgia State Guards. Atlanta.
Lieutenant William O. Gwyn, 31st Georgia Infantry. Pike County.
Private William A. Hyers, 29th Georgia Cavalry. Thomasville.
Private Noah H. McGinnis, 2nd Georgia Cavalry. Gordon County.
Private James P. Mooney, 18th Georgia Infantry. Rome.
Sergeant Benjamin D. Morgan, 13th Georgia Infantry. Milledgeville.
Private Mansel W. Rasbury, Cobb's Georgia Legion. Atlanta.

Kentucky

Private George Freeman, 7th Kentucky Cavalry. Versailles.
Lieutenant Cornelius M. Hendricks, 2nd Kentucky Mounted Infantry. Lexington.
Colonel Thomas W. Napier, 6th Kentucky Cavalry. Lincoln County.
Sergeant William W. Weatherhead, 2nd Kentucky Cavalry. Lexington.
Private Robert L. West, 3rd Georgia Reserves. Hopkinsville.

Louisiana

Private Joshua Baker Hare, 5th Louisiana Infantry. Baton Rouge.

Mississippi

Private Thaddeus B. Gillis, 22nd Mississippi Infantry. Summit

Missouri

Lieutenant John B. Benham, Clardy's Missouri Cavalry. St. Francois County.
Corporal Lander A. Boone, 2nd Missouri Cavalry. St. Louis.
Captain George W. Law, 1st Missouri Cavalry. Callaway County.
Private Frederick J. Palmore, 39th Virginia Cavalry. Springfield.

North Carolina

Private Francis J. Baker, 21st North Carolina Infantry. Stokes County.
Private Thomas DeVane, 3rd North Carolina Artillery. Wilmington.
Private John L. Greene, 28th North Carolina Infantry. Rutherford County.
Sergeant Henry C. Owen, 6th North Carolina Infantry. Rowan County.

South Carolina

Private Cotesworth P. Fishburne, 3rd South Carolina Cavalry. Ravenel.

Tennessee

Sergeant James M. Breedlove, 2nd Kentucky Cavalry. Henry County.
Private Enock Cooksey, 16th Tennessee Infantry. McMinnville.
Private John M. Claridge, 154th Tennessee Senior Infantry. Memphis.
Private John M. Fenton, Tobin's (Tennessee) Light Artillery. Memphis.
Corporal William J. Fraley, 34th Tennessee Infantry. Hardin County.
First Lieutenant Jason W. Fussell, Co. E, 6th Tennessee Infantry. Madison County.
Private John M. Gear, 30th Tennessee Infantry. Memphis.
Corporal Willoughby H. Nelson, 19th Tennessee Cavalry. Tracy City.
Lieutenant Newton C. Perkins, 13th Tennessee Infantry. Jackson.
Private Milton H. Stephens, 4th Tennessee Cavalry. Williamson County.
Private Daniel Summit, 2nd Tennessee Cavalry. Nashville.

Texas

Lieutenant John H. Adams, 11th Alabama Infantry. Hempstead.
Private Jackson T. Barfield, 15th Arkansas Infantry. Worthan.
Private John C. Birdwell, 17th Consolidated Texas Cavalry. Nacogdoches County.
Private Burwell J. Blankenship Jr., 6th Texas Cavalry. McLennan County.
Private Nathan Busby, 36th Texas Cavalry. Milam County.
Sergeant Joseph A. Campion, 2nd Texas Cavalry. Lavaca County.
Private Wesley Cherry, 5th Texas Infantry. Lampasas County.
Private William A. Clark, 3rd Alabama Cavalry. Jacksonville.
Private Jasper N. Coghlan, 14th Mississippi Infantry. Wise County.
Private Marion M. Coleman, Giddings' Battalion Texas Cavalry. Marlin.
Private James M. Daniels, Griffin's Regiment Texas Infantry. Lampasas County.
Lieutenant John Q. Daugherty, 15th Texas Infantry. Uvalde County.
Lieutenant Rufus H. Day, 12th Arkansas Infantry. Henderson County.

Captain Leonard C. DeLisle, 34th Texas Cavalry. Harrison County.
Private Isaac B. Heffington, 12th Texas Cavalry. Lee County.
Private Laban J. Hoffman, 30th Texas Cavalry. Waco.
Corporal Josiah J. Jordan, 13th Texas Cavalry. Orange.
Private John W. Love, 6th Texas Cavalry. Limestone County.
Sergeant Absalom K. McCarty, 19th Tennessee Infantry. Denison.
Lieutenant William R. McMullen, 13th Texas Cavalry. Homer.
Private William L. "Brack" Mitchell, 19th Texas Infantry. Fisher County.
Private Uel Musick, 16th Texas Cavalry. Vernon.
Private Elias T. Mussett, 3rd Texas Cavalry. Corpus Christi.
Private John D. Nelson, Jones' Texas Light Artillery. Kerr County.
Private Silas B. Newcomb, Waller's Regiment Texas Cavalry. Victoria.
Colonel Charles H. Nichols, Jackman's Missouri Cavalry. Dallas County.
Sergeant Jackson M. Phillips, 2nd Texas Cavalry. Bandera County.
Private James K. Phillips, 55th Georgia Infantry. Tyler County.
Private John H. Spalding, 19th Texas Cavalry. Waxahachie.
Private Eli Stalllings, 10th Mississippi Infantry. Bastrop.
Private Alexander C. Starks, 3rd Kentucky Cavalry. Rockwall County.
Captain Edward A. Stevens, 36th Texas Cavalry. Bexar County.
Sergeant Albertus Sweet, 17th Texas Infantry. Belton.
Private George W. Taylor, 24th Texas Cavalry. Rusk.
Private George V. Vise, 19th Georgia Infantry. Dallas County.
Private Marion D. Wallace, 34th Alabama Infantry. Young County.
Private Isaac Ward, 1st Indian Regiment Texas Cavalry. Jack County.
Corporal Duff G. Williams, 17th Texas Cavalry. Smith County.
Corporal Benjamin Wilson, 40th Mississippi Infantry. Rusk.
Private Moses L. Wright, 19th Texas Cavalry. McLennan County.
Private Addison Wyser, 35th Texas Cavalry. Robertson County.
Private Herman H. Young, 26th Texas Cavalry. Houston.

Virginia

Private William A. Cook, Danville Artillery. Danville.
Private James T. Cox, 46th Virginia Infantry. Richmond.
Private John J. DeHart, 54th Virginia Infantry. Floyd County.
Private John B. Drummond, 21st Virginia Infantry. Brunswick County.
Private John Minetree, Jr., 12th Virginia Infantry. Petersburg.
Private John W. Saunders, 13th Virginia Cavalry. Greensville County.
Private Lewis F. Webb, Carroll County Home Guard. Carroll County.

Bibliography

BOOKS

Allardice, Bruce S., *More Generals in Gray*. Baton Rouge, LA and London: Louisiana State University Press, 1995.

Atwater, Isaac, *History of the City of Minneapolis Minnesota, Part II*. New York: Munsell & Company Publishers, 1893.

Collins, R. M., *Chapters from the Unwritten History of the War between the States, or, the Incidents in the Life of a Confederate Soldier*. St. Louis, MO: Nixon-Jones Printing Co., 1893.

Connon, David, *Iowa Confederates in the Civil War*. Charleston, SC: Fonthill Media, 2019.

Cosmos, Graham A., *An Army for Empire: The United States Army and the Spanish- American War*, College Station, TX: Texas A&M University Press, 1998.

Couper, William, *The Corps Forward: Biographical Sketches of the VMI Cadets who Fought in the Battle of New Market*. Buena Vista, VA: The Mariner Companies, Inc., 2005.

Davis, William C., Pohanka, Brian C., Troiani, Don, editors, *Civil War Journal: The Leaders*. Nashville, TN: Rutledge Hill Press, 1997.

Freeman, Robert C., *Civil War Saints*. Provo, UT: Deseret Book, 2012.

Gallagher, Gary W. and Glatthaar, Joseph T., editors, *Leaders of the Lost Cause: New Perspectives on the Confederate High Command*. Mechanicsburg, PA: Stackpole Books, 2004.

Hughes, Nathaniel Cheairs, Jr. *Yale's Confederates: A Biographical Dictionary*. Knoxville, TN: The University of Tennessee Press, 2008.

Johnson, Rossiter and Brown, John Howard, editors, *The Twentieth Century Biographical Directory of Notable Americans*. Norwood, MA: Plimpton Press, 1904.

Junkin, Nettie DuBose, *For the Glory of God, Memoirs of Dr. and Mrs. H. C. DuBose of Soochow, China*. Lewisburg, WV: The Children of Dr. and Mrs. DuBose, 1920.

Krick, Robert E. L., *Staff Officers in Gray: A Biographical Register of the Staff Officers in the Army of Northern Virginia*. Chapel Hill, NC: The University of North Carolina Press, 2003.

Pollard, Edward Alfred, *The Lost Cause: A New Southern History of the War of the Confederates*. New York: E. B. Treat & Co., 1866.

Rosen, Robert N., *The Jewish Confederates*. Columbia, SC: University of South Carolina Press, 2000.

Toney, Marcus B., *The Privations of a Private: Campaigning with the First Tennessee, C.S.A., and Life Thereafter*, Fire Ant Books, 2005.

Trimpi, Helen P., *Crimson Confederates: Harvard Men Who Fought for the South*. Knoxville, TN: The University of Tennessee Press, 2010.

Waring, J. I., *A History of Medicine in South Carolina, 1825-1900*. Columbia, SC: R. L. Bryan Co., 1967.

Warner, Ezra J., *Generals in Gray: Lives of the Confederate Commanders*. Baton Rouge, LA and London: Louisiana State University Press, 1959.

ARTICLES

"A Confederate in the Capitol: Samuel D. Shannon," Wyomingstate archives.wordpress.com, Carl V. Hallberg, December 11, 2015.

"Colonel Mottrom Dulany Ball: A Founding Father of the State of Alaska," William P. Johnson, II. *The Fare Facs Gazette: The Newsletter of Historic Fairfax City, Inc.*, vol. 12, issue 4, Fall 2015.

"Great Success of the Evansville Blue and Gray Reunion," *The Wisconsin State Register* (Portage, WI) Saturday, September 24, 1887, issue 32.

"Milwaukee's Monument to be Erected in Memory of her Sons Fallen in the Civil War." *The Milwaukee Sentinel*, April 7, 1898, issue 9.

"Obituary of William M. Polk, M.D," *Cornell Alumni News*, vol. XX, Nos. 38, 39, July 1918.

"Presidents Who Were Civil War Veterans." Robert McNamara. *ThoughtCo*, July 3, 2019, thoughtco.com/presidents-who-were-civil-war-veterans-1773443.

"Reunited Veterans Annual Encampment of the Illinois Department of the Grand Army of the Republic." *The Daily Inter Ocean* (Chicago, IL), January 29, 1880, issue 257.

"The South to the North: Piedmont Exposition Directors Invite Old Soldiers to a Reunion of Blue and Gray," in *The Daily Inter Ocean* (Chicago, IL) Sunday, August 28, 1887, issue 157.

"Well-born Lt. Col. Paul Francois de Gournay was the South's adopted 'marquis in gray'." *America's Civil War*, Mauriel Joslyn, September 1995.

FILMS

The Civil War: A Film by Ken Burns. Public Broadcasting System, 2002.

ONLINE SOURCES

State Historical Organizations

Alabama: www.encyclopediaofalabama.org
Arkansas: www.encyclopediaofarkansas.net
Georgia: www.georgiaencyclopedia.org
Mississippi: www.mississippiencyclopedia.org
North Carolina: www.northcarolinahistory.org
South Carolina: www.scencyclopedia.org
Tennessee: tennesseeencyclopedia.net
Texas: www.tshaonline.org
Virginia: www.encyclopediavirginia.org

Colleges/Universities

Agnes Scott College: www.agnesscott.edu

Auburn University: www.auburn.edu

Citadel: www.citadel.edu

Clemson University: www.clemson.edu

Duke University: www.duke.edu

Georgia Southern University: www.georgiasouthern.edu

Louisiana State University: www.lsu.edu

Medical College of the State of South Carolina: www.waring.library.musc.edu

Millsaps College: www.millsaps.edu

Shepherd University: www.shepherd.edu

Tulane University: www.tulane.edu

United States Military Academy: www.westpoint.edu

University of Alabama: www.ua.edu, www.mallet-assembly.org

University of Arkansas for Medical Sciences: www.uams.edu

University of California, Berkeley: www.lib.berkeley.edu

University of Maryland: www.umd.edu

University of Mississippi: www.inauguration.olemiss.edu

University of North Carolina at Greensboro: www.uncg.edu

University of Texas at Austin: www.president.utexas.edu

University of Texas System: www.utsystem.edu

University of Virginia: www.virginia.edu

Virginia Military Institute: www.vmi.edu

Virginia Tech: www.president.vt.edu

OTHER

"Act of Kindness 40 Years Later - 23rd New Jersey & 8th Alabama: Soldier's Tales." American Civil War Forums, May 9, 2017. Https://civilwartalk.com/threads/act-of- kindness-40-years-later-23rd-new-jersey-8th-alabama.130341/#post-1456173

Admin. "Chester A. Arthur Presidential Library and Museum Blog." Chester A. Arthur Presidential Library and Museum Blog, July 3, 2018. www.chester arthurlibrary.org/.

"Alabama Department of Archives and History." Alabama Department of Archives and History. www.archives.state.al.us/.

"AMA." American Medical Association, n.d. www.ama-assn.org/.

"American Bar Association." American Bar Association. www.americanbar.org/

"America's Lost Colleges." www.lostcolleges.com/.

Anderson, P. C. (n.d.). Capers, Ellison. www.scencyclopedia.org/sce/entries/ capers- ellison/

"Benjamin Morgan Harrod." Benjamin Morgan Harrod | The Cultural Landscape Foundation. https://tclf.org/pioneer/benjamin-morgan-harrod.

Bierce, Ambrose, "A Bivouac of the Dead" (1903), describing the unmarked graves of some Confederate dead in Pocahontas County, West Virginia.

Biographical and Historical Memoirs of Louisiana, Vol. II, Chicago, Goodspeed Publishing, 1892, pp. 278-79 (Author not given.)

Boggs, William Ellison (1838-1920), Find A Grave (n.d.). Retrieved from www.findagrave.com/memorial/33358282/william-ellison-boggs

Brett Schulte blog, Short Takes, by Fred Ray on December 15, 2017.

Breysacher, Augustus L. (n.d.). //medicine.uams.edu/about-the-college/college- of-medicine-history/founders/augustus-l-breysacher-m-d/.

"Brig. General Thomas Jordan (CSA), General-in-Chief of the Cuban Liberation Army (CLA)." geni_family_tree, February 24, 2015. www.geni.com/people/Brig-General-Thomas-Jordan-CSA-General-in-Chief-of-the-Cuban-Liberation-Army-CLA/6000000017018497422.

Byrd, Dr Harvey Leonidas (1820-1884). Find A Grave (n.d.). Www.findagrave.com/memorial/91909456/harvey-leonidas-byrd.

Carroll, G. L. E. (n.d.). Dinwiddie, James. Www.ncpedia.org/biography/ dinwiddie- james.

Causey, Donna R. (May 29, 2019). www.alabamapioneers.com/old-southern- university-greensboro/.

Chancellors of UM. (n.d.). Retrieved from https://inauguration.olemiss.edu/ about-um/chancellors/.

Clemson, Thomas Green. (n.d.). www.clemson.edu/about/history/bios/ thomas- g-clemson.html

Coker, Maj James Lide (1837-1918). Find A Grave (n.d.). www.findagrave.com/memorial/12291661/james-lide-coker.

Connon, David. "From Confederate POW to Officer in Spanish-American War." Confederates from Iowa: June 18, 2018. www.confederatesfromiowa.com/from- confederate-pow-to-officer-in-spanish-american-war/.

Cox, R., & University Libraries. (n.d.). http://library.uncg.edu/map/details/ Curry_ Building.aspx.

Dancy, Col. Francis L. Dancy. (n.d.). https://floridacitrushalloffame.com/inductees /col-francis-l-dancy/.

Daniel, J. (2010, June 15). Merchant, Claiborne Walker. https://tshaonline.org/handbook/online/articles/fme26.

D. Cockrell, T. (September 24, 2019). Mark Perrin Lowrey. https://mississippi encyclopedia.org/entries/mark-perrin-lowry/.

Department of Justice: "Front Page." The United States Department of Justice, www.justice.gov/.

Department of State: www.history.state.gov, U.S. Department of State.

Douglass, J., and Thomas, S. (n.d.). U.C. Presidents Overview. www.lib.berkeley. Edu/uchistory/general_history/overview/presidents/index.html#leconte.

Dudley, Thomas Underwood. (September 30, 2019). https://en.wikipedia.org/ wiki/Thomas_Underwood_Dudley.

"Educator Turned Soldier Saved Virginia's Oldest College from Wartime Ruin." https://web.archive.org/web/20070724173142/http://vaudc.org/ewell.html.

Forney, William. (n.d.). www.encyclopediaofalabama.org/article/h-3321.

Gardner, Katie. "About Us." Preserving History, October 29, 2014. www.donning.com/2014/10/29/benjamin-azariah-colonna-a-biography/.

Garland, Augustus Hill. (n.d.). https://encyclopediaofarkansas.net/entries/ augustus -hill-garland-106/.

Hardy, Michael. "Confederates beyond the War—Governors." January 1, 1970. Http://michaelchardy.blogspot.com/2017/02/confederates-beyond-war-governors.html.

Harris, Nathaniel Edwin. (n.d.). February 16, 2020, www.nga.org/governor/ nathaniel-edwin-harris/.

Hill, Daniel Harvey (1821-1889). Https://northcarolinahistory.org/encyclopedia/ daniel-harvey-hill-1821-1889/.

"Historical Military Records." Fold3. http://www.fold3.com/.

"History & Traditions." (n.d.). www.agnesscott.edu/about/history-traditions/ index.html.

"History of the city of Minneapolis, Minnesota." https://archive.org/stream/history ofcityofm02 atwa#page/800/mode/1up.

"Home." American Battlefield Trust. www.battlefields.org/.

"Homepage: Choctaw Nation." www.choctawnation.com/.

House of Representatives: www.history.house.gov.

Jewish Confederates. www.jewishencyclopedia.com/.

James, W. (June 15, 2010). Waggener, Leslie. Https://tshaonline.org/handbook/ online/articles/fwa06.

Jarvis, Thomas Jordan. (n.d.). Www.ncpedia.org/biography/governors/jarvis- thomas-jordan.

Judson College. (n.d.). www.encyclopediaofalabama.org/article/h-2492.

Kestenbaum, Lawrence. "The Political Graveyard." www.politicalgraveyard.com/.

Klein, and Kara. (n.d.). Colonel Asbury Coward, CSA (1890-1908), The Citadel, Charleston, SC. www.citadel.edu/root/president-past-presidents/107-info/administration/office-of-the-president/20867-colonel-asbury-coward,-csa-1890-1908.

Kohn, Edward P. "Teddy Roosevelt's Confederate Uncles." *The New York Times*, June 25, 2014. https://opinionator.blogs.nytimes.com/2014/06/25/teddy-roosevelts- confederate-uncles/.

List of Presidents of the University of South Carolina (August 6, 2019). https://en. Wikipedia. org/wiki/List_of_Presidents_of_the_University_of_South_Carolina.

Los Angeles Public Library, Local History Collection, Biography, Cameron Erskine Thom. https://dbase1.lapl.org/webpics/calindex/documents/16/523517.pdf.

Louisiana State University. www.lsu.edu/president/history.php.

"Main Page." www.wikipedia.org/.

Maness, L. E. (March 1, 2018). Alexander P. Stewart. https://tennesseeencyclopedia. Net/entries /alexander-p-stewart/.

McNamara, Robert. "The Presidents Who Served In the Civil War." *ThoughtCo*, July 3, 2019. www.thoughtco. com/presidents-who-were-civil-war-veterans-1773443.

Millsaps, Major Reuben Webster. (n.d.). www.millsaps.edu/admissions/major- reuben-webster-millsaps.php.

"National Governors Association." National Governors Association. www.nga.org/.

National Oceanographic & Atmospheric Administration: www.history.noaa.gov. "NOAA History—Main Page." NOAA History - Main Page. www.history.noaa.gov/.

Nott, Josiah C. (n.d.). www.encyclopediaofalabama.org/article/h-1484.

Obenchain, Maj William Alexander (1841-1916). Find A Grave (n.d.). www.findagrave.com/ memorial/88919198/william-alexander-obenchain.

Past Presidents. (n.d.). https://tulane.edu/past-presidents.

Past Presidents. (n.d.). www.president.vt.edu/presidents.html.

Presidential biographies on WhiteHouse.gov.

Rutherford B. Hayes Presidential Library & Museums. www.rbhayes.org/.

Sansing G., D. (April 13, 2018). James Lusk Alcorn. https://mississippiencyclopedia. Org/ entries/ james-lusk-alcorn/.

SchoolandCollegeListings. www.schoolandcollegelistings.com/.

Scott, Charles Lewis, Biographical Information. http://bioguide.congress.gov/ scripts/biodisplay. pl?index=S000167.

Seay, Thomas (1886-90). (n.d.). www.encyclopediaofalabama.org/article/h-1533.

Senate: "Floor Proceedings." www.senate.gov.

"Serve, Preserve, Inspire." Architect of the Capitol. (September 25, 2019). www.aoc.gov/.

Smith, Ashbel (n.d.). Www.utsystem.edu/board-of-regents/former-regents/ ashbel-smith-md.

Smith, Edmund Kirby (n.d.). www.aoc.gov/art/national-statuary-hall-collection/ edmund-kirby-smith.

Supreme Court: Supreme Court Historical Society. www.supremecourthistory.org/.

Sutori. (n.d.). Www.sutori.com/story/southern-education-foundation-150-years-TESC3sQUoEEo8DD 863cfUJte

Taylor, R. H. (n.d.). Scarborough, John Catre. Www.ncpedia.org/biography/ scarborough-john-catre.

Thecivilwarproject, The Civil War Project (TCWP). https://thecivilwarproject.com/ tag/elizabeth-herndon-maury/.

"The Latin Library." The Latin Library. www.thelatinlibrary.com/.

"The Reconciliation Movement." Gale Library of Daily Life: Civil War. Encyclopedia.com. (August 10, 2019). www.encyclopedia.com/history/applied-and-social-sciences-magazines/reconciliation- movement.

Ulysses S. Grant Presidential Library. http://www.usgrantlibrary.org/.

The University of Alabama. (n.d.). Retrieved from www.ua.edu/legends/list_ presidents.php.

University of Arkansas for Medical Sciences (UAMS). (n.d.). https://encyclopediaof arkansas.net/entries /university-of-arkansas-for-medical-sciences-uams-2395/.

University Presidents. (January 18, 2018). www.umd.edu/history-and-mission/ university-presidents.

United States Army: www.history.army.mil.

Waggener, Leslie. (December 3, 2019). https://president.utexas.edu/past-presidents /leslie-waggener.

"Welcome to VictorianVilla.com!" www.victorianvilla.com/.

"Well Known Confederate Veterans and Their War Records." Genealogy Trails. Http://genealogytrails. com/main/military/confederatevets_wellknown.html.

Whitehead, Dr William Riddick (1831-1902). Find A Grave (n.d.). www.findagrave. com/memorial/120221997/william-riddick-whitehead.

"Who's Who in TN." www.tngenweb.org/whos-who.

"William Freret: From Folly to War to Success." Emerging Civil War, June 8, 2018. https://emergingcivilwar.com/2018/06/09/william-freret-from-folly-to-war-to-success/#more-175135.

"Williamson County Historical Commission." www.williamson-county-texas- history.org/.

Willson, Dr. John Owens (1845-1923), Find A Grave (n.d.). www.findagrave.com/memorial/ 116770168/john-owens-willson.

Wilson, D. B. (n.d.). Martin, William Joseph. www.ncpedia.org/biography/martin- william-joseph.

Wilson, William Lyne. Www.wvculture.org/hiStory/government/wilsonwilliam 04.html.

ALPHABETICAL BY KEYWORD

www.academia.edu/34991390/Shelby_Foote_Memphis_and_the_Civil_War_in_American_Memory.

www.lib.auburn.edu/archive/find-aid/533/wlb-bio.htm

www.maxinkuckee.history.pasttracker.com/cef__cma_hartman_pdf/fleet_alexander_frederick.pdf.

www.schoolandcollegelistings.com/US/Bartow/103785712993560/South-Florida-Military-College.

www.sefatl.org/1878.html. (n.d.).

www.thelatinlibrary.com/chron/civilwarnotes/johnson1.html. (n.d.)

www.tulane.edu/~matas/historical/medschool/doctors/richardson.htm. (n.d.)

https://web.archive.org/web/20070724173142/http://vaudc.org/ewell.html

www.wvculture.org/hiStory/government/wilsonwilliam04.html. (n.d.).

Index

attorney general of the U.S., Office of the Solicitor General, U.S. Department of Justice, 35-37

Cook, Pvt. Virgil Y., 12th Kentucky Cavalry, Maj. Gen., Arkansas State Guard, Col., 2nd Regiment of Volunteers (Spanish-American War), governing board (University of Arkansas), 84, 211

Cook, Pvt. William A., Danville Artillery, law enforcement (Virginia), 215

Cooksey, Pvt. Enock, 16th Tennessee Infantry, law enfocement, 213

Coward, Col. Asbury, 5th South Carolina Infantry, superintendent of the Citadel, 127

Cox, Pvt. James T., 46th Virginia Infantry, law enforcement, 215

Cox, Col. Nicholas N., 10th Tennessee Cavalry, member U.S. House of Representatives, 204

Cox, Brig. Gen. William R., member U.S. House of Representatives (North Carolina), Secretary of the U.S. Senate, 201, 203

Cravens, Col. Jordan E., 1st Arkansas Consolidated Infantry, member U.S. House of Representatives, 201

Creek Military Units, 1st Creek Mounted Volunteers, 181; 2nd Creek Mounted Volunteers, 181

Croft, Col. Edward, 14th South Carolina Infantry, member U.S. House of Representatives, 203

Croft, Col. George William, Citadel Battalion of Cadets, member U.S. House of Representatives, 203

Crossland, Edward, Capt. 1st Kentucky Infantry, Col. 7th Kentucky Mounted Infantry, member U.S. House of Representatives, 70, 202

Crow, H. L., co-founder (city of Glendale, California), 98

Culberson, Col. David B., 18th Texas Cavalry, member U.S. House of Representatives, 204

Cumming, Brig. Gen. Alfred, Army of Tennessee, U.S. Military Commission to Korea, 40

Curry, Col. Jabez L. M., staff officer to generals Joseph E. Johnston and Joe Wheeler, instructor and president (Samford University), teacher, ordained minister and founder (University of North Carolina at Greensboro), established (Southern Education Boar, 40-41, 147, 168; photo, 41

Dabney, Maj. Robert L., staff of General Thomas J. Stonewall Jackson, professor of history (University of Texas), professor (Union Theological Seminary), 207

Dabney, Capt. Virginius Sr., staff of Gen. John B. Gordon, president (American Newspaper

Publishers Association), Collector of the Port of New York, 184

Dancy, Col. Francis L., quartermaster general of Florida, engineer, geologist, agronomist, Florida state engineer and geologist, 185

Daniel, Maj. John W., staff of Gen. Jubal Early, U.S. senator, member House of Representatives (Virginia), 200, 204

Daniels, Pvt. James M., Griffin's Regiment Texas Infantry, law enforcement, 214

Dargan, Pvt. George W., Citadel Battalion of Cadets, member U.S. House of Representatives, 204

Daugherty, Lt. John Q., 15th Texas Infantry, law enforcement, 214

Day, Lt. Rufus H., 12 Arkansas Infantry, law enforcement (Texas), 214

Deering, Dr. John R., surgeon, 20th Tennessee Infantry, chairman Department of Physiology and Clinical Medicine, chairman Medical Department and Department of Theory and Practice of Medicine (University of the South), postwar physician of the Tennessee St, 102, 208-209

DeHart, Pvt. John J., 54th Virginia Infantry, law enforcement, 215

DeLisle, Capt. Leonard C., 34th Texas Cavalry, law enforcement, 214

DeVane, Pvt. Thomas, 3rd North Carolina Artillery, law enforcement, 213

Dibrell, Brig. Gen. George G., member U.S. House of Representatives (Georgia), 204

Dibrell, James A. Jr., founder (University of Arkansas College of Medicine), 156

Dickson, Pvt. Jesse W., 1st Florida Infantry, law enforcement, 212

Dinwiddie, Hardaway H., VMI cadet, professor, faculty chairman and president (Texas A&M University), co-founder (Texas Military Institute), 149

Dinwiddie, James, Brig. Gen., Henry, Wise's Legion and the Charlottesville Light Artillery, educator and president (Peace College), professor (University of Tennessee), principal (Sayre School), 177

Dooley, Pvt. William, 1st Georgia Cavalry, law enforcement, 212

Douglas, Henry K., 183

Douglas, Col. Henry T., engineer on the staffs of generals John B. Magruder, A. P. Hill, and E. Kirby Smith, Civil engineer and chief engineer (Baltimore and Ohio Railroad), engineering commssioner (City of Baltimore), Brig. Gen. 4th Illinois Regiment of U.S. Volunteers (Spanish-American War), chief engineer (New York Rapid Transit Railroad), 78-79, 81

Stephen M. "Sam" Hood graduated from Kentucky Military Institute, Marshall University (BBA, 1976), and is a veteran of the U.S. Marine Corps Reserve. A collateral descendant of Confederate General John Bell Hood, Sam is a retired industrial construction company owner, past member of the Board of Directors of the Blue Gray Education Society, and a past president of the Board of Directors of Confederate Memorial Hall Museum in New Orleans.

Sam is the author of two award-winning titles: *John Bell Hood: The Rise, Fall, and Resurrection of a Confederate General* (Savas Beatie, 2014), and *The Lost Papers of Confederate General John Bell Hood* (Savas Beatie, 2015).

He lives in Myrtle Beach, South Carolina, with his wife of 43 years, Martha, and is the proud father of two sons: Derek Hood of Winchester, Kentucky, and Taylor Hood of Huntington, West Virginia.